Gallery Books
Editor Peter Fallon
QUESTIONING IRELAND

Thomas McCarthy

QUESTIONING IRELAND

Gallery Books

Questioning Ireland
is first published
simultaneously in paperback
and in a clothbound edition
on 5 September 2024.

The Gallery Press
Loughcrew
Oldcastle
County Meath
Ireland

www.gallerypress.com

*All rights reserved. For permission
to reprint or broadcast this work,
write to The Gallery Press:*
books@gallerypress.com

© Thomas McCarthy 2024

The right of Thomas McCarthy to be identified as Author of this Work has been asserted in accordance with Section 77 of the Copyright, Designs and Patents Act 1988.

ISBN 978 1 91133 868 0 *paperback*
      978 1 91133 869 7 *clothbound*

A CIP catalogue record for this book
is available from the British Library.

Questioning Ireland receives financial assistance
from the Arts Council of Ireland.

Contents

PART ONE: THAT IRISH QUESTION
  Five Women and Three Men: 1991-2016 13
  Poets, The Ireland They Dreamt Of 25
  A 1916 Foreword 31
  Celtic Tiger, Irish Climate 39
  The Cappoquin Cricket XI 48
  The Years of Forgetting: 2006-2011 52
  Fianna Fáil, The Waiting Game 60
  Luck and the Irish: A Brief History of Change,
    1970-2000 by R F Foster 66

PART TWO: THE QUESTION OF WOMEN'S POETRY
  'The outrage of people': Why Men Should Study
    Women's Poetry 75
  Herself 83
  Eavan Boland's Daring Integrity 86
  Eavan Boland By Jody Allen Randolph 93
  From a woman on a train to 'Formal Feeling' 96
  'None of us well fixed' 105
  The Bears and the Bees 117
  'We could be in any city' 123
  Echoes from the Cistern 140
  Saturated with Light 145
  The Flower Master and Other Poems by Medbh
    McGuckian 150
  This is Yarrow by Tara Bergin 153
  The Poison Glen by Annemarie Ní Churreáin 155
  Life Saving: Why We Need Poetry 158
  For the Desert Air 161

PART THREE: QUESTIONS FROM AN ASCENDANCY
  Snow, Göring's Train, Hofstetter's Serenade 169
  Mrs Victor Rickard 172
  Monument to Inner Space 176

The Death of a Fox 181
Reading Molly Keane's Papers on Christmas Eve 187
Elizabeth Bowen and Molly Keane 199
Bowen's Court, an Introduction 205

PART FOUR: THAT ULSTER QUESTION
  The Outsider of Irish Poetry 215
  Documents of Exclusion 219
  Incorrigibly Plural 227
  Northman 231
  Derek Mahon's 'Ophelia' 233
  A Shell Case Full of Flowers 235
  Your Beautiful Life 238
  Heroes and Nasties 242
  Tides Revisited 246
  Poet of Exile and Return 249
  John Montague 256
  The Prince of the Quotidian by Paul Muldoon 259
  Seamus Heaney's First Anniversary 262
  The Translations of Seamus Heaney 265
  Collected Poems: Volumes One and Two by
    Ciaran Carson 273

PART FIVE: THE QUESTION OF CORK
  James Barry, 'Self-Portrait as Timanthes' 287
  'Like Maginn, A Corkagion': Bad Company for
    Daniel Maclise 291
  A Quiet Voice that Lingers On 306
  Seán Dunne: A Memory 309
  Selected Poems: Seán Ó Ríordáin 312
  Nine Bright Shiners by Theo Dorgan 317
  Quarryman: A New Generation Takes Control 321
  Gerald Y Goldberg and Cork 326
  Memoir of an Irish Jew by Lionel Cohen 331
  Preface to a Planning Document 334
  The Lonely Voice by Frank O'Connor 337

University College Cork Conferring Address 343

PART SIX: A QUESTION OF RESPONDING
Poetry and the Memory of Fame 351
Praise in Which I Live and Move and Have
  My Being by Paul Durcan 363
Collected Poems of Dennis O'Driscoll 367
Blind Man's Bluff by Aidan Higgins 373
The Last Peacock by Gerald Dawe 375
Sharp Words from Elsewhere 377
August Kleinzahler and the American World 382
Peter Fallon: Poet, Publisher, Translator, Editor 386
Sinking Ships 391
John Keats by Nicholas Roe 394
Michael D Higgins, Poet 398
A Rebel Act 402
Memoir and Celebration 406
Speckled Bird of the North 409
Desmond O'Grady and Federico Fellini 412
The Last Cold Day by Sara Berkeley/Company by
  Tom French 416

Acknowledgements 423

PART ONE
THAT IRISH QUESTION

Five Women and Three Men: 1991-2016

When I think of Ireland since 1991 I think of five women and three men, all brilliant, important, central to my thoughts, healers of my own unsettled soul. Through their work I found doors into other kinds of perception, new ways of looking at the world, and a definite view of what Irish life contains in terms of its human and literary possibilities and limitations. I see the last twenty-five years as an anthology of their works. All three men are poets, Seamus Heaney, Patrick Galvin and Paul Durcan; and three of the women of my era are also poets, Eavan Boland, Nuala Ní Dhomhnaill and Paula Meehan. But the era itself, those silver years, are bookended by two women whose genius rests in magnificent bursts of prose: Kathy Sheridan of *The Irish Times* and Martina Devlin of the *Irish Independent*. I will never forget the extraordinary reports of Kathy Sheridan as she followed Seamus Heaney to Stockholm in the mid 1990s, reporting daily in *The Irish Times*, sometimes on the front page, on the Nobel progress of our Ulster hero. In those days, in those weeks, Heaney became our Winter King, hauling the entire retinue of Irish dreamers and fantasists behind him as he turned and spoke to nations. Day after day Sheridan captured those golden, or gilded, moments with fabulous élan and an *Irish Times* thoroughness: 'On a moonlit, snowbound Stockholm evening, Seamus Heaney stepped up to the podium where Yeats, Shaw and Beckett* once stood before him. In the blue and gold splendour of the 200-year-old Swedish Academy's Great Hall he began his Nobel Lecture by recalling that as a child in rural County Derry in the 1940s he had

*In fact neither Shaw nor Beckett attended the prizegiving.

Thomas McCarthy

first encountered the word "Stockholm" on the face of the radio dial.' She reported on that Ulster formation, the vigilance and harder realism of the North, the putting down of any extravagant aspirations. The decade had opened, remember, with Heaney's influential 1991 *Seeing Things*, a collection that included 'Markings', 'Glanmore Revisited' and brief lyrical raids into the *Inferno* and the *Aeneid*: 'I pray for one look, one face-to-face meeting with my dear father / Teach me the way and open the holy doors wide.' That year of *Seeing Things* was also the year of Heaney's Oxford Professorship, with its sense of an Irish dog winning the Waterloo Cup. It was the holy door of fame that had burst wide open and all of us, whether Terry Kavanagh writing in the *Irish Independent* or Ciaran Carty writing in the *Sunday Tribune* or Eileen Battersby and Douglas Dunn writing in *The Irish Times*, all looked on in delighted amazement.

But it is Kathy Sheridan, faithful still with pen and perception, who also bookends these twenty-five years with another perfect piece of prose, an encounter with the dedicated Socialist, Joe Higgins TD. In February of 2016 she wrote in her paper: 'The venue is a suburban house on the edge of Blanchardstown village, headquarters of the Anti-Austerity Alliance's campaign to keep the vote for Ruth Coppinger, in the Dublin West constituency carved out over decades by Joe Higgins.' She describes this tireless Socialist TD at a point of retirement from the fray of elected politics, retiring like a Senator of ancient Rome to the distant sunlit vineyard where he will have time to read the documents, to indulge his love of music and the arts, an honest, still poor man for whom even the hope of modest travel is too much. Some lives are exemplary. One thinks of James Connolly or Peadar O'Donnell; and Higgins, retiring, had made the final modest gestures that will, by being lived out, set a political agenda around what an honest public life might be. The instinct to teach is as deeply felt in a good politician as in a good poet and Sheridan captures this insight in what is

Five Women and Three Men: 1991-2016

ostensibly a conventional interview for a newspaper. And out of this personal portrait, inevitably, correctly, a description is achieved of something vitally important in Irish politics — an alternative, truly dissenting viewpoint. It was difficult for Joe Higgins, as it was for others, to be Socialist during those Irish years of boom, to carve out a Socialist identity in a conservative society, a society where there is constant dismissal of any left-wing argument by 'what he calls the financial and political elite as well as the media'. Sheridan's journalism here is a crucial document, a witness document of the moment of transition when the older generation leaves the battlefield and the newly radicalized young enter. Her journalism here is part of a great feminist intellectual tradition, a tradition birthed and fostered by an august sisterhood that included June Levine, Nell McCafferty, Nuala O'Faolain, Terry Keane and Mary Kenny. O'Faolain's *Are You Somebody?* and Levine's *Sisters* are key texts of that new radicalism among women: for women to claim some public space for themselves was in itself a hugely radical act. Their books should be read by every young Irishman; they are as radically different from the dominant discourse of the South as, say, the Ulster Protestant literary memoirs, Robert Greacen's *Even Without Irene*, George Buchanan's *Green Seacoast* and Forrest Reid's *Apostate*. To read these is a radical education for any Southern reader; it is a first glance at strange materials. It is not to be sniffed at, as the earliest texts by women writers were either sniffed at or ignored. The omission of women writers from the canonical *Field Day Anthology* was the most public act of male episcopal arrogance in contemporary Irish literary criticism. But it was a timely reminder of how things really stood. The Field Day lark did a huge public service to intelligence by coming out into the open with egg all over its face; it was the literary equivalent to those TV 'specials' we have to suffer where withered old rock stars and poets seem to be surrounded by females who are clearly younger than their granddaughters.

Thomas McCarthy

What are they doing? For God's sake, where are their wives, their sisters? The fact is this is male power at work, delivering visual fantasies of youth and in precisely the way Nuala O'Faolain describes it in *Are You Somebody?*

There is a very real and distinctive thing, a vital, life-affirming experience, called friendship between women. It is unlike anything else and it never involves men. In the last twenty-five years I feel blessed to have seen the fruits of these friendships. Working in the Public Library Service for all of these years I witnessed at first hand the empowering spark of creativity in such deep friendships between creative women: time after time I have watched such literary friendships grow at the Lending Desk, friendships as rich as that of Elizabeth Bowen and Molly Keane, or Vera Brittain and Winifred Holtby. It was in such friendships, such radicalizing power, that Eavan Boland could continue the work of *In Her Own Image*, could extend her enriched consciousness, into three of the key poetry books of the 1990s, *Outside History, In a Time of Violence* and *The Lost Land*. Boland was more than capable of writing for herself and, in an era still dominated by maleness, her complex explanations of her female self became an important literary narrative for at least two generations of women writers. As we know from Irish history (the Irish poets in Corkery's *Hidden Ireland*, the fearsome ballad-writing of Young Irelanders) excluded groups will eventually create a counter-narrative where they may raise their voices. This is precisely what happened in women's writing in the last twenty-five years, and Boland's poetry and essay making mapped a new territory that had lain outside the Yeatsian core narrative, that male Pale, like an Irish town at the edge of an English or New England city. In all these years Boland has meant what she said and has written what she meant. It has taken us a long time to register the weight of these female voices, as crucial in literature as in politics. One of the further developments of this growing power will be, I hope, an entire generation of female editors who will be given the task of

Five Women and Three Men: 1991-2016

editing not more anthologies of women's poetry, but the future Faber Books and Penguin Anthologies of Irish Poetry. I look forward to this and I expect it to happen: 'My gifts / are nightly, / shifty, bookish' as Boland wrote in 1980 or, as she explained more fully in 1998: 'This is what language is: / a habitual grief . . .'

Then again, walking to work in Cork in the 1990s, through wet streets and narrow lanes or, even, in lucky moments of bright sunshine, at the Number 6 bus stop on South Mall I would sometimes bump into him, that towering poetic presence among Cork poets, Patrick Galvin. There he is, carrying a bunch of mixed flowers from Roches Stores for Mary, holding a glass of red wine at a reading, fidgeting impatiently at his pack of twenty Major, smiling on with a wry, dramatist's eye, a poet of pure instinct and music. The poet Gregory O'Donoghue would shift his willowy frame to offer a seat, the poet Gerry Murphy would think of something provocative to set the older poet laughing, a serious young arts administrator would hover anxiously as if something might go wrong, as if something might explode. But the explosions were on the page and on the stage of Galvin's belovèd Lyric Theatre of Belfast. Galvin was a poet of the old school, a kind of Southern John Hewitt, left-wing, internationalist, a believer in communities of poetry rather than the individual poet, believing always that good work would come from any assembly of radicals. Galvin always wanted assemblies of poets to be battalions of working men rather than trade associations of small-shopkeepers. His voice, his self-assurance, his London-Irish accent, his humour and mischief, there was nothing like that combination in any other poet: Galvin was unique. Our poet-Professor at UCC, Seán Lucy, would stand to attention and recite, in the perfect Received Pronunciation of a British army officer:

In Patrick Street
In Grattan Street

Thomas McCarthy

> In Ireland Rising Liberty Street
> The Kings are out.
>
> Along the Mall
> The Union Quay
> In every street along the Lee
> The Kings are out.

There was something timeless, out of this world, poetic, Andalusian, about Galvin, an atmosphere that he knew he had. His was not a cerebral poetry but an emotion that explained itself by working outward from a feeling about being in the world, a pure, confident, emotional poetry. He developed this persona further in wonderful articles, 'Rainbows in Evergreen', his weekly column in *The Cork Examiner*. His audience was enraptured. Strangers would find his work in *Cyphers* or *The Tablet*, his two faithful publishing friends. But for us, the truly blessed, we had the company of the man who wrote *Christ in London, Song for a Poor Boy* and *Folk Tales for the General*. If there was goodness in the air in Irish poetry of the last twenty-five years it hovered very close to Patrick Galvin; you only had to stand beside him to feel an effect called poetry. I feel his absence terribly, a kind of narrowing of the air. His life is a reminder that we shouldn't worry too much about creating 'space' for a writer; a writer asserts and claims his or her own territory, a stake is driven into solid ground that wasn't even visible before the poet arrived. Chill, don't worry about it, Patrick Galvin might say to a worried young poet, you can always take in washing for a living.

I first met Nuala Ní Dhomhnaill on the day that her first book, *An Dealg Droighin*, was published. That must have been in the foyer of the Listowel Arms Hotel in 1981, the year before Caitlín Maude died. Our conversation was about those multi-talented poets, Maude and Hartnett, Maude's pure, clear voice and Hartnett's attempts at acting on stage. I think we spoke about Maude's voice in her Gael Linn recording of 'Dónall Óg', a haunting track, and of Maude's insistent voice in the poem 'Aimhréidh'. At the time an atmosphere of everyone in the Irish world being in love with Caitlín Maude was still very strong. Ní Dhomhnaill herself had just emerged from the drenching surf of exile and family estrangement. Her power was technically and spiritually immense. Her poetry in the following two decades would soar above every other talent of the Gael, transforming her into an Irish Akhmatova with collections like *The Astrakhan Cloak* and *Pharaoh's Daughter*. In the mid 1990s I stood before a class of Seniors at Macalester College, Minnesota, wealthy children of the lakes and prairies, a class of mainly Lutherans, Episcopalians and Quakers with hardly a drop of Irish blood in them, and read 'Féar Suaithinseach' and 'Ceist na Teangan' with their Heaney and Muldoon translations. The students were enthralled by the work, the strange demands of a poetry and a culture that was registering with them for the first time. It was difficult to move on to another text because the questions kept coming, the duality of the poet's existence in Irish and in translation, the Muse-object suddenly become sexually independent, the idea that a consecration of terrible experience could be embodied in an Irish Catholic Communion wafer or that all one's hope could be placed in a little boat of language: such things thrilled them and made them wonder whether all poems are, in effect, an act of translation. In the true spiritual sense of that word an act of transubstantiation had occurred in the lived experience of a female Irish poet.

It is a truism that we can be sure a new talent is abroad when something settled is disturbed and when areas of experience that have been locked are picked open. Ní Dhomhnaill's work, following the iconoclastic energy of the Cork *Innti* crowd, unsettled a language culture that was becoming too deliberate, too programmatic, too sanctioned. But her real genius lies in her ability to archaeologically and forensically (she is, after all, the daughter of medical doctors) examine hidden areas of sexuality. The human body is her isle of folklore, the poems are the stories her body has told her; her technical instruments are both *dinnseanchas* and Jung. Hers is certainly a Jungian *dinnseanchas*. As Denise Levertov once wrote, speaking of Ginsberg and Creeley, 'it's one's own body, the primal, the instinctive, and the intuitive basics one started with, that is being spoken of.' Ní Dhomhnaill has never ceased to be amazing in all of the last thirty years and I can't imagine a definition of those years in her absence.

Another poet of this era whose rise parallels that of Ní Dhomhnaill is Paul Durcan, a poet of Dublin and Mayo who also spent a number of de-formative rather than formative years in Cork before he re-collected himself poetically back in Dublin. He had supplemented and later succeeded Patrick Galvin with a regular column in *The Cork Examiner*. Durcan's *The Berlin Wall Café* and *Going Home to Russia* are two of the most important collections by an Irish poet in the post-War era. Despite what the idle may think Durcan is the most unfairly neglected poet of modern Ireland. His voice is distinctive, his genius beyond dispute, his social themes distinctly Irish and utterly crucial, yet one finds very little detailed analysis of his work or his context. His dramatic public readings, marvellous performances in themselves, may have actually worked against his reputation among scholars while simultaneously electrifying audiences: scholars don't readily forgive a public success. It is difficult to describe the effect of those two earlier books; they are lyrical, tightly structured, vectored against the hostile world, explosive emotionally and heartrending. They are a kind of crucifixion in verse or, at least, a long stay at Calvary, the log books of an escape from Golgotha, from the place where love was found and lost again. In Durcan the homestead of love and attachment is set ablaze and a life of wandering begins, a life that continues to produce collections of tremendous power like

Five Women and Three Men: 1991-2016

Cries of an Irish Caveman and *Praise In Which I Live and Move and Have My Being*. In the latter work, published in 2012, Durcan writes in 'The Annual January Nervous Breakdown':

> *Why do Christmas and the Epiphany*
> *Always end in tears — in such bile-black, bilges-beige,*
> *Canary-yellow tears?*

I first met the poet Paula Meehan, in the company of Hugh McFadden and John Borrowman, at Joyce's Tower in Sandycove on a blustery day in June 1984. The occasion was the launch of *Poetry Ireland Review* Number 10 and a set of Beaver Row books. Beaver Row, like Co-Op Books, seemed to be the future of Irish writing at the time. Little did I realize then that it wasn't to be the publisher but the poet who held the future in her young brain. Community-driven, justice-saturated, feminist and maker of perfect lyrics, Meehan was only at the beginning of a crowded busy career. In a photograph of her young self, published next day in the *Irish Press*, the poet seemed guarded and apprehensive. Two decades of writing and political action later the poet is not only unguarded, but wise and open-hearted, sanguine and deeply centred. I now find an extraordinary calm in her work, a nurturing calm that invites others in, a world created by good grandmothers, a world confirmed by the company of women. In her all the promises of Máire Mhac an tSaoi and Eavan Boland find a lyric confirmation. In *The Man Who Was Marked By Winter* (1991) she wrote:

> *Didn't I rob you of your eyes, father,*
> *and her of her smile? No dark blood*
> *but the simple need to lose an uneasy love*
> *drove me down unknown roads...*

Her journey, like Eavan Boland's, has been a process of mapping while voyaging. The early 1990s volume itself was a mapping and re-ordering gesture as it collected the best poems from her two earliest books and added others. But it is in the most recent books, in *Dharmakaya* and *Painting Rain*, that a prodigious shift from localized inner-city family memory to a travelled communal memory occurs. Here her focus becomes a Buddhist humanism, a universal anxiety captured in poems like 'On Howth Head' and 'The Following Message Will Be Deleted from Your Mailbox'. In her Zen-like poems, in page after page, it is the one tree of humankind that struggles to survive, and Meehan turns to the world from an altar of poems in communion with, and receiving transmissions from, Rinpoche's *The Tibetan Book of the Dead* or Gary Snyder's *Regarding Wave*. Earth is suddenly frail as a watercolour, and the poet is a poet become watercolourist, painting the rain black and ultramarine. This painter is a wonderful author and her words now have a Pound-like certainty. She has arrived at a point of silence, a kind of hillside shrine from where her climb continues. Each of these poets, Ní Dhomhnaill in her Jungian boat of language, Boland in her recovered country, Meehan the Zen watercolourist, Patrick Galvin the gypsy Corkman saturated with *duende*, Durcan tempting a father's judgement upon us all, advances the possibility of the poem by manipulating the materials available to them: each survived by constantly singing inside the capsule of the last two decades. Sometimes, when I worry too much that I left myself isolated from the swim of things by continuing a day job in a city library for too long, I recall all the books of these authors. I handled all of these lustrous materials, shelving and date-stamping and recommending. Their books remind me that we are not isolated as long as we read. Our primary community is a community of readers. We know each other through reading each other, and such reading is not a kind of polemic: it is, rather, a shared meal on the hard shoulder of a highway.

We tend to underestimate the power of great journalism,

Five Women and Three Men: 1991-2016

forgetting that Yeats and Shaw wrote for newspapers constantly and that the preoccupations of their journalism became the materials of their plays and dramatic poems. We live inside a discourse, we add to it in different ways through reading newspapers. Omagh-born Martina Devlin is now best known as a novelist, a successful one at that, with the visionary, futuristic ambition of her latest work, *About Sisterland*, creating a great stir. But it's for her golden journalism that I'm most grateful in the last two decades. Her regular columns in the years when Ireland entered deeper and deeper into crisis were a consolation to me and kept me sane. 'Day Our Bewildered Bankers Entered the Twilight Zone' was clipped from the *Indo* and pinned to my kitchen noticeboard in May 2009 and, six weeks later, her narrative of the beginnings of social collapse under austerity, 'Cuts mean that writing is on the wall for our literacy rates', was noted and added to the dreaded utility bills and threatening bank letters stuck to the same board. The state of our nation wasn't a sudden obsession with her because she'd been commenting on our divided society for years. Eleven years before the banking collapse she'd written about the dangers of national delusion: 'We're delighted with ourselves' (6 July 1998) and 'Is the Celtic Tiger Mutating into the Celtic Ostrich?' (17 November 1998); and in September 2001 she'd ominously written the column 'Wall Street Wipe-out'.

Few creative writers have been so close to the day-by-day action of society and matters of public concern. I think of Martina Devlin as a writer of the roaring twenties, a Scott Fitzgerald watching the tickertape in mounting horror and probably planning an escape into the movie business. The best journalists make a journey with you, inviting you into an almost therapeutic attachment to them, creating an agreed reality day-by-day. It is interesting, now, to go through what the young Devlin wrote, how clear-headed she was, how uncannily intelligent. I'm just glad that the Reference cataloguing staff at Cork City Libraries were aware of her too. Here in this public workplace there are more than eighty catalogued references to her journalism, including the ominous library File 72A, with her article of 12 October, 2013: 'Bank Guarantee — A Night of Drama'. The fact is: Ireland 1991-2016, you couldn't make it up. In the end, and for the sake of the people, Ireland must continue to be a task for great journalists as well as a source for poetry.

Beyond the Centre: Writers in their own Words,
An Irish Writers' Centre Anthology,
2016

Poets, The Ireland They Dreamt Of

More than 17% of people born in Ireland now live abroad. Ireland has exported a greater proportion of its young people than any other country in Europe. We have just suffered an invisible lower middle-class mass migration, the quietest excision in our history, as quiet as the disappearance of quarter of a million Ulster Presbyterians in the decade after Catholic Emancipation and the hegemony of O'Connell's Repeal Movement in 1829. At this moment in history around one and a half million Irish citizens live on welfare; another million earn less than €20,000 a year. But around 100,000 people earn between €125,000 and €200,000 a year. They are the salaried elite, 'the seriously comfortable' in 2016, as my poor mother might euphemistically say. This elite of 100,000 take home more than ten times what half the nation's population take home — and probably more, because elites tend to inter-marry. They are the objects of every populist envy. In truth, while 17% of us went away, that 100,000 are the ones who have inherited our patriotic dream called 'Ireland' — our country exists for their intense benefit and through this poetic construct called 'Ireland' their children will be the true beneficiaries of the Easter Rising. That is a simple, social fact. To prosper undisturbed has been the dream of every Irish father and mother. Easter 1916 was a poets' Rising, certainly, but the upper middle-class always inherit the earth, whether that Irish earth is in Dublin, Cork, Limerick or Galway. It doesn't matter that poets dreamed of this new country, it was always the significant owners of land and property who would inherit it.

Though we may have emerged from the land the whole

future of Ireland lies in its cities; there is no getting away from this. The entire population of the world, from China to the West of Ireland, is moving into cities. The romance of the countryside, a 1960s' fantasy, is dead and it's important for poets as well as political scientists to acknowledge this. Those working in climate science already know this truth. But some victory more general in Ireland, a sense of achievement felt more widely in society, was surely intended by our 1916 Proclamation: 'The Republic guarantees religious and civil liberty, equal rights and equal opportunities to all its citizens, and declares its resolve to pursue the happiness and prosperity of the whole nation and of all its parts, cherishing all the children of the nation equally ... '

Like James Connolly I love plain facts as well as the sound of them. They are a marvellous antidote to abstract fanaticism. Facts, like literature itself, can never be subordinated to politics, but in a country like Ireland we love a fanatical diversion: think Blueshirts, Clann na Talmhan, Farmers' Freedom Force, League of Decency etc. Poetry is grand but, for the poor, bread is more essential: bread, housing and winter heat. If only we could write a set of poems that might cover the homeless with a roof, poems that build social housing, poems that reimagine our National Assets Management Agency and turn it back into a Congested Districts Board, a Board that built cottages, canals and island quaysides before it mutated into a mere Land Commission after our independence. Our 1916 revolutionaries were poets, certainly. The Ireland they dreamt of was noble, democratic, socially inclusive and more or less Gaelic. Almost immediately the latter dream would cause fierce ructions in the body politic. There was that small matter of one and a half million persons who were followers of kirk and Covenant in Ulster, persons who had devoured Michael McCarthy's scarifying *Priests and People in Ireland* in the years between 1902 and 1912 — the first two editions of McCarthy's prosecution case against Catholic power sold out within a fortnight. The signed Covenant

Poets, The Ireland They Dreamt Of

declared, 'Being convinced in our consciences that Home Rule would be disastrous to the material well-being of Ulster as well as of the whole of Ireland, subversive of our civil and religious freedom, destructive of our citizenship and perilous to the unity of the Empire, we, whose names are underwritten, men of Ulster, loyal subjects of His Gracious Majesty King George V humbly relying on the God whom our fathers in days of stress and trial confidently trusted, do hereby pledge ourselves in solemn Covenant, throughout this our time of threatened calamity . . . ' James Connolly must have known these anxieties. Did he think that a full-scale Socialist revolution would overcome, or cover over, real sectarian divisions? He must have thought so; the others, being poets dedicated to a charmed national programme, couldn't have cared less. I'm just guessing about this but I've never seen any evidence to disabuse me. Connolly had had his own problems with Catholic power, sparring in print with several priestly counter-revolutionaries. But the poets, being in love in various demented ways, were already a kind of priesthood; in the way the dead Rupert Brooke was the leader of a new British priesthood of sacrifice and patriotism:

> *If I should die, think only this of me:*
> *That there's some corner of a foreign field*
> *That is forever England. There shall be*
> *In that rich earth a richer dust concealed . . .*

The hundreds upon hundreds of literary idealists who marched to their slaughter in the Somme trenches must have had those lines in their hearts — as surely as Irish patriots, facing firing squad or damp misery in Frongoch or on Beara Island, must have had the words of Pádraig Pearse's 'The Mother' on their lips:

> *I do not grudge them: Lord, I do not grudge*
> *My two strong sons that I have seen go out*

27

Thomas McCarthy

> *To break their strength and die, they and a few,*
> *In bloody protest for a glorious thing,*
> *They shall be spoken of among their people,*
> *The generations shall remember them . . .*

There was, therefore, our Irish war, a private matter — or, at least, something that only mattered to us — and there was a huge war on elsewhere that would fatten the capitalists of Manchester and Catalunya, that would drag as many poets as 1916 into its cruel industrial vortex — by the end of that war, the Great War, many poets would also be dead, Wilfred Owen, Tom Kettle, Rupert Brooke, Francis Ledwidge and Philip Little. Many other writers would never really recover, Patrick McGill and Siegfried Sassoon, Robert Graves and Robert Gibbings. If there's anything that distinguishes the first two decades of the twentieth century it must be this wholesale slaughter of good poets. No wonder people went mad in the 1920s; no wonder men took to Fascism and women took to hard liquor. This gloom that was to come is described uncannily by Osbert Sitwell in his brilliant memoir, *Great Morning*:

> *'Something else that might have been an indication, I recall. Nearly all the brother-officers of my age had been, two or three months earlier in the year, to see a celebrated palmist of the period whom, I remember, it was said, with what justification I am not aware, that Mr Winston Churchill used sometimes to consult. My friends, of course, used to visit her in the hope of being told that their love affairs would prosper, when they would marry, or the direction in which their later careers would develop. In each instance, it appeared, the clairvoyant had just begun to read their fortunes, when, in sudden bewilderment, she had thrown the outstretched hand from her, crying "I don't understand it! It's the same thing again! After*

two or three months the line of life stops short, and I can read nothing". To each individual to whom it was said, this seemed merely an excuse she had improvised for her failure: but when I was told by four or five persons of the same experience, I wondered what it could portend . . . '

By the end of that first year all of Sitwell's companions were dead, slaughtered in the most useless of useless wars ever fought on earth. Commentators often complain about the appalling blood-sacrifice cult of Irish Nationalists in 1916, but I think in the history of mankind the bloodlust of upper-class England and Germany between 1914 and 1918 is incomparable in its wickedness. It is something from which the human spirit has never recovered. Compared to the dead of Europe our Easter Rebellion was but a minor skirmish. But not for us. All revolutions are a form of definition and the 1916 Rising offered a definition of independent Irishness that was accepted by the Irish electorate in several General Elections between 1918 and 1924. Another electorate also developed elsewhere under the jurisdiction of Stormont. Two kinds of public realm, two sets of tax payers, two arrangements of public and cultural life, now governed our one island, whether we liked it or not.

So, they began to make a poetry like Ireland, led by Austin Clarke and Robert Farren, because they thought a deeper Ireland was inside that poetry. This literature soon found its dissenters from the embarrassing narrowness in Joyce, Beckett and Thomas McCreevy. Over the border a new life, for which we never felt imaginatively responsible, was also forming. It's important to remember, to credit, that for our national culture, being truly faithful to the insights contained in the 1916 Rebellion, we chose the narrower path. The marvellous campaigns against this new narrowness by W B Yeats are wonderfully documented by Roy Foster in his masterpiece *The Arch Poet*, Volume II of his Yeats biography.

Thomas McCarthy

Yeats's terrific career in the Senate, a useful, practical political life that included contributions on Education, Culture, Coinage, Censorship and Divorce, remains for all of us poets an exemplary life. His later, cranky flirtation with Fascism should not blind us to the liberalism and tolerance of his years in the Senate. He accepted the Ireland that the forces of nationalism had delivered to its people; he would do everything in his power to enrich the public realm for which he was responsible. He worked doggedly for Ireland. He wore himself out and probably shortened his life in the service of his nation.

So that when I think of 1916, that Rebellion of the Poets, I think not of Pearse and Plunkett whose work was over quickly, but of poets like Yeats who carried the prodigious optimism of nation building forward into the public realm. The ones who carried on, the idealists turned editors and agitators like Seán Ó Faoláin or Peadar O'Donnell, these are my heroes who worked in the long shadow cast by fallen heroes. To live for Ireland is the very best thing, to live long enough to pay taxes; to live long enough to see a proper distribution of wealth, a levelling of life chances across the broad spectrum of society. To die is too easy. Once there were over half a million landless farm labourers, trapped and humiliated or patronized in their native parishes. As a poet it is the children of the one and a half million Irish living on welfare that I think about today. When art and poetry reaches them in their Council terraces and labourers' cottages then the promises of 1916 will be complete.

1916-2016: An Anthology of Reactions,
Limerick Writers' Centre,
2016

A 1916 Foreword

When Cork City Libraries and the city's Arts Office asked four writers of distinction to respond to the 1916 Proclamation they can't have imagined the brilliance and variety of the responses found here. These reports from four personal realms, of Hugo Hamilton, Leanne O'Sullivan, Theo Dorgan and Doireann Ní Ghríofa, are as varied as one could ever have imagined and yet as precisely personal as one could only have dreamed. The Republic that followed the 1916 Proclamation and Rising was not a friend of the literary imagination; even writers who had proven their patriotism, Seán Ó Faoláin, Frank O'Connor and Liam O'Flaherty, for example, saw their books banned and their cosmopolitanism stifled. Joyce's bitter words, forged in exile, that Ireland was the sow that eats her farrow, still seems apt and fully justified. When Sir John Keane rose in the Seanad and called the Censorship Board a 'moral Gestapo' he was echoing the feelings of an entire generation of poets and artists. Yet our Republic has had its successes — it would be dishonest to deny the internal politics of Ireland completely. There have been good men and women who gave everything to Ireland, who carried the land safely through a World War and who had to deal with undercapitalized native industry as well as the loss of over half a million farm-labouring jobs as agriculture became mechanized. But emigration, social inequality, inadequate housing provision, and the long baleful authority of one particular Church hierarchy, all seemed beyond improvement or control. Writers like the writers here do continue to scrutinize the fruits of freedom and the persistence of social crisis in our Republic.

Reflections towards a solution continue, and creative

writers are an important repository of such reflections. Here Hamilton's intimate yet cosmopolitan day in the life of Dublin, Dorgan's characteristic, searing political analysis, O'Sullivan's backward flip into a cave of Beara habitation, Ní Ghríofa's yellow bittern-poetic gymnastics, all cohere into the widest possible contemporary response to the matter of a Republic.

Hugo Hamilton brings us on a wonderful journey, so characteristic of his personal manner, so quietly stylish, where we see the conscious and unconscious inheritors of the Republic promised by our 1916 Proclamation. On an April day, one hundred years after the Rebellion, he meets a German journalist, Susanne Kippenberger, and they walk together in the rain through streets that are now inadequate for the prodigious footfall of a booming European capital city. He thinks of a self-portrait by Susanne's brother, a sad modern portrait, a work full of the sadness of dislocation, of a post-War Germany where many may never reach home, where home may never be more than a memory. Such a work of art resonates with Hamilton, it reminds him of his own nationally mixed origins. Ironically, these two rain-drenched walkers pass the windows of a German-owned shop that's displaying photographs of the 1916 leaders. They carry on down to Moore Street where Pearse surrendered, a surrender that was decided upon in order to avoid the further slaughter of innocent civilians. While they stand under the Dealz archway he thinks of the meaning of this Revolution in 1916, of the sense of betrayal that was felt among the thousands of Irish serving in the Somme trenches, of the madness of the quick military executions that swung public opinion and altered the course of history. Hamilton, as always, has his ear to the ground and his eye on what's contemporary — he notices the Money Transfer services, offering simple connections with Lagos, Entebbe and Manila. This is a reminder that we now share the hallowed space of Dublin and Ireland with non-nationals, with persons who have emerged from entirely different historic traumas

A 1916 Foreword

to share their lives with us: to make a home. 'So much has changed,' he writes, 'and so has our way of gazing back at the past — it takes a hundred years to understand what happened a hundred years ago.'

In Moore Street Hamilton finds a perfect example of old and new Irish communities, all inheritors of our Republic, all working in a new spirit of live and let live. He discovers that the old established fruit sellers of Moore Street continue to sell their apples and oranges and yellow bananas, while the new community fruit sellers handle only the exotic fruits — and green bananas. Thus, a very real kind of courteous non-interference is at play commercially, a communal harmony, a true Republican spirit. This happy commercial situation becomes, for Hugo Hamilton, a metaphor that contains within it the seeds of national salvation, the sense of 'home' becomes really powerful because it is a new kind of Irish home that natives and immigrants now create together. He goes on to describe the great debates about the past in Germany in the 1970s, a profound, very public encounter that became known as *Historikerstreit* — the clash of historians. He sees in this German debate lessons for Ireland, lessons on how to guide people through historical denial and come to an acceptance of the past or, at least, a proper settlement of the past within the present so that a country can go on and develop a truly contemporary life. Hamilton's writing here is beautiful, considered, humanist. His essay is a treasure.

Leanne O'Sullivan creates a uniquely different encounter with the materials of the Irish past. Her world is the world of the Beara Peninsula, that place of final refuge, the stomping ground of Fenians and the impregnable fortress of Irish resistance where the vast ocean offered the final escape route for patriots. The poet tells us how she would question her own mother on the exploits of the IRB and the Easter Rising, only to be met with a wall of silence. Her mother's silence made her wonder if there was a twofold caution at work — a fear of saying too much, but also an unspoken reverence for the great traumas of the past. There was, and is, in Beara a great respect for invisible worlds. After all it is a landscape of no less than two-hundred-and-eighty-four circular forts, fifteen wedge tombs and twenty-four habitation caves:

> '*A place becomes muscular when we give it dramatic purchase, recreate it through matter and memory. In fact, it tells us more about our present selves, our imaginations, and how we think about our origins and our ends. The mythologies we build around our fears and identities endure in the landscape and weather the test of superstition.*'

And the poet reminds us here that 'it's a matter of minding your own business and whatever spirit is in the place will do the same.' O'Sullivan writes passionately and openly, in poetry and prose, knowing full well the effects of that mythical twilight zone of Irish being. Life in the Beara Peninsula is a mixture of topography and family story, of real landscape such as the Hag of Beara rock and silenced, unreachable habitation caves. If these caves could tell their story it would be terrible, telling us of the Tudor clearances through burning, murder and exile, a narrative captured by the colonist Edmund Spenser in his *View of the Present State of Ireland*, a view that so reeks of anti-Irish racism that it cannot be treated with a grain of respect, yet it contributed to a key colonial attitude to the 'mere' Irish. It was attitudes such as Spenser's and competing truths known by the makers of Beara myth that set alight a deadly fight for possession of land and facts, a fight for definition that would end in flames in 1916. A poet like O'Sullivan, a female poet and thus placed outside history (as Eavan Boland has written) can only leap backwards into the dark cave of the Irish past, and this has been Leanne O'Sullivan's method in dealing with the atavistic materials of our Irish history. 'Fair? Don't talk to me about fair. / When I came to the river in spate / I could only carry one of

A 1916 Foreword

my two / companions across it with me,' she writes in 'The Cailleach to the Widow'. In writing like this she has combined both a repossessive instinct for myth-making and a humane, social consciousness. The truth of the Proclamation for her lies somewhere in that space created by a silent mother and a mother's myth-creating daughter. The past lies beneath everything, to be discovered like this:

*A penny dropped
a hundred years ago
turns up beneath
our sweetheart cabbage.*
                              ('Heirloom')

Those who have followed the work of Theo Dorgan over the past decades, this poet of voyages and praxis, this poet of public service and high aestheticism, will know what to expect in terms of commitment and definition when it comes to the matter of Ireland. His Ireland is a clearly and completely defined republic, a place worthy of James Connolly. He begins his own response by tackling the contests of definition that have plagued Republican life in Ireland:

'*As is all too common in Irish politics there are absurdities at work here: the actually existing but formally unclaimed Republic is at odds with the theological Republic-to-be-established. We have a Republic that decries 'Republicans', and 'Republicans' who disdain and grant only a partial legitimacy to the Republic most of us think we live in.*'

Dorgan goes on to outline the sad neglect, the public avoidance of any definitions of the Republic, by the intellectual and administrative elites in Ireland. When he published a major collection of essays on a possible future Republic-defining constitution he was met with a wall of silence; only

Thomas McCarthy

SIPTU's paper reviewed the work. He surmises, correctly, that the powers-that-be in our Republic avoid the embarrassment of such defining efforts. He goes on to recall that the Democratic Programme of the first Dáil had been drawn up by Thomas Johnson and William O'Brien, with the participation of Cathal O'Shannon. Ironically, it was that great advocate of later massive Public Housing programmes, Seán T O'Kelly, who toned down the more Socialist elements in this programme. The radicalism implicit in the words of the 1916 Proclamation could not survive the proprietorial Nationalist cadres who have always been the bulwark of Irish separatism. Any tendency towards Bolshevism within the Irish political family in 1916-1923 needed to be eradicated, or at least rendered neutral.

Dorgan, first and foremost a Socialist poet since early youth, tries to bridge that gap between 1916 radicalism and the comfortable bourgeois laissez-faire of current Irish politics. He has always tried to bridge this gap by an honest effort of theorizing, theory and policy expression being the only options open to a democratic Socialist operating upon the *res publica*, the matters public. Dorgan has worked tirelessly to add value and depth to our political discourse; his brilliant effort here is yet another example of heavy lifting on behalf of the nation. 'In our stalled republic,' he writes, 'the political class has continued in the habit of pretending they mean certain things while we, the electorate, happily pretend to believe them. This corrosive ambiguity, on both sides, from the very start laid the foundations for the emergence of a disdainful state-management class of professional politicians and senior civil servants, and at the same time for mass defection from political responsibility on the part of a citizenry reduced to a rubber stamp electorate.' All of which defies the programme implicit in the words of the Proclamation, 'to pursue the happiness and prosperity of the whole nation and of all its parts, cherishing all the children of the nation equally'. Dorgan's historical sweep, his understanding

A 1916 Foreword

of 1916 combined with his ability to detect the cumulative effect of national hypocrisy, makes his essay an important witness document.

The couplets of Doireann Ní Ghríofa call us back into an intensely personal response to what was proclaimed in 1916: 'Its capitals call still, to IRISHMEN AND IRISHWOMEN / in mismatched fonts, just as it did in its beginning.' The frail paper upon which the words of Connolly and Pearse are printed become, for the poet Ní Ghríofa, a metaphor for all humble origins. Humble origins when they cohere become a powerful new force; this is one of the first messages contained in her lyrical response. In 'For Our Sisters, Another Proclamation' Ní Ghríofa freeze-dries the Proclamation, sparing only the inky parts that cohere into a gender-relevant witness document; what is essential survives in her postmodern text. The code words contained in Witness Statement 94 of the Bureau of Military History, the statement of young Mary McLoughlin, that strange 'Béalrún,' was the final instruction she received from Thomas MacDonagh:

> *It was only four syllables — Yellow Bittern —*
> *the title of a poem he had translated*
>
> *based on the poem An Bonnán Buí. These, the last words*
> *chosen by MacDonagh to send to his friend*
> *as their battle drew to its end: a bird that died of thirst,*
> *its body left stretched on a frozen lake.*

Her work here is a marvellous response to the meaning of MacDonagh's encoded message. Her linguistic playfulness (she is a poet in both Irish and English) combined with an instinctive feminism creates a unique document. Hers is a fabulous response made uniquely useful by the intervention of a woman's voice from that day of Irish surrender and definition. What is personal seems vulnerable when placed against the juggernaut of history and peer-reviewed historical commentary, but Ní Ghríofa sees history not as a sounding board for the declared Republic but as a sounding board for the heart of Mary McLoughlin. The work in its entirety becomes the most intense artistic response possible. It is a triumph of the human over the historical; it believes in anecdote rather than theory. In the end what is good for a Republic is not a metaphysical question, but a personal one.

These essays with their four distinct yet fully developed personal voices are a tribute not just to a theory of our Republic, but to the endurance of the human spirit. They are four blessings upon the heart of our enduring nation.

Cork City Libraries,
September 2016

Celtic Tiger, Irish Climate

Here, in the late spring of 1997, we begin the long happy slide toward summer and the annual ritual of celebrating ourselves with workshops and summer schools. This year we feel lucky to have made it out of the winter. February was a cruel month, breeding storm after storm out of the far from dead Atlantic. Cork City in the South has borne the brunt of these storms. My neighbours in Montenotte, a hilly eighteenth-century suburb, emerged each February morning with a mixture of fear and relief on their dear faces, picking their way through shattered slates, dislodged dustbins, expired shrubs and choked storm drains. The citizens in the 'flat of the city' had an easier winter, apart from a few days of Lee floodwater. Despite the weeks of beautiful sunshine in April I think of this as one of the stormiest winters of my twenty-six-year sojourn in Cork. Winter has served to remind me, yet again, that rain is a weak metaphor for the Irish experience. Rain is too soft. In the past two decades our Irish character has moved from one of soft rain to one of hard weather. We live in an island now that is well rigged for heavy cruising. Whatever about the political future the weather will be worse.

Yet, like the weather, we have changed. I am old enough to remember an Ireland of the late 1950s. I remember the smells of the houses — especially the labourers' houses of Twig Bog Lane and the Barrack Street terrace of houses that was owned by the convent. I was five years old in 1959, throwing sods of wet turf over the half door of an old woman's house in Twig Bog and letting my older brother, Michael, take the blame. The distinctive smell of clothes that were worn and worn and never washed, because the young wearer had no spare set of clothes, the heavy smell of stale tobacco mingled with the distant whiff of dry toilets: the small town of my childhood had hardly changed since the Great War. In fact it had not substantially changed since the Great Famine of 1847. Irish Catholic society had stood still. A kind of vapour of indolence hung over the smaller shops, the kind of indolence that has been captured so well in books like *The Valley of the Squinting Windows* or *The Country Girls* or even in Cork City novels like *The Threshold of Quiet* and *Bird Alone*. Sociology never quite captures what Ireland was like: to know that Ireland you have to use the more precise sciences of fiction and poetry.

It is now seventeen years since many of us attended the Sense of Ireland festival in London. I notice that some arts organization in the South is organizing A Sense of Cork week this summer. We do have a tendency to cling to old labels. How reassuring they are. One might have hoped, though, that after seventeen years a new kind of expression, a new concept, would have been found. Maybe we don't want new labels in Ireland because we fear that offering of a new experience. If we go for a new form of words the Celtic Tiger might devour us! And so we recycle what's familiar, hoping thereby to recapture the excitement of an old feeling. How long will the 'Celtic Tiger' label survive, I wonder? At any moment I expect someone on the radio to announce that a Sense of the Celtic Tiger festival has been organized for Prague or Paris, Boise or Boston. We are that shameless. But let me get back to London, in 1980, and to that row of labourers' cottages in Cappoquin in 1959. After I read poems at the Poetry Society there was a reception at the Irish Club. I was soon buttonholed by a middle-aged man carrying a pint of Guinness. 'Yoosir, so you're the Capperken pote,' he said, very annoyed. He had an interesting accent, half-Waterford, half-Kilburn, like so many of my relatives. 'Tell may, do da fokine nuns and the fokine Major still run de town a Capperken, do dey?' It was more than a question. An

Celtic Tiger, Irish Climate

educated person might call it 'rhetorical'. On that night in 1980 I was conscious only that the man was pure blind drunk. I really dislike drunks. I've cleaned up after drunks, both in my childhood and in my student days. But I could see rage in the question. It registered with me. It was an essay in sociology.

That man was an exile from my home town, one of the hundreds of thousands who fled the sinking ship of Éire in the post-War years. The Celtic world he knew was a dead cow rather than a wild tiger. The Cappoquin he fled was depressed, poor and congested since the mid-nineteenth century, or at least the poor man's part of it was. The 'nuns and the Major' when spoken in the same sentence was a hate euphemism for the town's two dominant presences — the Convent of Mercy and Cappoquin House, the home of the Keane baronets. At that moment in the Irish Club in London I could feel the force of these two different Irelands. Here was just one schism in our cultural consciousness. In terms of class origins that exile and I were as brothers — absolutely one being. But something had happened in less than a generation to cause us to remember Cappoquin in utterly different ways. What had happened was that first Celtic surge, Ireland of the 60s with its better social welfare system and its free education. I didn't have to leave Cappoquin Station as a teenager like my cousin John who left for Coventry in 1963. I was able to spend five years in the local convent secondary school, St Anne's High School as it was grandly called, among teaching nuns whom I absolutely adored, and who adored me in return. And then, on to university, a rare treat for a working-class boy. The drunk man who had stood over me so unsteadily in the Irish Club had never had a chance to look twice at his own native land. At the age of twenty-six in 1980 I had already had a first, a second, and even a third look at Cappoquin and my native country.

In a way, for someone born poor in Ireland, even from a warm Fianna Fáil neighbourhood, a university education was as spiritual and as useful as a long prison sentence: university gave me some 'time out' to think about myself and my background. University College Cork in the 70s was a revisionist paradise in more ways than one. Many of my College friends were following Conor Cruise O'Brien into the Labour Party. I didn't quite 'go over' to the side of the thinking middle class, but poems I wrote then — 'State Funeral,' 'Last Days in the Party' — show a sufficient distance from Fianna Fáil national thought as to be almost 70s Labour lyrics.

I see these lyrics now as efforts to impress the imaginary keeper at the prison gate. There was no prison. There was no keeper. But the belief that there were forces arrayed against me was a powerful kind of belief. It is the kind of belief that makes 40% of the Irish population vote for Fianna Fáil, the party of origins, rather than for the Labour Party, the party of policies. I am interested in those voices of origins: irrational, atavistic, overwhelming. And for that reason I listened to my Cappoquin exile. He wasn't interested in my poem about Micheál Mac Liammóir at Cappoquin, or in the fact that James Joyce had namechecked Cappoquin as the home town of Molly Bloom's lover at Gibraltar. What my Irish exile wanted to hear was a litany of the names he hated so that he could expectorate his sense of betrayal and grind it into the floor of the Irish Club. I failed him as I failed all the angry fathers in my life. But I cannot forget him. The pain of exile must be worse than the frustrations of living in the Irish Republic. The success of the Irish economy today comes from the voluntary self-exile of surplus labourers over a long period — and not just labourers, but doctors, technicians, even educated children from — God forbid! — respectable families.

So, when I hear the expression 'Celtic Tiger' I don't reach for my revolver. I reach for my handkerchief. I weep. I weep at the birth of yet another neat cliché of Irishness that will prevent outsiders from knowing us. Like the United States or Canada Ireland is a tentative compromise of interests. The

Celtic Tiger, Irish Climate

welfare state that educated me is slowly being withdrawn from working-class terraces. The tax codes are revised so that the rich can keep more of their money, while welfare legislation becomes more complex and difficult to understand. It is not yet a sin to have no job, but we are getting there. Privatization is on the agenda. The social capital of mighty companies like Bus Éireann or Bord na Móna has been removed from the balance sheet. In a marvellous twist the Dáil has just ceded authority for its citizens' wellbeing to the European Commission, having just recently wrenched such authority from the clutches of the Catholic hierarchy. Perhaps we never wanted national independence in the first place. Perhaps that is the nub of our nature, and this has driven our national and international policy for two decades.

And, now, today a surprise phone call. My brother, Michael, wants me to come back to my native town for a committee meeting. This will be a meeting to discuss the editing and publication of a book to mark the millennium in Cappoquin — such a book, therefore, to haul together all the strands of Cappoquin memory. Is such a book possible? I mean, is it possible to publish a non-fiction book that would say everything about the past of an Irish parish? My brother tells me that the meeting will be attended by all those who write things down, the parish priest, a highly educated man, and the school teachers, those scriveners of every Irish townland, as well as Cappoquin's most famous son, the intellectual Dr Michael Olden, now a parish priest of the diocese, but formerly a president of Maynooth. Absent will be that drunk man of the Irish Club, a Plenipotentiary of the Exiled who left nothing behind him in Ireland but a society that oppressed him and an economy without promise. Should poets represent him? Should we light a candle in the committee room? Or should the memory of the *spailpín fánach*, of the wandering Irish labourer — like the memory of the millworkers of New Hampshire or the fishermen of Minnesota's north shore — be allowed to run its course and die of irrelevance? So, we return to the vital questions of remembrance and the 'Celtic Tiger'. Has an excess of memory weakened us? Should we open the umbrella of a new electronics factory between us and our discomforting past? Isn't this what we have hoped for and planned for with astonishing confidence?

The question has rarely been asked: to whose advantage have we revised our past? Who has this weakened, who has it made strong? Is it true that since 1969 or 1970 we have come to live in a new continuous present that began with the new Ulster 'Troubles' and the 'Arms Trial', and continues with political violence and the reactive teaching of a revisionist history? The teaching of history involves a strong socialization process, but this has not often been properly interrogated by our sociologists or historians. The past of Ireland belongs to its educated middle class. Yes, there has been a change in memory. The software of our past has been re-bundled to suit the present task of Irishness. The current idea of prosperity has overwhelmed the idea of nationhood. All the exiles who left our shores contribute now to that new propaganda of prosperity, just as the exiles in the old IRB, Clann na nGael, and AOH once sharpened and deepened our sense of nationhood.

The 'Celtic Tiger' is our great new invention. It should stifle social envy and unrest with the same thoroughness as the old idea of nationhood. But it can also get us into trouble. At a recent meeting of European Ministers, for example, the ugly face of continental envy began to reveal itself. Danish and Belgian Ministers grumbled that Ireland had breached European Union guidelines in attracting inward investment. Somebody was very sore about the establishment of a new facility for Boston Scientific in Galway. In Ireland we consider this European reaction to be slightly daft. After all the German company, Siemens AG, had decided to site a huge wafer fabrication facility in the North of England, and this just after the UK had rejected new EU regulations on working conditions. Much bitterness had been felt in Ireland around that decision, especially in Cork where Siemens executives had looked at the Cork harbour area as a probable location.

Another aspect of this rivalry for jobs between European countries — an area that has never been discussed freely in Ireland, as if we didn't want to upset the shrewd Dutch or the compliant Danes — is the negative impact the European Union has had on jobs in Ireland. From my house atop the hill of Montenotte I look across the river Lee each day at a site where three to four thousand men were once employed in highly skilled industrial jobs. All of these jobs were lost after 1973 as a result of Ireland opening its trade borders with Europe. There's not space enough here to list all the footwear factories, bakeries, flour mills and car assembly plants that were lost to Cork City as a direct result of Ireland's membership of the European Union. The fact that we raised our little tiger from the ruins of these factories has been lost on all of our European partners. Most of the people — mainly men — who lost good jobs in the 1970s and 1980s never worked again in Ireland. As a public librarian in Cork I've been serving these people since the day they lost their jobs. I've witnessed their physical and mental deterioration. Just today I spoke to one of those men. I remember this man's wasted middle age. Now he is an old age pensioner. He laughed when I mentioned our 'Celtic Tiger'.

'Another shaggin' smokescreen,' he joked. He still lives in a corporation housing estate in Cork's northside. He has four children, two boys and two girls. His eldest child, a boy, landed a job as a clerical officer in the Dublin civil service ten years ago. That amazing stroke of luck was one of those miracles of de Maupassant proportions that sometimes fall upon a working-class family. His youngest child is now twenty-three but she has never had a job though she is well educated with diplomas in various business disciplines. The other son and daughter are also on the dole. So, that family whose breadwinner became redundant in 1977 has a second-generation unemployment rate of 75%. What is unusual about that man's family is that one member actually has a permanent job. The industrial trauma created by our membership of the EU has never been properly catalogued. Our administrative and political class is too heavily invested in the European idea to catalogue those negative aspects of European membership. To raise them in public is to be labelled 'anti-Europe'. A pariah. This Stalinization of political thinking in Europe has become increasingly alarming. A mental Europe is being created in both the European Parliament and the Commission that begins to look like the 'democratic centralism' of old Soviet political thought. In future Ireland's duty in the EU may be to become more American rather than more European. The American nature of Irish life may be our greatest contribution to Europe in future years. It may save our democracy, if not Europe's.

This is why the 'Celtic Tiger' label is such a dishonest one. Ireland is much more than that — fluid, tantalizing, varied, hopeful and despairing, uplifting and depressing, all at the same time. Like any other country we have myths and national delusions that orientate our character and even determine our responses to social and political events. Despite this we are probably unique in that the greater part of our literary/intellectual life seems to take place outside the jurisdiction of the state. Influential outsiders speak for us, tell us how we should live on our island, even wanting to correct us when we tell them how we truly live. Imagine if all the English and American journals were published in Ireland, or if all the influential publishers, Faber, Oxford, FSG and Knopf, were based in Dublin or Cork? 70% of everything manufactured here has to be sold outside Ireland. I should think that the same percentage of Irish thought is edited and consumed abroad as well. What should this mean for our daily life in Ireland, and for writers like me who live here, year round?

Every idea I have about my country is not conceived for

the seminar or lecture circuit but, rather, as part of my way of life, as part of my living here. To live in an Irish place, metaphorically smack in the middle of the Anglo-American Atlantic, is to be part of a constant struggle between the local and the international, between the parochial and the modernist. Our native land is more than a seminar or a clever phrase. All one can say for certain is that the same Irish present continues — from the Arms Trial of 1970 to the McCracken Tribunal of 1997.

New Hibernia Review,
1997

The Cappoquin Cricket XI

Here is a summer photograph from the long ago in County Waterford. Older Cappoquin people will recognize the family likenesses in many faces. At the centre-back of this photo are the towering figures of Mick Sargent, Jack McCarthy and Paddy Mullane, Mick Sargent of the legendary Sargent's Garage, and Jack McCarthy, then a Professor at Mount Melleray Abbey with its third-level seminary. There's Jimmy Lacey too, and Dominic Dunne, Jack Smith, Capt Jameson of Tourin, Ion Villiers-Stuart of Dromana House, shopkeeper Charlie Mansfield, and the handsome Bobby Keane who would go on to marry the novelist Molly Skrine and briefly bring great happiness into her life. The

The Cappoquin Cricket XI

pursuit of cricket persisted in Cappoquin well into the 1930s, with practice every Monday, Wednesday and Friday during the season and with matches played in the local Sports Field. The main challengers in competition for the Cappoquin Cricket XI were Cahir Park, County Tipperary, Lismore Castle Cricket Team and Hearne's of Waterford City. Around 1935 a number of the team members were banned by the Gaelic Athletic Association for playing 'foreign games', but like many cricketers in Waterford and Kilkenny several players were reinstated during the 'Emergency' of 1939-1945 and went on to contribute hugely to hurling in the South East. Not that there was any shortage of sports in Cappoquin: these cricketers were also keen tennis players. There were two grass courts and one hard court at the Cappoquin Sports Field and the more prosperous tenants of Cappoquin Estate and Cappoquin Bacon Factory were always free to use the tennis courts at Belleville House when Bobby Keane lived there with his wife, Molly. Also, the competitive fours and eights of Cappoquin Rowing Club, the Old Dark Blues, were hugely successful, and enthusiastically supported by the Keane, Chearnley and Villiers-Stuart families. This being County Waterford a number of cricketers were also competitive and champion cyclists and track and field enthusiasts, as well as champion open road bowlers, always using the heavy 32oz bowl rather than the lighter 28oz bowl used in Cork.

Captain T O Jameson of Tourin House and the whiskey family was a highly competitive cricketer. Two of his regular house guests at Tourin House, Cappoquin, were Sir George Oswald Browning Allen, or 'Gubby' Allen, the right-arm fast bowler who played for Middlesex and captained England in eleven test matches, and Lionel Hallam Lord Tennyson, grandson of the poet, who captained Hampshire and England, and played his last Test match in 1921 against Australia. So the Cappoquin Cricket XI were keeping good company and benefited from several coaching sessions with these famous cricketers at Cappoquin Sports Field.

Thomas McCarthy

In the golden Edwardian age of Cappoquin cricket between 1905 and 1914 Harry Keane had founded in 1907 the Cappoquin Bacon Factory on the site of a former sawmill on the banks of the Blackwater River, a business that employed nearly a hundred men. The factory was set up deliberately and determinedly to give employment to able-bodied sportsmen, especially good rowing men. 'There's no reason why any man should emigrate from Cappoquin, and there's no need for it,' was what Harry Keane said. The aristocratic Keanes themselves were an intriguing family, not English planters at all, but an Irish family, the Catholic Ó Catháins of Derry, many of whom fought with King James at the Battle of the Boyne. After the defeat at the Boyne all their Ulster lands were confiscated. But one, Seoirse Ó Catháin, converted to the Protestant faith and practised as a barrister for years. When he retired from the Bar he leased lands at Cappoquin from the Earl of Cork in 1737. The family prospered and consolidated its holdings in West Waterford, collecting a Baronetcy for voting for the Act of Union, all going well for them until 1847 when the non-payment of rent meant mounting estate debts, including a Tithe Bill of over £500. Under the Encumbered Estates Act the Keane Estate was put up for sale in 1855. At that time the estate consisted of 11,400 acres. The value of the estate didn't include the timbers of the Cappoquin Demesne: oak, elm, beech, horse chestnut, fir and larch. A private offer was made by Sir John Henry Keane for eight lots in the sale, comprising of 7,791 acres, the town of Cappoquin, the Big House and Demesne.

There were two hundred estate tenants in the town and nearly a hundred in the countryside. Twenty years later Sir John Henry Keane had increased the size of the estate yet again by more than a 1,000 acres. Sir Richard, the 4th Baronet, succeeded the father in 1881. He was Deputy Lieutenant and High Sheriff of Waterford. He set up the Foundry and Farm Implement Works at Cappoquin, a successful business that was eventually amalgamated with the Pierce Ironworks of

The Cappoquin Cricket XI

Wexford, with the Cappoquin part of the business shut down by the end of the nineteenth century. Cappoquin House was burned to the ground by Republicans in February 1923 because Sir John Keane was a Free State Senator.

Over the years, in both my memoir writing and in poems, I've emphasized the poverty that was widespread in Ireland up to the late 1960s but in fairness, it is important, also, to remember the prosperity of Cappoquin. Though our own childhood family is the filter through which we are likely to view all things the story of one luckless McCarthy family in this writer's life is never the full story of a town. The fact is, between 1962 and 1972, the high Fianna Fáil years before the oil crisis of '73, Cappoquin was a bustling, prosperous town where over a hundred able-bodied men, and many women, were constantly employed in retail hardware, railways, Co-Ops and bacon factories. As I grew older I began to see the evidence of history, the statistics, even the records and receipt books, of a hugely prosperous town where a simple comfort was widespread, not just held by a narrow elite. More than a hundred families did well in Cappoquin, more than a hundred played sport through their weekends and long summer evenings and more than a hundred human souls saved wages and bought cars, built houses and created healthy, active families. In other words many made a good life without leaving Ireland. This old image of the Cappoquin Cricket XI is such a telling reminder of that prosperous, settled Ireland that is hardly ever recorded in the memoirs of poets. When I look at the prosperous Cappoquin of this Cricket XI I thank God that I've outgrown the old bitterness of a poor beginning.

Facebook,
June 2020

The Years of Forgetting: 2006-2011

I am waiting at the gate at the top of our road with my new friends, Bashik and Stephane. It is a cold day in the South, unnatural cold of June made even more miserable by the persistence of Cork rain. Rain has settled in pools on plastic bags that are full of old newspapers and school or college notebooks going back to 1967. Bashik and Stephane came with a van after two or three weeks of our tidying, clearing out, trimming down, downsizing. Letting go. Not that we're leaving the house after twenty-six years. No, we're not going away. There is nowhere to go. But after four years of recession, of huge salary cutbacks and a general sense of failure in that very special political weather created by our Irish Catholic realm, we are doing the next best thing: we are shedding what we've hoarded. We have convinced ourselves that what we've hoarded now has no meaning. It seems to be a shared feeling in these parts. Many of our neighbours and relatives have had a skip parked on their streets since 2009. There really is a frenzy of lightening, a new-found disgust at accumulations of any kind. Soon our homes will be so empty they'll be full of echoes. There won't be a spare chair left in the house of Éire. It's as if all those blunt warnings so harshly annunciated by William Carson in his *Ulster and the Irish Republic* (1957) or by Paul Blanchard in his *The Irish and Catholic Power* (1953) have come true. Hugh Montgomery Hyde, in his Foreword to the latter book, could claim: 'I have already touched on some of the proven facts which show that the bishops in the hierarchy are the true rulers in the South. Mr Blanchard examines all the available evidence in detail and in doing so he has rendered a signal service to the English-speaking

The Years of Forgetting: 2006-2011

peoples. He has also demonstrated that, though it may possess some imperfections, the government in the North is fundamentally democratic, whereas that of the South is only superficially democratic.'

Maybe he was right — despite all the early serious talk of gerrymandering and B-Specials. How scary is that? Maybe he was right. Nowadays we look up to Ulster with its post-Good Friday Stormont that begins to look more and more like a commonwealth Assembly in old New England where the spoils of power are shared openly and equally among the accrued interests of permanent old enemies. And it still looks that way, despite the usual midsummer excitement about flags and symbols. Up there it's beginning to look like the little Presbyterian village of Villierstown in my native County Waterford. Presbyterians were imported South by Lord Grandison of Dromana who dreamed of a Munster linen industry to rival the North. The landlord gave each Presbyterian a field but told each weaver that he couldn't till it; rather, he'd have to rent it to a Catholic in the hinterland. The Catholics needed the grazing, so the two religions were locked in perpetual interdependence. It's as good a model as any for a successful society. This could be the road that Ulster has embarked upon, a future that will unlock value for each citizen or subject. This was also the promise implicit in the life of the early Dáil. The story goes that when Seán Lemass, upon assuming office as Minister for Justice in 1932, told the head of the Special Branch to burn the file with the names of the men who cruelly murdered his brother in the Dublin mountains, he added: 'We might have to do business with these men for the sake of Ireland.' To think, in those days, they knew nothing about the psychology of 'closure'.

So, these black plastic bags awaiting collection at the top of the road are a kind of closure. They say farewell to my mother's *Messenger of the Sacred Heart*, to *The Field*, to *Reality*, to *The Far East* (where I learned that Edson Arantes do Nascimento was nicknamed 'Pelé' by his Irish Christian

53

Brother teachers because he was always running away from class, *ag imirt peile* like any good Kerryman). But here's one I'd better hold on to, a journal I bought in the Lee Bookstore in 1977: *The Capuchin Annual 1976*, with its pious cover drawn by Seán O'Sullivan RHA, and its more than forty pages on the life and death of Mr de Valera. Ah, there it is, on page 285, T Ryle Dwyer's essay 'Canada and David Gray's Attempts to Discredit de Valera during World War Two'. And there, also, is that full-page portrait of Prince Rainier of Monaco and the glamorous Grace Kelly visiting our President at Áras an Uachtaráin in 1962. Here are the ads for Dubtex slacks and Tal-Kraft suits for boys, the Commodore Hotel in Cobh, the EBS Building Society ('Give Yourself Everything to Look Forward To') and photographs of the young Pádraic Fiacc, Dermot Keogh, Kevin Faller and Conleth Ellis — all of our Irish kind of life placed reassuringly between Lisavaird Co-Op Creamery and the Convoy Woollen Company of County Donegal. Better hang on to this, better temper this frenzy of wanting to forget.

This wanting to forget did begin a few years ago. It was an economist quoted in the *Sunday Independent* of 6 February 2005 who wished to nail those feelings of Catholic anxiety once and for all. This was before the banking/building crisis, many months before. Lara Bradley reported the words of the Economic and Social Research Council's senior economist, Danny McCoy:

> *'Admittedly there are individuals who are living beyond their means. They see others doing well and that puts pressure on them to overstretch themselves, but overall our economy is not out of control... The credit card numbers are actually piddlingly small in terms of the aggregate. Job prospects are a central confidence provider and the labour market remains very strong and shows no immediate sign of slowing down... Our aspiration must be to get the highest*

wages because we're worth it. So long as we continue to produce the goods we deserve the lifestyle. You'll get no Catholic guilt here.'

Mr McCoy used the expression 'benign paradigm' in explaining the great success of the 'Celtic Tiger'. He was adamant that we should accept our success and get over our Catholic guilt. So I became extravagant in the boom. I bought a second two-person tent and a battery radio, waterproof and tidy, and coloured markers so that I could write even in the rain. I sat in the tent at night and listened to the distant sound of waves crashing on the shore of West Kerry, listened to the wind in the marram grasses, the sound of animals rustling in the bushes. When my wife and I walked through the crowded, shopping-frenzied streets of Cork we spoke of the seashore, the quiet between-places. There was no property between the low watermark and the high watermark, and no rich man would be given permission to build in our sandy realm. Now I could only write about inanimate things, things that won't become a national embarrassment: stones, sand, water, cliffs, seaweed, the wind. The anchorite poets are my constant companions still, the ones who sought a solitude of stone and water — Michael Longley in his Connemara retreat, Richard Murphy braving the storms of High Island, troubled Theodore Roethke who walked alone across a far field. These are the poets who camp outdoors with me. In them is a companionship of the tested ordinary. They are the antithesis of every failed politics. Politics has saturated and ruined our brains: I need a salty cleansing. So, I relent. I carry *The Capuchin Annual* back indoors. But I wonder, while descending the wet steps, is there anyone out there who might start a new national conversation? No matter how hard we try a country will always be more than the sum of all its poems, even more than the sum of all its poets. When it comes to Ireland, including all of Ulster, we are in disputed parliaments of responsibility. Much of Ulster was elsewhere while all of Catholic Ireland became its all-singing, all house-building self. While Northern Ireland seemed to make itself into a rose-growing, golf-coaching, Fenian-excluding Liechtenstein of the Moyle Water, Saorstát Éireann became something else entirely. The entrenched bourgeoisie of the South grabbed a little country with the only power structure it could recognize. Now the 'Celtic Tiger' looks like one dreadful conspiracy, a Catholic nineteenth century that lasted nearly two hundred years, from the victory of Daniel O'Connell to the defeat of Taoiseach Brian Cowen. This era of one kind of power is neatly bookended by the Protestant banking crisis of the early nineteenth century and the very Catholic boys' club banking crisis of the early twenty-first century. Both crises left us with an excess of vain building projects, both utterly unsustainable within local economic activity: Georgian house and contemporary ghost estate. We have lived in that twilight zone of time, as Conor Cruise O'Brien put it in his wonderful essay on Seán Ó Faoláin in *Maria Cross* (1952), that zone of time that never quite belongs to the rest of history. Certainly, our elders have talked their memories into our memories: not that we might learn from the past, but that we might not notice the breach of planning regulations. So, twenty-seven black bags of everything now deemed irrelevant, old diaries, old calendars, old concert tickets, old newspapers (oh, except this other publication, a copy of *Hibernia* for 24 June 1977: 'Jack Swings Back!' with its picture of Jack Lynch swinging a hurling stick in front of a crowd of party followers after the famous 'Abolish Rates' victory that brought down the Cosgrave-Corish coalition of the mid-70s. The same *Hibernia* carries an advertisement for 'Macrobiotic Weekends' in Kilkenny and offers 16% on your funds, 'tax not deducted', from the Leinster Investment Society.

Now, in exchange for a reasonable fee and one-and-a-half thousand books from my library, Bashik and Stephane, citizens of the lands between the Danube and the Dnieper, are ready to clear the detritus of over twenty years of Irish family reading. When I thank the two men for lightening my load they are not sure what I mean. For Bashik these are his last few weeks in Ireland. He has been headhunted by a California games company who spotted his online game-development work, uploaded onto YouTube from his bedsit in Sunday's Well. He is a highly qualified programmer, but in a different programming language from that used by game designers in Ireland. Stephane and I will miss him when he goes. We've had a thousand conversations over the last eight years about corruption in Irish society and in Fianna Fáil. It has left us wondering if there's a peculiar kind of Catholic corruption, a teeming form of old-world life that is passing away in our own era, that both our native lands have had to work out of their systems. Like Bashik I sometimes feel I use the wrong programming language. The games of national life must be the same in every language, but I am still using the old Commodore-64 of Austin Clarke and Patrick Kavanagh while all the others have rushed forward using Beckett-style flash, or Leontia Flynn-style flashdrive? The human heart, though, is the same human heart in every kind of poem. In every poetic playground there are several generations at play together. Sometimes there is a conversation but most of the time they have nothing to do with each other. As David Thompson wrote in his marvellous book on Hollywood films: 'Here is proof that the most special effect in the movies is always the human face when its mind is being changed.' That is also the camera angle at which a nation's trauma is etched upon a line of poetry. It is the poet's duty to map those changes in the face of our nation(s). The wonderful thing about the coming generation of poets is that they haven't had our experiences, including our failures of nerve. Anxiety about the Republic, for example, if you're twenty years old and emerging into the daylight after a poetry workshop, may be as academic as anxiety about the lost GDR.

Before I consigned all the black bags and recycling boxes to Stephane's white van I typed up some of the notes I'd made years ago, at the very beginning of thinking about things. What these notes were for, these journal entries, or who they were written for, is irrelevant now. I must have imagined an audience, an engaged audience that I now believe has faded away as imperceptibly as the subscribers' list of *The Capuchin Annual*. Thirty years ago I was an assiduous reader of diaries: poets', statesmen's, artists', actors', reviewers' — all of human life was reduced to the naked witness of the personal journal. I bored colleagues at work in Cork City Library with quotes from Stendhal, Gide, Camus, Harold Nicolson, Richard Crossman, Evelyn Waugh, Arnold Bennett, Yeats and Gemma Hussey. Make a note, I used to say to myself, keep the habit of the pen, as Seferis says in his *Journals*. They were my scrawls on the wall as we passed through our Free State cave. The people we meet day-by-day are like the politicians we meet: as far as art is concerned they are a series of accidents. Diaries are accidents from elsewhere that we visit upon ourselves. So, here we are, at the narrow gate of 2011. We wait at the top of the steps as the white van is parked awkwardly. The black bags with their detritus from my life are placed hurriedly along double yellow lines. It is good to lighten one's life. There has been an unbearable weight in Irish life these last four years.

Our country has been undone. The national purpose is in a heap of fragments. We are living at the heart of a national catastrophe: the result of one or two key miscalculations by a brilliantly educated but ill — and ill-informed — Minister. If Ulster had been in charge, like the great Earl of Kildare, decisions would have been different. I'm sure of that. Ulster, the low-church accountant inside its soul, would have been able to hold all of Ireland steady. The citizens of the Dáil are now the indentured servants of European capitalists. We must all work like dogs, with less pay, to pay for our passage through this dark night of the Irish Nationalist soul. Scholars and historians worry on the radio. Theatre directors fret and form 'citizens' assemblies'. Poets worry: yes, the poets of my generation really worry. Was it a single process of national thinking that brought this catastrophe to pass? The misjudgements of Brian Lenihan TD have undone our South; a Minister hoodwinked by bank directors and economic risk analysts. The poor, hoodwinked, dying creature. Our hearts went out to him because a man with cancer will always have to make decisions in a hurry. Thank God the executives that advised him would never want to tamper with poetry. Auden was right: poets live in a parallel universe, a state where policy lives through the changing expressions of a human face. Yesterday I was full of rage with him, that dead Minister. But I was full of pity too, a raw and howling pity, because he was a very attractive and charismatic man, from a family of brilliant men and women. I tried to make a poem for him, for his memory, because there was something Parnell-like in his passing. He brought down an entire country; but death, the final Speaker, removed him from the house before he had time to recover his composure. I shake hands with my old Polish friend who will make a happier life in a sunnier country, those silicon valleys of Denise Levertov and Robert Duncan. The rain doesn't ease off as I fold this fragment of an unfinished poem. For the next decade let us be pleased merely to be alive. Let us be happy to live on fragments:

> *I can see more wreckage far out to sea;*
> *all receding still. The pilot boat*
> *with all its unused lifebelts*
> *has the mark on its prow where you*
> *were pushed, Brian. Black gulls return*
> *to their feeding grounds: Paris, Berlin.*

Irish Pages,
2012

Fianna Fáil, The Waiting Game

For that old Party a lot of water has flowed under the bridge since the dark days of the 2011 election. Actually a lot of water has passed *over* many a bridge in this long, wet winter. And, on this weekend in 2016, I find that one of our old pubs has closed; I mean the pub where I ran into a bevy of retreating and perplexed Party activists five years ago. My cousin has also emigrated, yet again. Not only is the old pub closed, but it is roofless. I wonder what happened to its seven-day licence; perhaps it was purchased and transferred to a city location by some incoming British pubs group. No sign of the Party activists, but I can bet that, wherever they've hidden, they're a happier lot right now. But at this moment there must be groups of perplexed and wounded Labour Party activists assembling in the coffee shops of Cork and Dublin, wondering, like the faithful of the Party in 2011, what happened precisely? What did happen precisely? As I motor around this part of County Waterford I notice that nearly all the posters have come down, apart from a few outlying Fine Gael and Anti-Austerity Alliance/PBP banners, blowing forlornly in the rural wind, calling time back the way posters do. But time, like an election result, cannot be undone. Strange, the Party faithful are not in public places, not yet; although you'd think, after having more than doubled their seat count, they'd be taking a few victory laps around the drinking circuit of Tallow, Cappoquin and Dungarvan. Not at all. Or not yet. We're living in a strange time, a time of uncanny quiet that might alarm those who have a tendency to panic. Few of these panicking people are Fianna Fáil activists, I must admit. The yearning for panic seems to belong to those who don't seem to want to be in any government. I mean these very, very kind young people, those handsome Tom Courtney/Pasha lookalikes, who now bother their poor elders in the Party like children wanting to hurry their parents into an Old Folks Home. 'Here, dad, mum, you'll be much happier in the Home, those Fine Gael people won't mind your taking up residence with them.' The old codgers of the Party can see through this. They can see that box of firelighters behind their children's backs; they have no intention of combusting together in a single conflagration so that the children can get the whole constituency. It's one thing to lend your votes to Fine Gael, it's another thing entirely to drop them into the paws of some elegant young Communist.

But these handsome young people in black, they may know something about history, notwithstanding John A Murphy, that great historian of our modern era, who reminded *Irish Times* readers last Tuesday about the permanent gulf of social empathy between the Party and Fine Gael (a name so constantly mispronounced by Willy O'Dea, as Professor Murphy shrewdly noted). Yes, some of these young Pashas may know a thing or two about war; they may know that in June of 1940, when Ireland faced certain invasion either from the British or the Germans, bitter memories of the Civil War were set aside. At that moment of crisis old Republicans like Tom Barry, Tom Crofts, Liam Deasy and Michael Kenny arrived at the gates of Collins Barracks in Cork to offer their services to the officers of the still Regular Army. They would not desert the Army of the Dáil, the only sovereign and legitimate army of Ireland, in its hour of danger. Colonel Costello welcomed Barry personally but couldn't persuade him to become an officer. Barry insisted on remaining with the ranks where he lasted all of twenty-eight days. The aloof Florence O'Donoghue, former adjutant of the Cork No.1 Brigade, became an invaluable asset to G2, the Army intelligence service. These Old IRA men would serve faithfully and loyally for the five years while a danger to Ireland lasted. The conversations in the Officers' Mess must have been electric. But they would resume their Civil War differences after the Emergency had passed. Today, oddly, that sense of emergency has faded: the invasion forces of the Troika and the ECB have withdrawn behind their Channel ports. Our insular island has survived yet again. This ill-advised Election of 2016 produced a result that comes five years too late. More's the pity because there's so much important national work to be done in Ireland.

This result in 2016 has foxed more than the experts and historians. The mood here, picked up in conversations at filling stations, gossiping in the mist by the bridge at Lismore, falling into conversation at two cafés in Dungarvan's bustling building site of a new Square, is still one of puzzlement; and the firm expectation among ordinary Party folk is that there will be another election within two years. But the realization, when pushed, that two years cannot be spent in idle uncertainty. It is astonishing how aware people are of the deterioration of confidence abroad, the daft project of Brexit, the Syrian refugees, the lacking of social housing. Suddenly the whole world seems to need a new house. Dungarvan is still bustling. Its cafés are busy, the streets are crowded: I dare not use the word 'recovery' — but I think that its use was not entirely a dishonest slogan. One feels that if towns like Dungarvan, Dingle, Westport or Nenagh begin to bustle, especially on weekend shopping days, then all need not be lost in rural Ireland. The ordinary folk I spoke to, and I spoke to many this week, can see how the Irregulars may have to keep the commissioned Officers at their command for a few years. If only for Ireland, as they say.

I turn back at the Master McGrath monument near Dungarvan, beneath the few orphans of surviving election posters, and travel back through a landscape where, in the latest estimate, more than twenty million euros will be needed to repair the roads after several winters of flooding and where money will be needed to reopen closed branch libraries, restore book funds and set the clockwork of a brilliant public

Fianna Fáil, The Waiting Game

service going again. In a county like Waterford that has had excellent public roads since the days of John Redmond it is heartbreaking to see roads that need urgent repair. Waterford has always been blessed in its Engineers and Managers, really blessed — and I don't exaggerate — in the incredibly high level of its infrastructure. When Martin Cullen built his brilliant motorways he was only carrying on a long Waterford tradition. Now, in the twilight, I drive past Arland Ussher's gates at Cappagh, Molly Keane's old mansion at Belleville, F X O'Leary's town house in Cappoquin, Dervla Murphy's den in Lismore, driving on through a rural landscape of unsurpassable beauty, even at the dead end of winter. These are noble places, this rural Ireland. These places deserve the life blood of political attention, even if my Party cousin has flown. We live in a waiting time, a time of uncertainty. The countryside here, flooded and expectant, waits for some decent and honest person to make the first move. Waiting is a game, certainly, but too long a wait is as disastrous as a Troika visit.

Fianna Fáil, instinctively, are less unnerved by this waiting and uncertainty; deep in the FF soul is that almost Russian acceptance of a society held together by safety pins and binder twine. The important thing is to survive any long political winter. A Fine Gael mindset is more narrowly focused, both socially and politically; that haut bourgeois instinct for order and discipline, a world more familiar to army officers and *monsignori* of the Church. It is ironically an IRB world, a world of discretion and professionalism where to be unqualified or not spoken for is to be considered almost illegitimate. But this other mindset, this Russian passivity, allows Fianna Fáil to float, to wait for a kind of mindfulness to develop, a mindfulness harvested from its betters on the Left or Right. It was de Valera's method to keep talking, to talk and talk until others died from boredom or surrendered. In the end most FF leaders will collapse from intolerable blandness rather than error. FG leaders, assertive and with a fuller sense of ownership of authority, will always make a determined and stubborn public mistake — cutting the old age pension, taxing children's shoes, calling an election in the middle of winter while half of the Shannon basin is under water.

Why was the election not called before Christmas? It's a mystery to people I talk to in a garage beside one of the many Dungarvan roundabouts. It's as if the experiences of people we don't meet socially don't matter. The very assertiveness that comes from long and honest ownership always leaves Fine Gael open to attack. The fact is most people in Ireland have to scramble to make a life and, amazingly, most people will make some kind of life for themselves if given a few decent chances. As a rule people feel good only momentarily. Constituents vote not for those who do right but for those who seem to do right by them. Empathy is everything. Those who live on lack, to use a phrase from Austin Clarke's poetry, don't need to be told why they must live like this; they need to be told when and how the tide will turn for them. It was either Micheál Martin's political genius or his innate sense of decency that made him say that the people needed a break. Everyone could see that, even if they couldn't yet see the recovery. Those of us who were born poor in the 60s will remember the introduction of Free Education and that astonishing era of hope. Perhaps fewer will remember how our brand new secondary schools were flooded with thousands of blue Careers leaflets describing, for all of us whose families had scrambled to make a living, how if one studied hard one could become a Teacher, a Meteorologist, a Chemist, a Physicist, an ESB Engineer (the ultimate 1960s glory for a boy or girl). These leaflets were as ubiquitous as Ladybird books or broken Marietta biscuits. Six or seven years before the first oil crisis these leaflets offered a limitless future by introducing children of no background into a career conversation that was once only held in middle-class homes. It was a stroke of genius politically, expanding the psychology of advancement right into working-class and rural hinterlands.

Even now, half a century later, I can recall the emotional effect of those blue leaflets, that feeling of a limitless future. It was wonderful to have a future one could believe in. Young Irish people need to experience that feeling again; they need to see a rising tide. Surely if housing and health are matters of public concern then an emergency programme to deal with these concerns is the least a nation can hope for. This hope is more important than any budget, any programme, or any Troika. Counter-intuitively, I mean from a right-wing economist's point of view, it is this very feeling that lifts all boats and creates consumer demand. How to create this feeling must surely be the single most important political task of the modern era. That good feeling is waiting impatiently to come back, and it will return when someone announces a restoration of Public Service recruitment, the building of one hundred thousand social homes, the recovery of lost hospital beds, the restoration of funding in arts and public libraries. In other words the restoration of our national self respect. It is a truism, my Party cousin tells me on the phone from West Norwood, that political hope always pays its own way in the end through increased tax revenue. As the wily Micheál Martin and the impatient young Socialists scratch their heads and wonder what to do next they must surely know that, unlike bailing out private banks, helping the poor to complete their journey out of poverty never ruined a country.

The Irish Times,
2016

Luck and the Irish: A Brief History of Change, 1970-2000 by R F Foster

Roy Foster's new book is a timely, erudite, and extremely witty personal essay on the condition of Irish political and social life in the contemporary era. It is a benign and patrician attempt, in the manner of Hubert Butler, Arland Ussher and Seán Ó Faoláin, to come to terms with the almost constantly contradictory facts of recent life in Ireland. Just at that point where civil rancour might have certainly torn the land apart another set of forces was at work that delivered success and prosperity. 'When did the future present itself to be grabbed? Looking back, we can see that certain statistics suggest where change was likely to begin,' writes Foster on page three, but by page 181 he has widened his forensic investigation:

> *'The options of Irishness at the end of the twentieth century reflect a great dislocation. Looking at the new motorway encircling Dublin, the cultural commentator Ann Marie Hourihane caustically pronounced: "History is finished here. Now we are going to live like everybody else." But it is not that simple.'*

Indeed Ireland was never that simple. What country is? As Foster observes: 'A certain amount of good luck was maximized by good management.' His book is a commentary on that management, a multilayered commentary that had its origins in Foster's Wiles Lectures at the Queen's University, Belfast, in 2004 — and the simultaneous duty of adding a catch-up section to his definitive 1988 volume, *Modern Ireland 1600-1972*. He is aware of the limitations and anxieties created

Luck and the Irish: A Brief History of Change, 1970-2000

by such commentaries and recognizes that a work on such recent happenings will surely be interspersed with opinion and speculation. But Foster is convinced that what he is writing is 'history none the less'. That 'none the less' is a warning to the reader — a warning that historians who engage in the kind of material that might be the stuff of journalism and opinion are acting as agents of history. An historian so close to material of this kind is also a political agent, more or less, effecting the direction of things with that ability to report upon vast quantities of current information and to create patterns for contemporary action and response. Ireland has always generated this kind of historical writing: such writing reflects the yearning of our country to find a workable pattern, a paradigm by which it might engage all contradictory forces at work in Irish life. Foster captures one of these emerging forces brilliantly in the chapter, 'How the Catholics became Protestants'. Here he traces the decline of Catholic influence in Irish education, the decline of Mass-going, and the empowering influence of Bishop Empey in Dublin, culminating in that famous gesture of the devoutly Catholic President McAleese taking communion at the Protestant Cathedral. These developments have led to a position in Ireland where, as Foster observes, 'The recognition that Northern Unionism had a voice worth listening to has come slowly, but it is one of the striking reversals of approach over the last thirty years.' All of this is part of what might be seen broadly as a coming to terms with the entirety of the cultural memory of Ireland.

After 9/11, says Foster, any notion of a benign world order is speciously unhistorical. While he praises the management of Ireland, the seven National Wage Agreements between 1970 and 1978, the sunny expectations of a liberal future, and the differentiation of 'politics' from 'policy', he shrewdly notes the persistent negative feelings towards the European Union — a national hesitation that has led to the postponement of the future with our recent rejection of the Lisbon

Treaty. The difference between 'politics' and 'policy' is particularly striking here as Foster continues a forensic scrutiny that was usefully initiated by the historian and broadcaster, John Bowman, who identified de Valera's continued use of the 'Ulster Issue' to advance a Fianna Fáil electoral advantage. By emphasizing the 'politics' of the matter rather than addressing the more complex 'policy' implications of Ulster de Valera rallied his troops before the polling stations. It was a cynical exercise, a Balkanized vote-gathering, but it always worked for Fianna Fáil.

The chapter 'The Party Fight and the Funeral' reads like a suite of poems or a novel that I myself might have written. Taking his dislocated narrative viewpoint from William Carleton he reports — sharply and with no little mischief — on the doings of that marvellous power circus, Fianna Fáil. He might be telling the story of my own childhood and youth in West Waterford: fist fights in Lawlor's Hotel in Dungarvan, the unbelievable and bizarre Charles Haughey, hungry figures from the West like Pádraig Flynn and Seán Doherty and, again, Mr Haughey who 'never lost his sense of entitlement. In some ways he kept it to the end of his life.' Indeed he did, as did Daniel O'Connell, our Liberator, who kept the same sense of entitlement, collecting twenty thousand pounds from the shillings of the rural poor at the height of the Great Famine (a gesture of ravenous greed that was roundly condemned by the sublime Father Prout of Cork in verse and prose. For a picture of Irish corruption similar to the worst excess of the Haughey era every historian should read Father Prout's *Facts and Figures from Italy* with its portrayal of Dandelione, the rogue of the Two Sicilys). Yes, the seeds of corruption were sown early in Irish public life. For that matter the average historian might well look at the exchequer debates of the Protestant Irish Parliament of 1795 when four unnamed individuals were given the licence for a public lottery. It makes for familiar and bitter reading. Foster's Haughey chapter is a portrait of something dreadful and

Luck and the Irish: A Brief History of Change, 1970-2000

recurrent, a consequence of de Valera not having eaten Parnell's heart. We are now at the fag end of an era of tribunals that began in 1992. These tribunals were a kind of Truth Commission, a persistent and hugely expensive public washing of Party linen that had undermined all legitimate opposition, destroyed the effectiveness of the Fine Gael Party, and flattened almost every work of political poetry and fiction for over two decades.

In discussing the Arms Trial of the 1970s Foster correctly remembers that devoted and loyal servant of the Dáil, Captain James Kelly, 'fall-guy for the politicians', as one of the victims of that bad time. I remember debating politics with the same Captain Kelly in my flat in Cork in the 1980s, a time when the good Captain was hoping to be elected to the Fianna Fáil national executive in an effort to clear his name. His ill treatment at the hands of his masters in the Irish Department of Defence will forever remain a blight on the good name of the Irish establishment. Another visitor to my flat in those dark days of the 1980s, following quick on the heels of Captain Kelly, was Vincent Buckley, the Australian poet who was writing *Memory Ireland* (1985), having already written *Cutting Green Hay* (1983), a book about the political Irish in Australia, the Sisters of Mercy and the Australian Labour Party. 'Political tourism and reinvented Irishness were much in vogue in the 1980s,' as Foster observes caustically in his chapter 'How the Short Stories became Novels'. The poet Buckley was a first-rate intellectual whose critical skills were finely honed in the forge of Melbourne University but he despaired of us young Irish Southerners. He thought that, with one or two honourable exceptions, we had all gone soft on basic Republican principles. He was right: we had. Or most of us had. Foster's achievement in *Luck and the Irish* is the chronicling of that collapse of our Republican convictions and pious family values: the admission, by us, of our doubts and contradictions. Foster, here, moves from Vincent Buckley to Tom Hayden in a withering critique. But the writer who most fits the new mould, a 'new man', as it were, is Colm Tóibín, the Wexford novelist. His *Walking Along the Border* (1987) and *The Heather Blazing* (1992) reflect a more humane, holistic Southern viewpoint, offering a seriousness and relevance like that of Frank O'Connor in the 1940s. A pity Foster hadn't read my own novel of the same period, *Asya and Christine* (1992), where he would have found a similar resonant opening of political consciousness. In terms of reading Foster is up to date in an impressive way, mentioning the wonderful Ulster novelist, David Park, whose *Swallowing the Sun* (2007) and *The Truth Commissioner* (2008) are among the finest socio-political novels of the modern era.

Foster's chronicle of the Irish Women's Liberation Movement, the founding of the Council for the Status of Women under the brave Hilda Tweedy, the Women's Right to Choose campaign, and the rise and rise of Mary Robinson, is a *précis* of the most relevant issues at stake for all liberals in the Ireland of the 1970s and 1980s. As Ann Marie Hourihane remarked, 'You didn't have to be a Socialist to be a member of the Irish Left, you just had to want contraception.' Foster has edited these times astutely in this book, identifying agents of change such as Gay Byrne and Garret FitzGerald, while also admitting the reactionary power of the New Right that had now been inserted into these debates. It is important to remember, also, the incredible flowering of women's writing in the South, a bloom of literature in the bog of Southern politics that paralleled the eruption of creativity in Ulster. When I edited *Poetry Ireland Review* in the 1980s the mailbag was ablaze with women's creativity. At that time, as well, the Cork Women's Poetry Circle was founded by the indefatigable Máire Bradshaw, with its journal, *The Box Under The Bed*. The title came from one woman who had to hide her productions from her husband, rather like the Palestinian novelist I met in Iowa, Sahar Kalifeh. The women who formed Garret FitzGerald's inner circle, who were empowered and encouraged by him and his wife, Joan, have yet to tell their story. My own memory of that time, from working in the

Luck and the Irish: A Brief History of Change, 1970-2000

Public Library system, is that the most important publication of that era was not a novel or a collection of poems but *Women Mean Business*, published by Nuala Fennell, that sincere and hard-working Minister for women's affairs. Her empowering business and legal booklet was lent many thousands of times in the Cork City Library system. Multiple copies disappeared and had to be constantly replaced. I remember the desperation of Library staff on behalf of women borrowers when we couldn't get our hands on any more copies. Who now remembers Nuala Fennell, or Joan FitzGerald, or Hilda Tweedy, or Máire Bradshaw, in these self-serving times?

In general books such as the one Foster has written prove unsatisfactory for a number of reasons, not least because each Irish reader will have his or her own autobiographical interjections to skew any learned narrator. Each Irish memory is an accusation, an affront to someone, and every scholarly insight is cornered and battered by the polemics of the moment. Foster has written a very fine book — decent, fair, sometimes quirky, and always provocatively informing. As readers of his Yeats biographies will know, his prose style is superb, yet the stylishness is never overbearing. A gentleman, he records the crimes lightly and adroitly like that other famous Waterfordman, Raymond Chandler.

New Hibernia Review,
Autumn 2008

PART TWO

THE QUESTION OF WOMEN'S POETRY

'The outrage of people': Why Men Should Study Women's Poetry

When I was in my early twenties poetry had an extraordinary physical sweetness. It was like sugar hardened or honey solidified into flaky whitish wafers on the printed page. Its sweetness has come back to me in recent years. I am now more conscious than ever of its private power, its hoarded treasures, and this consciousness has made me even quieter. But I love breaking off bits of this rich coagulant and sharing the pleasure of poems read slowly. There is a huge connection between slow reading and good writing, and poetry workshops lie in this creative hinterland, this hinterland where poems get written. I trust poetry workshops more than any other activity in poetry, more than lectures, more than readings, more than performance. At a workshop where the facilitator has created a trusting space new poets speak to us without fear of bullying and with the certainty of a hearing. In such a space we hear the full, welcomed voice of the poem's maker.

The certainty of a hearing. When did women poets first achieve this certainty of a hearing in the world of Irish poetry? It was in answering this question, but in this quiet mood, that I spoke about Irish Women's Poetry to the Mid-Western professors, about a poetry that begins in the modern era for me with Máire Mhac an tSaoi's wonderful 'Cré na Mná Tí' or 'Housewife's Creed':

> *Keep the household bright*
> *and the family disciplined,*
> *washing, scrubbing, cleaning,*
> *meals arranged and milking,*

Thomas McCarthy

> *mattress turned and carpet beaten —*
> *but, in the manner of Scheherazade,*
> *you must, in fairness, do poems.*

Or, from the same great poet of the Gael, more daring, more personal, more sexual, the great poem 'Ceathrúintí Mháire Ní Ógáin':

> *I care little for the outrage of people,*
> *the disapproval of priests,*
> *for anything except to be stretched*
> *between you and the wall —*
>
> *indifferent to the night's cold,*
> *to the lash, the lash of rain,*
> *I lie in our narrow, secretive world*
> *within the confines of our bed.*

This was our great poet, one of the greatest Irish poets of the last two centuries, mapping a private world in the fearsome cold of the 1950s. As that decade went on the passions of women were invisible. Women were love objects, not lovers — indeed the male poets and novelists turned women of passion into lunatics or objects of derision. Novelist Brian Moore gave us *The Lonely Passion of Judith Hearne* while Austin Clarke gave us 'Martha Blake'. Men appropriated the private lives of women in an act of breathtaking presumption. Novelists such as Honor Tracy and Edna O'Brien would defy this male hegemony in their writings, but the poets fell silent until, one day in early 1980, a young woman returned to Ireland from her home in Anatolia, a woman who would transform and enchant the 1980s in Ireland with beautiful, flamboyant, radiant poetry in the Irish language:

> *I place my hope on water*
> *in this little boat of language*

'The outrage of people': Why Men Should Study Women's Poetry

the way a mother might place
her little infant

in a basket woven of
iris leaves all intertwined,
its base water-proofed
with pitch and bitumen,

setting the whole of her world
among sedge and bulrushes...

This small poem, 'Ceist na Teangan' ('The Language Issue' or 'The Language Question') by the young Nuala Ní Dhomhnaill created comment and commentary everywhere in Ireland, dealing, as it seemed, with the burning issue of the Irish language in an increasingly Anglophone world. Now we can re-read this text in a different context — perhaps it is about an even deeper issue, the issue of woman's voice and sensibility, placed tentatively in the woven basket of a woman's poem. Like Máire Mhac an tSaoi before her Ní Dhomhnaill is a creature of passion and assertive yearning. Her breathtaking poem 'Maidin sa Domhain Toir' ('Morning in the Eastern World' or 'Oriental Morning') is one of the greatest personal poems written in the Irish language:

Ní foláir ag teacht ar an saol so
go rabhas róchraosach; gur roghnaíos
an bhullóg mhór is mallacht mo mháthar
in ionad na bullóige bige is a beannacht...

There's no doubt in coming to this place
I was too ravenous: that I chose
The full loaf (of life) and my mother's hatred
Instead of a half-loaf and her blessing...

In this poem the poet has fled abroad with her lover despite

Thomas McCarthy

every effort from her professional, haut bourgeois parents — including an attempt to make her a ward of court — to prevent her from leaving Ireland. The poem opens at dawn on the plains of Anatolia where the poet has made a new life with her Muslim husband and baby. She thinks of the great founder of Turkish hegemony, Mehmet I, and how in his moment of sorrow he recognizes the future flag of his country in the bloody pool of a horse's hoofmark. She thinks of her own smaller heroisms, of personal exile and motherhood. The poem is a triumph of human will and artistic grandeur. There is no poem like it in the Irish canon.

In those same years, those early years of a mean decade, the 1980s, another already respected young poet, Eavan Boland, also stepped forward and declared a new kind of feminist, person-centred, woman-centred poetry in a series of poems with unexpected titles like 'Menses', 'Anorexic', and 'Mastectomy'. Boland became an urgent new map-maker, mapping the body that had been excluded from history, from the political masculine history of Ireland. Male critics simply did not know how to cope with such new materials. Her project of reimagining Ireland was met with silence, cynical commentary, sometimes with open hostility. It would take many years and many books, such as *Night Feed* (1980), *In Her Own Image* (1980), *The Journey* (1987) and *Outside History* (1990), before Boland's new perception and sensibility would find purchase in the Irish critical world:

> *I was standing there*
> *at the end of a reading*
> *or at a workshop or whatever*
> *watching people heading*
> *out into the weather,*
>
> *only half-wondering*
> *what becomes of words,*
> *the brisk herbs of language,*

'The outrage of people': Why Men Should Study Women's Poetry

*the fragrances we think we sing,
if anything.*
      ('The Oral Tradition')

Nuala Ní Dhomhnaill and Eavan Boland were the beginning of that new wave in Irish women's poetry. The example they set, the courage with which they began, eviscerated male categories of thinking and circumvented the gatekeepers of the Irish canon. We have had two and a half decades of marvellous writing and publishing by women. The list of names is impressive: Áine Ní Glinn, Bríd Ní Mhóráin, Medbh McGuckian, Sinéad Morrissey, the astonishing Paula Meehan, the wonderful Mary O'Donnell, the sublime Vona Groarke, the hypnotic Martina Evans, the gifted Enda Wyley, Annemarie Ní Churreáin; all marvellous poets with distinctive and important voices. And there are others. When I was a young student in University College Cork the two dominant poets of the campus were John Montague and Seán Ó Tuama; one the great old voice of Ulster, the other the sparkling Gaelic voice of Munster. But recently the same University has appointed two new poets, young voices of the South, to lectureships in its English and Irish Departments — the wheel of life has turned and now two young female poets rule the roost in that place. Time, it seems, has begun to sift the canon. The first of these poets, Leanne O'Sullivan, has already achieved great things in her elaborate and passionate poetry. Her first collection, *Waiting for My Clothes* (2004) was published when she was just twenty years old. Since then she has published wonderful work in *Cailleach: The Hag of Beara* (2009) and, more recently, in that beautiful, heartrending collection *A Quarter of an Hour* (2018). The latter book is an astonishing poetic diary of the hours, days and months spent waiting at her comatose young husband's bedside while he recovered from a severe brain infection. The poems are an impressive record of the power and terror of human attachment:

Thomas McCarthy

> *The eyelash that drifted down the broad plane*
> *of your cheekbone comforts me. Is it the archer*
> *travelling across the night-sky of your un-*
> *consciousness...*
>   ('Prayer')

'Now an old truth rises to its zenith / in my adult life,' she writes in 'Oracle'; and in 'Note' she paints a picture of comatose drifting, separation, survival: 'If we become separated from each other / this evening try to remember the last time / you saw me, and go back and wait for me there...'

In poem after poem, in 'Tracheotomy', 'Lightning', 'Morning Poem' and many others, she creates an utterly believable picture of that pain of human attachment, such a picture that places her achievement in the tradition of the great Irish lament, the County Cork tradition of poems such as 'The Lament for Art O'Leary' by Eibhlín Dubh Ní Chonaill: 'Mo ghrá go daingean tu! / Lá dá bhfaca thu / Ag ceann tí an mhargaidh.' The power of a wife's attachment; the passionate, possessive nature of such love is wonderfully expressed by O'Sullivan in *A Quarter of an Hour*.

The other, equally marvellous, young female poet who graces UCC's thriving campus is the Irish-language poet, Ailbhe Ní Ghearbhuigh. She is a native of Tralee, County Kerry, now living in the Lough neighbourhood of Cork (a neighbourhood that features in the novel *The Threshold of Quiet* by the legendary Daniel Corkery) with her husband, the poet Billy Ramsell. Energetic, mischievous, provocative and witty, Ní Ghearbhuigh has recently published a selection of her original and translated work, *The Coast Road*, with Ireland's premier poetry publisher, The Gallery Press. The book brings to a wider, English-speaking audience the confirmed achievement of her two collections in the Irish language, *Péacadh* (2008) and *Tost agus Allagar* (2016). Here is a poetry of lust, loss, travel, folklore and philosophy:

'The outrage of people': Why Men Should Study Women's Poetry

Tógtar túr eile!
Túr na himní
Tuar an uafáis
Túr na tarcaisne
Tuar na tubaiste.

Let's build another tower!
Tower of anxiety
Omen of horror
The tower of insult
Omen of disaster.
(trans. Peter Sirr)

A poet of sure, confident feeling, a poet with the easy familiarity of love and love of the familiar and familial, Ní Ghearbhuigh has created a distinctive, thoughtful new style inside the Irish language. Her work is beyond politics; it is the voice of an entirely new generation, a new sensibility that's sociable and unshackled from Irish conventions and worries. The delight in her voice within the Irish language is unmistakable. Her youthful confidence remoulds old ways of thinking in an old tongue. She is unquestionably original and completely her own woman, owing nothing to anyone else in the field: 'Níl ann ach gur / thug mo shúil / taitneamh éigin duit, / a stróinséir . . . '

It's just that
my eyes lit
up at the sight
of you,
someone
out of the blue,
that I left behind
at the end of the night

before I came to
with an aftertaste

Thomas McCarthy

>*of Guinness
>and something
>little less than remorse
>in the light*
>
>*of the morning after.*
>   (trans. Peter Fallon)

The voice is so contemporary, so young, so free of the chains that bound us to the task of Irish poetry forty years ago. It is a joy to think that these very young poets, O'Sullivan and Ní Ghearbhuigh, now walking the campus of University College Cork as permanent members of its teaching staff, secure in their lives, making a new Irish future, that they have decades, even generations, of life ahead of them. They don't just occupy spaces vacated by lost male poets of the same campus, they create a new kind of space with new kinds of meanings and challenges for poetry. They are not just map-makers, they are creators of a new poetic landscape. And this is the reason why we should read them. Yes, it is the reason why men should read women poets — we should read them for the landscapes we once excluded from our own thought processes, we should read them for that 'new territory' as Eavan Boland described it so many years ago. It is not just the story of the long struggle to reach the full story of poetry, it is not just that long struggle that gives women's poetry its moral power. It is something more ordinary than that, something obvious to those who pay attention to texts and contexts: it is just that Irish women's poetry in the last forty years has created a new, larger aesthetic, a larger way of thinking about Irish poetry as well as a new way of thinking about Irish life itself.

*Encounters: Poetry and Writing,
December 2018*

Herself
In Her Own Image *by Eavan Boland. With drawings by Constance Short.*

Having just enjoyed a novel by that chauvinist Evelyn Waugh I hesitated before entering into the minefield of Eavan Boland's new book. Ms Boland has protested that she doesn't see herself as a feminist poet, but I know from her broadcasts over the last three years that she has suffered a feminist vision: that she had discovered exclusive female experience as a value in itself. *In Her Own Image* is the first serious attempt in Ireland to make a body of poems that arise out of the contemporary female consciousness. There is nothing in Eavan Boland's earlier books that will help the reader to unravel these new poems. All of the ten long poems that make this collection arise from the domestic micro-world of woman, from their body consciousness, their mother consciousness, etc. Putting it in a literary way one could say that Eavan Boland wasn't satisfied to go on looking at herself through the muse-mirror of Kinsella. She has chosen to construct her own mirror that will allow her to say 'not renewable, but *woman*':

> *I look*
> *in the glass . . .*
>
> *Myths*
> *are made by men.*

Whether Ms Boland believes that she's a feminist or not is irrelevant here; she has written a collection that addresses itself to feminist experience. Her poems, therefore, are so new on the Irish scene that they push questions of literary excellence, of correct construction or accepted modes of expression, to one side. There is a triumphant affirmation of womanhood throughout the book that seems to burst through old forms with confidence:

> *then I begin to know*
> *that I am bright and original*
> *and that my light's my own.*

or

> *I'll singe*
>
> *a page*
> *of history*
> *for these my sisters.*

One couldn't read a book such as this without being infected by the moral force of its protest. To find raw female thoughts like these one would have to turn to prose, to the recent stories of Kate Cruise O'Brien who also writes out of an upper-class experience where the most intense female angers seem to fester.

If you really want to get into Ms Boland's new book you should read it as part of a reading triangle with Kate Cruise O'Brien's *A Gift Horse* and Adrienne Rich's *Of Woman Born*. Surely it's more than a coincidence that some of the poems in the Boland book ('Mastectomy', 'Menses', 'Witching') are dramatic monologues on the subjects dealt with by Adrienne Rich. In particular the Boland poem on infanticide could have arisen from Rich's recollection of an evening spent with women poets (many of them mothers) in 1975 when they talked about a local woman who had murdered and decapitated her two youngest children. In her book Rich

Herself

recalled: 'Every woman in that room who had children, every poet, could identify with her ... The words are being spoken now, are being written down; the taboos are broken, the masks of motherhood are cracking through.'

In this very carefully constructed book Eavan Boland has tried to speak with the voice of a disembodied female consciousness. She has tried honestly to write down the tension between femaleness as an institution and femaleness as an experience. It will be interesting to see whether she carries on down the thematically limiting road of the Sisterhood or whether she will dance again upon the more general iambic table.

The Irish Times,
17 May 1980

Eavan Boland's Daring Integrity

There are many competing versions of Irishness. Every one of them is a distraction, dragging us back into a dialogue of atavisms. In poetry what matters are achievements of imagination. It is not a matter of what is appropriate or what is inappropriate. All kinds of orthodoxies fetter the imagination — social expectations, political attachments of Left and Right, religious training, academic canons, those inevitable limitations set by commercial anthologists — all are sent to persecute us, to disrupt the stuff we're made of. As Louis MacNeice wrote in *Autumn Sequel*: 'Which some explain by reference to God / And others find an inexplicable fact, / But fact it is, as downright as a clod, // As unremitting as a cataract.' Irishness can be a technical advantage, as some novelists and poets have discovered, but only in the context of the company we keep in the English language. It is only advantageous in terms of its relationship with Englishness — in any other context it is disastrously limiting, allowing the writer to make no great effort in order to create a literary effect. It offers an Irish writer the easy notoriety of rhetoric and bombast. Many have made good use of it, most especially those writing for the Anglophone theatre.

Frank O'Connor spent a lifetime trying to escape from narrow versions of Irishness. He lived at a time when the keys of the State had been handed over to the Catholic pietistic authorities, a situation that had been predicted a hundred years earlier by another Cork writer, Francis Sylvester Mahony, author of the *Reliques of Father Prout*. Writing as an invented clerical persona Father Prout, the wealthy and Jesuit-educated Rev Frank Mahony, never relented in his journalistic campaign against Daniel O'Connell and his Repeal Movement. He could see the corrupt combination of O'Connell's 'place men' and how Mammon had made a deal with the Divine:

> *'This arch-lawyer's name was Dandeleone [sic], of the old Carthaginian family of the Smugglêri, settled on the south-west coast, towards the Spanish port of Valentia. Always disaffected to the government in Turin, they were of course ineligible to posts of emolument in Sardinia, but they helped themselves to wealth in rather an off-hand manner. This is rather a delicate topic, which I would rather avoid, but the "immaculate" party having adopted the bullying system in every minute matter, will insist on our not only reverencing a hero himself, but his grandfather and his grandchildren, his ox and his ass, and everything belonging to him. To drive a coach and four, or a "six-oared gig", through Sardinian* law, *was an exploit therefore to him of instinct and hereditary transmission.'*
> — 'Don Jeremy Savonarola' in *Final Reliques of Father Prout*, (1876).

Mahony's campaign against the social and imaginative limitations of Catholic power (he also reported on the banning of stethoscopes in hospitals of the Vatican states) was understood by both Joyce and Beckett, and Mahony remains as a vibrant presence in their work.

It is interesting that Frank O'Connor, another Corkman who would bang his head against the brick wall of a provincial Irish influence, could not comprehend Mahony/Prout's centrality. That he couldn't do so is a sure sign that clerical control not only of private morals but of public history was complete. The controlling narrative had been established. The controlling essence of Irish imagination has been in the provinces: County Cork, depraved, as Beckett's Murphy

Thomas McCarthy

growls, thinking, no doubt, of Daniel Corkery's crowd at a Munster Hurling Final rather than Miss Counihan's lover upon the tomb of Father Prout in *Murphy*. Such provincial culture (think stories of Daniel Corkery, plays of T C Murray or paintings of Seán Keating) is male, sporting, homespun as a Connemara holiday and, sometimes, stupid with alcohol. It is what every Irishwoman has had to negotiate, that lethal conjunction of laddish politics and 'national feeling' — a feeling so alarmingly identified by Yeats in his Journal of 14 March 1909:

> 'So long as all is ordered for attack, and that alone, leaders will instinctively increase the number of enemies that they may give their followers something to do, and Irish enemies rather than English because they are the more easily injured, and because the greater the enemy the greater the hatred and therefore the greater the power. They would give a nation the frenzy of a sect.'

And all of this so aptly captured by an Editorial in *An Camán* of 6 January 1934:

> 'We of the Irish-Ireland movement are wholeheartedly behind this anti-jazz campaign. In these columns we have never ceased to stress the dangers, morally and nationally, which jazz music and jazz dance hold for our people, especially in rural areas. The false tolerance towards jazz, speciously advanced in argument by those who advocate freedom of choice in pastimes and recreations, has had its corrosive influence on all phases of national thought.'

Little over a year after our *An Camán* Editorial Frank O'Connor would write one of his great stories, 'In The Train'. The central character, a woman who'd been found not guilty of her husband's murder, is placed at the periphery of the story. Her destiny is a reminder that the short story is primarily an achievement of forms of constraint.

It is interesting to note, in the context of so much that Eavan Boland has written, how quickly 'freedom of choice' became something un-Irish, un-patriotic. The seeds of our Stasi-like Republic that diminished women were sown long, long ago, and the trail of that national stain goes all the way back to the shrewd and ambitious 'place men' of Daniel O'Connell, the resurgence of Catholic power, that Ibsen-like inertia so brilliantly captured by Joyce. It created a mindset that dominates Irish commentary to this very day. If I linger too long in any Irish pub I meet Daniel Corkerys thirty years younger than I, and their political and moral certainties frighten me. You must understand this: in Ireland the cowed and conventional still laugh loudest for they are relieved from the burden of conscience. Developing and protecting the national conscience has been the major Nationalist project since the Act of Union. We still act as if we were all Repealers. It is best to see Eavan Boland's work as a singular, visual leap of conscience, away from those curators of national narrative, into a new studio, in order to act upon a fresh canvas. In this great leap of artistic conscience she was most like the visual artists, Norah McGuinness, Mainie Jellett and Evie Hone, who abandoned the dead dialogue of national representation in art and discovered a new conversation with modernism, with Cubism. But, as Paula McCarthy notes in the Ní Chuilleanáin-edited *Irish Women: Image and Achievement*: 'Despite Mainie Jellett's enormous influence, Cubism was never fully accepted in Ireland.' A firm and powerfully-resourced Nationalist viewpoint had its icy grip upon Irish imagination; it would be decades before that grip was even slightly eased.

There was always something slightly off-centre about the young Boland, an intensity and restlessness that gave her views of history more precision and much less sentimentality. Coming from a cradle of record keepers, two generations back, who administered to over a thousand souls at Clonmel Workhouse, it was in Boland's inherited nature to keep records straight, to eschew what was easy, colloquial, congenial. She began very early to be a rapporteur for immortality. From this beginning she lived in 'exile or arrival / And be at home in both'. As early as *New Territory*, in 'Athene's Song', the poet lives within the pain of a secondary yearning, that yearning for pipe and music left behind in order to conform to a mythic purpose, a confirmation of art by men. The stillness of this beginning is disrupted a few short years later by a sound now famous in the annals of Irish poetry — the sound of a straying Dundrum horse: 'clip, clop, casual // Iron of his shoes as he stamps death / Like a mint on the innocent coinage of earth.' Something is broken by this sound, the winged horse of Poesy is grounded, literally. In a very real sense that war horse is the harbinger of a major disintegration: the bond of authority that bound Eavan Boland to accepted Irish themes and lyric forms will collapse very quickly now — in the space of three or four years she will have migrated, emotionally and politically, from Ó Rathaille and Yeats to Lowell and Plath. It was an important leap for freedom: 'For the senses arise from the essences, they have their origin from the sting of desire, from the sourness; they are the bitterness, and run always in the mind,' as Levertov wrote to Robert Duncan in 1959. For Boland Adrienne Rich and Denise Levertov were the Albert Gleizes and André Lhote of the revelatory moment. Reviewing the correspondence of Duncan and Levertov years later Boland wrote, 'Duncan's way of becoming a poet was essentially — as was Pound's — collaborative. He needed witnesses, companions, an audience.' The great irony of Boland's brave career is that the Irish audience, that crucial parish of rich women, needed her more than she needed them.

The audience *yearned* and Boland *became*. In becoming herself she created an entirely new field of poetic activity. I was an early witness to her profound effect upon a generation of new women writers. In Cork City in the bleak 1980s she was a pivotal, Messiah-like presence from afar. The poets and fiction writers of the Cork Women's Poetry Circle found in her work, poems and commentary, an enabling, moral presence. And she responded to the responsibilities set up by the new expectations in her work; in the mid-80s she encouraged women leaders like Máire Bradshaw in Cork by making the long journey south to give readings and preside over workshops. She carried other writers with her, from this land of Ireland to the better land of ideas. The act was gender aware only because of exclusions based upon gender, for she has always understood, as Robert Graves wrote in his essay '-Ess' that 'poetry should not be an affair of sex any more than, for example, surgery. One says: "Mary Smith is a surgeon," not "Mary Smith is a surgeoness," or even "Mary Smith is a lady surgeon." Sex has no place in the operating theatre. Poetry is a sort of operating theatre.'

For poetry is where we dwell. It is a second country that requires the second map; or, to quote Graves again, 'This nobleman is at home anywhere / His castle being, the valet says, his title' ('The Cloak'). *Object Lessons* and *A Journey with Two Maps* is the double map of that title 'Poet'. It is her attempt at integration, cultural and psychological integration, beginning at an estranged starting point, that title 'Irish Poet', and ending with political arrival, as described in her essay on Paula Meehan, 'The emergence of women has now made a new space in the Irish poem.' It was Boland, working alone and constantly derided by the male of the species, who created that new space for poetry. She created a new masterpiece with her own name upon it. In writing prose, such work as we find in both *A Journey with Two Maps* and *Object Lessons*, Eavan Boland is answering Yeats's command to the lyric poet; the command that the lyric poet should do everything to explain the life behind the lyrics. The motive of her autobiographical writing is not autobiographical. There is no desperate effort of explanation or personal redress such as one finds in Frank O'Connor's *An Only Child* or Frank McCourt's *Angela's Ashes*. It is exploratory explication, an act of exemplary remembrance. Socially Boland has no need to explain herself. Like Beckett she has been blessed with an *un*fractured upper middle-class Dublin life. An artist-mother carried her in her womb and she has grown into the full adult life of art. In 1988, in a regular *Observer* review, Anita Brookner wrote:

> '*Autobiography is traditionally a genre peculiar to the upwardly mobile, the socially insecure, those who have no context to explain them. Its purpose is to expunge pain, but more than this, to create a life myth, an alternative support system. In rewriting history and establishing causation a measure of control over circumstances is achieved. It is a daring and agonizing task which may not fulfil its intended purpose.*'

Boland's daring and agonizing task has been to call back Irish life, that poor Free State of Austin Clarke living on lack, and to feed it retrospectively with insights of liberation; it is a prodigious effort not just to make the poem but to make the audience learn a little jazz. She has chosen to take on, politically, a society that made boors of educated men and modest creatures of all women. If her mother was an artist then she is the prodigy, creating a vast studio of new work. She belongs with Mainie Jellett and Evie Hone as they scramble to put the last few centimes together for a second Paris latté. She belongs among such Irishwomen, the instinctive and the first rate who strive for a second kind of representative art.

PN Review,
2014

Eavan Boland by Jody Allen Randolph

Scholarship, and particularly gender scholarship, now teaches us that there is no such thing as the simple act of reading or writing, however much your public librarian will want you to believe in it. You come to the page drunk or rabid with prejudice: 'Boland's work has been tested by various critiques, from the feminist to the postcolonial, from the postmodern to the environmental, from visual studies to film theory, from trauma theory to diaspora theory,' writes a brilliant Research Fellow from UCD, Jody Allen Randolph, as she sets up the dissecting table under this floodlight of theories.

What distinguishes the complex and intellectually trenchant Boland is her respectful relationship with such theorists: academic by nature and nurture she trusts the process of intellectual dialogue. No Irish poet, not even Seamus Heaney, was so prepared for a lifelong dialogue with a highly motivated readership. One of the great delights of this book, part of the Cork University Press series on Irish writers, is that it provides an exhausting and thrilling narrative of that intellectual, mainly feminist, dialogue between the poet and her demanding congregation of listeners. These chapters are singed with controversy and a great ferment in the public domain; the smell of a public burning comes off the pages.

As scholar and theorist Allen Randolph would eschew the poet Brodsky's warning that a writer has but a life and a work. The new scholarship has ensured that we now read poems through the highly glazed window of theory. In Allen Randolph's and Boland's case this is a happy and perfect match: the book itself is a powerful monument to a long relationship. Here is Boland's Boswell, or Joseph Hone. By the age of thirty Eavan Boland had abandoned the simplistic Brodsky viewpoint; she reorientated entirely her own conventional thinking. In an act of defiance, mainly against herself, she abandoned the poet-woman of the old aisling, the woman as national metaphor, and embraced the body imperfect. Womanhood, motherhood, sisterhood, bodily function, rather than the table-tapping Theosophists of Yeats, became the basis for her new theory of art. A new architecture of historic and personal feeling was born that was every bit as radical as the concave house of her famous architect godfather, Michael Scott, a place from which Boland remembers gazing upon Joyce's Martello tower. Joyce, of course, is the great untoppled omphalos of fearful Jesuits and exploitative male ambition.

The resistance to Boland's recentring, the creation of her own self as the centre of a canon, was both heated and illuminating. Most of the commentary in Ireland between 1980 and 1990 has never found its way into print. It was snide commentary and nasty put-down, a shrewd short selling of what she was attempting to do. Regressive elements in a culture rarely want to be placed on the record but always hope, like the cowards they are, that some ill-advised fool will do the hatchet job for them. By 1990, certainly by 1994, Boland's trajectory had sent her well beyond the reach of Irish hatchets, regressive or otherwise. Her eyes were always on the main prize, which was to come into full possession of her fully integrated self. Allen Randolph, here, follows Ms Boland's marvellous journey, from suburban *The War Horse* to mystical *Night Feed* to the kitchen and shadow kitchen of *Domestic Violence*: 'nothing we said / not then, not later, / fathomed what it is / is wrong in the lives of those who hate each other.'

But with Eavan Boland it is always more than the poems. The theoretical garden where the poems grow is a product of invented belonging, a deliberate Yeats-like act by someone who was never completely at home in a simply defined Irish house. Her greatest years of personal happiness and fulfilment

Eavan Boland by Jody Allen Randolph

were the years when the poet created an invented territory that became the poetry of *The Journey*. Those were years of living poetry rather than living a theory. Allen Randolph charts this old territory and new territory in her very early discussion of Boland's two collections of essays, *Object Lessons* and *A Journey with Two Maps*: 'While *Object Lessons* was a book by a woman poet negotiating with a national tradition, *A Journey with Two Maps* is transnational in reach, engaging the question of how women poets are made, and what goes into that making . . . '

Indeed, in the early 80s, I remember reciting a group of Boland poems to mainly female tyro-poets at Iowa University: their response to her work was wonder-filled, welcoming, thrilled. I had to put away my own two books and talk of poor old de Valera away and instead field a torrent of questions on *Night Feed* and *In Her Own Image*. I remember thinking at that time, 'I hope this woman finds this audience.' The narrative of Jody Allen Randolph's book is how such a first-rate poet found such a first-rate readership, despite a distance of air miles and cultural background. Allen Randolph comes across here as a generous, expansive intelligence, both analytical and affirming, in a ground-marking work of literary synthesis.

Irish Examiner,
2014

From a woman on a train to 'Formal Feeling'
Eavan Boland, Frank O'Connor and our Troubled Irish Journey

'Aengus and Etain lived for each other's pleasure, / With gold for the head of Aengus as king / And gold so intricate in Etain's hair / No one could guess if the light scattering / Were a woman's beauty or a queen's treasure' — these lines are part of Eavan Boland's 'The Winning of Etain', published in *New Territory*, her very accomplished, and not in the least tentative, 1967 volume. This poem, a formal masterpiece of thirty-eight stanzas, was a real attention grabber in the settled, formalized milieu of a settled and self-regarding Ireland. By 1967, one year after the 1916 Golden Jubilee, two years after the Yeats Centenary and four years after a Kennedy Presidency, there were congratulations all round in the good old Emerald Isle. We were all living imaginatively, even those of us born poor, on a plush Youghal carpet with Celtic designs. Even the literature was becoming a little unctuous: when the existential Thomas Kinsella told us that life was an ordeal and existence a misfortune we knew he didn't mean it. But even at that moment of Irish national contentment before Ulster broke, comparable to that golden summer of 1914 in England, there were already many competing versions of Irishness: Behan, Kavanagh, Frank O'Connor, Conradh na Gaeilge or The Legion of Mary. The possibilities for public rhetoric were everywhere.

Stitching the golden threads of Etain and Aengus into the deep woolly pile of the translated Anglo-Irish tradition was one way of establishing a stall in this throbbing bazaar of Irish poetry.

The Ireland of what can best be described as the de Valera

From a woman on a train to 'Formal Feeling'

years, 1927-1967, was a land of established piety, legitimacy, conformity, a land of cowed intelligence. There were flashes of brilliance in this land, of course, from Kate O'Brien's *That Lady*, Máire Mhac an tSaoi's 'Ceathrúintí Mháire Ní Ógáin' in *Margadh na Saoire* to Edna O'Brien's *The Country Girls*. Such brilliance would be excluded from polite discourse, would be banned and rendered 'foreign'. As in all comfortably established tyrannies what was immoral could not be considered 'national' or 'normal'. One of the most illuminating tropes or fictional constructs of that era is the invented suffering female as central character in the work of writers like Brian Moore, Austin Clarke, John Montague and Frank O'Connor. The hearts of these male writers were in the right place, I assume, but the effects they create reek of a sexist ventriloquism. No such ventriloquism was intended, I'm sure, but the assumption of authority over female victimhood, the audacity to speak for silenced experiences, to colonize a distinct territory of threatened Irish being — Moore's *Judith Hearne*, Clarke's 'Martha Blake', Montague's mother of Jimmy Drummond ('Her only revenge on her hasty lovers / Was to call each child after its father') — was surely the clearest example of our masculine hegemony. Looking back now, I mean as a male writer, such a pervasive literary presumption is simply breathtaking.

No female victim was ever so poignantly drawn by Frank O'Connor as the character of Helena Maguire in 'In the Train', Helena who joins her fellow villagers for the terrifying return train journey to Farranchreesht after her acquittal. The villagers had perjured themselves in a collective effort to clear Helena's name — not because they loved or pitied her but only because they wanted to bring her home to punish her for the rest of her days: 'Then, just as the train was about to start, a young woman in a brown shawl rushed through the barrier. The shawl, which came low enough to hide her eyes, she held firmly across her mouth, leaving visible only a long thin nose with a hint of pale flesh at either side.' Helena's destiny has a cinematic, Hitchcock-like overtone; and in his extraordinary story O'Connor creates an astonishing portrait of trapped and punished victimhood. The fiction is of such humanity and magnitude that it almost leaps across gender categories. High art such as 'In the Train' is very nearly genderless in its common humanity — except that it isn't. Our focus here is on O'Connor, the genius storyteller. The denouement is his, not Helena Maguire's. In the end we will never know her voice, its quality or ambiguity, in the same way that we will never have but an elliptical knowledge of the life of Judith Hearne or Martha Blake. Such writing by men is, in the end, a *Black and White Minstrel Show*. For the true voice of any community literature has to wait for the arrival of the community itself. I am certain that in Irish poetry this community arrived in 1980 with the publication of *In Her Own Image* and *Night Feed*. The young everywoman, such an object of desire in the erotic work of Montague and Kennelly in the previous decade, now spoke of anorexia, menses, mastectomy and solitude. It was as if the love object in Montague's 'Life Class' turned to the reader and spoke in her own voice:

> Or when I moan
> for him between the sheets,
> then I begin to know
> that I am bright and original
> and that my light's my own.

In the chapter 'From Patria to Matria', published in her Cork University Press study of Boland (2014), Jody Allen Randolph maps both the political and sociological background to Boland's moment of insight: '*In Her Own Image* was written in the late 1970s, parallel to the emergence of feminist poststructuralist theory. The French feminist movement, as it was called at the time, began with the work of women theorists — Hélène Cixous, Julia Kristeva, Luce Irigary, Monique Wittig — who made bold restatements of theories linking sexuality to textuality. Their theories were gathered under the banner of *écriture feminine*, a term popularized by Hélène Cixous in "The Laugh of the Medusa" (1975).'

Ironically, in 1975, the year of the Cixous text, and just a few busy parenting years before she created the founding texts of Irish feminist poetry, Boland published *The War Horse*. The collection contained poetry of real achievement, structured brilliantly, robust and lyrical. I was with a group of young male poets when a copy of Boland's new collection came into the hands of John Montague, then our mentor and the uber-poet at UCC. The book was passed round in Montague's sitting room at Grattan Hill, Cork, and a male verdict was pronounced: this was terrific, unexpected stuff from Ms Boland. All agreed that it was as good as anything by Hartnett who, at that very moment, in his *A Farewell to English*, had decided to bid farewell to the English language, and who might then have been the leading poet of the South. Part of the shock of her subsequent 1980s texts was that embedded literary memory of her real achievement in conventional work between 1967 and 1975, and an inability in the male establishment to see how a poet could go outside history so irresponsibly, so recklessly. Her 1980s volumes were so unexpected that they were received and read as evidence of a technical breakdown rather than a breakout. In truth Eavan Boland's first major achievement, born of innate character, was her ability to centre herself against a prevailing wind, to orientate her being with an inner gyroscope. As a poet, with the seas hostile and the deck heaving, she had an ability to balance in this storm of masculinities. Thomas Kinsella in his 1963 *Irish Press* review of her early *23 Poems* (1962) was among the first to spot this capacity for orientation: 'Eavan Boland has already the gift of setting the scene as in 'Illusion at Shanganagh' or 'The Moon-Tree' or 'Dream of Cathleen' which begins:

Thomas McCarthy

> *Here is the bridge; four swans inside*
> *The midnight, ovaled in stone*
> *And darkness, are asleep . . .*

None of these reviewed poems would survive into *New Collected Poems*, though the Liffey, water and bridge, would be retained. Stones, water, flight, swans, fleeing lovers, Yeats, Etain, Kings and Earls: the poet might easily have settled into a narrow Austin Clarke-like mythology. A lesser imagination, so highly educated and socially placed, might have settled for the more settled, more worthy, discourse. But there was something more fiercesome inside, some compelling discomfort, that is the basis of the original art in Boland's poetry. Her ability to centre the self combined with a capacity to ignite the narrative outward; that was what made her uniquely complete: 'I will be here / til midnight, cross-legged in the dining room, / logging triangles and diamonds, / cutting and aligning, / finding greens in pinks / and burgundies in whites / until I finish it. // There's no reason in it.' She has always written from the emotional place where the self is adamant. She is more than aware of the presumptions of our human knowing, as she states clearly in that same 'Patchwork or the Poet's Craft':

> *I have been thinking at random*
> *on the universe*
> *or rather, how nothing in the universe*
> *is random.*

In a marvellous essay 'Evie Hone: Stained Glass Artist 1894-1955', first published in *Studies*, Summer 1955, and reprinted in *A Tribute to Evie Hone and Mainie Jellett*, edited by Stella Frost, C P Curran describes a turning point in the artistic life of Irishwomen, a first encounter between the Cubist Albert Gleizes and two Irishwomen in search of new knowledge:

> 'Gleizes has left an entertaining account of this first encounter from which I venture to quote. The date was 1921 when he was still immersed in his own technical problems with nothing further from his mind than the idea of teaching. The two friends said they wished to work along his lines and asked for lessons. Their quiet assurance and decided tone threw him into an agony of embarrassment. "Give you lessons? But it is I who want lessons. What do you want me to teach you? I have the greatest trouble in clearing up my own difficulties. How do you think I can tackle yours? What have you done? Where have you come from?" They told him and went on to say that his work corresponded exactly with what they were looking for... He pleaded his friendly relations with Lhote: he would not steal his pupils. "But we are at perfect liberty to choose our own master."'

In the weeks that followed Gleizes' teaching and their powerful responses would transform both master and pupils. What the three worked towards was a fulsome repudiation of the idea of a single viewpoint. Art would not succumb to the given viewpoint but would disturb it, rotate it, making inertia dynamic. Some years later Evie Hone would hold a joint exhibition at the Dublin Painters' Gallery with Mainie Jellett, but her innovative stained glass designs would still have to fight for their light until she met Wilhelmina Geddes in London.

What happens in visual art would also happen in literature. After ten years of Irish self-government the hegemony of the one little nation was complete. Even a cursory look at the lavish *Saorstát Éireann* Official Handbook (Dublin, 1932) will show that what was modern or modernist was not welcome: 'The Free State has not yet been established for a sufficient time to redeem the promise of those Irish artists who, in the eighth century, won for their country a preeminence

Thomas McCarthy

in illuminated manuscripts and precious metal work over all other nations of Europe. The intervening dark years of turmoil and misery effectively prevented the development of a distinctly Irish School of Fine Art.' The ignorance of this statement is simply astonishing, how it glosses over nearly three hundred years of landscape and portraiture of great beauty — but one can see why, politically. The ownership of studios and art in those centuries was mainly in the hands of Protestant Irishmen, persons seen in 1932 as a garrison population with alien interests. That the facts of art can be denied shows the power of a political atmosphere. And, as for literature, the same Handbook was adamant: 'Irish literature in English can scarcely be said to have become fully national til about the time of the Young Ireland in the forties of the nineteenth century. It has often been said that a new soul was born into Ireland at this time as a result of the inspiration of Thomas Davis and the "Nation" group. It is equally certain that a new soul was born into Irish poetry.' This new modest orthodoxy, a national chauvinism, now ruled the public realm. With honourable exceptions, tiny pockets of bohemia created by *Ireland Today* or *The Bell*, a modest and quietly satisfied Catholic Ireland purred splendidly for nearly half a century. Let us not forget that Boland's beginnings on paper were as orthodox and conventional as any other Irish poet of her era, a yearning for more history, a nod to the Celtic stuff, a go at gods or concepts scavenged from history or translations, that Irish naming of names that belong to the familiar:

> *Son of Lir as lonely are you now*
> *as the leaf when lightning strikes the tree*
> *and the bird when thunder breaks his bough.*
> *Now is lost, as bird and leaf and tree*
> *Son of Lir, your humanity.*
> ('Malediction')

Ah, Lir, bird, leaf, tree, even a broken bough. Here is someone who had heard Austin Clarke, President Douglas Hyde or Frank O'Connor speak. By the mid-twentieth century there had been an uncanny settling of orthodoxies in poetry: in Ireland it was a bird, a leaf, a Lir and in, let's say, Russia it was 'peace', 'commune', 'worker', 'pylon'. But there was always something slightly off-centre about the young Boland, an intensity and restlessness that gave her view of history more precision and much less sentimentality. The love of precision always contains a dangerous political risk in a comfort zone like Ireland:

> *maybe*
> *for those imprisoned here this was a small*
> *consoling inland symbol — how could their way be*
> *otherwise...*
>   ('A Cynic at Kilmainham Gaol')

It's not that such a woman poet finds herself outside History but that History has detained her for retraining so that she may be able to create a new History out of the materials she had found once she'd escaped from the cultural beginnings of our Free State. She rewrites the Handbook. The social realism of O'Connor, hot-headed idealist, vituperative and incandescent critic of the petit-bourgeois narrative of de Valera's Ireland, such pained realism would be cooled into a counter-narrative by Boland, nocturnally walking the corridors of a life more complex and humane:

> *Eros look down.*
> *See as a god sees*
> *what a myth says: how a woman still*
> *addresses the work of man in the dark of the night.*
>
> *The power of form. The plain*
> *evidence that stretch descended here once.*
> *And mortal pain. And even sexual glory.*

Thomas McCarthy

And see the difference.
This time — and this you did not ordain —
I am changing the story.
             ('Formal Feeling', *New Collected Poems*)

Eavan Boland: Inside History,
2017

'None of us well fixed'
Empathy and its Aesthetic Power in Paula Meehan's Poetry

'I'm no Buddhist: too attached to the world / of my six senses,' writes Paula Meehan in 'Sudden Rain', a brief lyric poem in *Dharmakaya* (2000). The statement is both true and untrue but its wavering distance from what is true and untrue is a dynamic aesthetic, a diary of oscillations, in the serious pilgrimage of this serious poet. It is now a quarter of a century since Beaver Row Press published *Return and No Blame* (1984), a book without packaging, a book without a blurb or biography, that fell upon us like an LP from Motown. Meehan's was a voice both unexpected and unheralded, yet polished and certain. It was still the early 80s in Ireland, a land of lightly trodden and unpaved roads in women's writing. Yes, Eavan Boland had recorded both her own image and her night feeds in brave, minimalist forms but Caitlín Maude was suddenly dead, and the achievements of Adrienne Rich, Carolyn Forché and Jane Cooper were but distant rumours.

Such rumours would never reach certain ossified male quarters of Irish poetry, but Meehan was already conversing with the gathered-in and the living. In 'The Apprentice' she wrote:

> *The poor become clowns*
> *In your private review.*
> *But when all is done and said*
>
> *Your swanlike women are dead,*
> *Stone dead. My women must be*

Thomas McCarthy

> *Hollow of cheek with poverty*
> *And the whippings of history!*
>
> (Return and No Blame)

That 'stone' before 'dead' is crucial, edgy, local, unheroic. In 'Journeys to My Sister's Kitchen' she catalogues the failed connections between her own vulnerabilities and the silences of her sister, domestic life as 'any small dead thing / In the arms of its mother' that acts as a mirror with its own narrative, a mirror that might trap her into a familiar slavery:

> *In your scullery*
> *You wash and you rinse*
> *Crockery, cutlery.*
> *You stack them, you dry them.*
> *The doors and the floors*
> *Are scrubbed, waxed, and polished —*
> *Hearth business.*

The sister of the poem might have been that of another Dublin poet, Máire Mhac an tSaoi, who had written, eleven years earlier in *Codladh an Ghaiscígh* (1973):

> *Nigh agus sciúr agus glan,*
> *Cóirigh proinn agus lacht,*
> *Iompaigh tochta, leag brat,*
> *Ach, ar nós Sheicheiriseáide,*
> *Ní mór duit an fhilíocht chomh maith!*
>
> ('Cré Na Mná Tí')

Meehan's first book is weighed down with instances of alienation and remembered failures to cohere. It is a scarred witness of Irish life, yet determinedly still standing and wanting to speak out. From 'T B Ward' with its 'Gobshite from Tuam' and 'Slimy little fucker' and 'Cronos / Time eating his children', to the child's return in 'Return and No Blame' with its 'room of my childhood' where the narrator can 'watch awhile the flames flicker / The story of our distance on the wall', the book's deepest impression is one of disturbance and dispersal and of love as the fleeting comfort of women on the run from threatening domestic scenarios.

Her first collection was a powerful debut and what followed was work of even greater power, work that would, over two decades, chronicle with honest indignation the war against the six senses of every Irish woman. Meehan's impulse is at all times sensual and political, a world where sisters not only walk into doors, but where art, too, is called to witness. In 'Woman Found Dead behind Salvation Army Hostel', Meehan submits narrative to a double discipline. It is not just death but an artist recording the image after 'the beast who maimed her':

> *You can make a quick sketch*
> *and later, in your studio, mix the colours,*
> *the purple, the eerie green of her bruises,*
> *the garish crimson of her broken mouth.*
> (The Man Who Was Marked by Winter)

In 'Night Walk' a living woman walks the streets late at night, walking out and away from love gone sour, but walking the gauntlet of eerie granite cobbles, Fumbally Lane, Blackpitts, Mount Street, past a night train of chemicals:

> Let her too get home safe, *your prayer,*
> not like that poor woman last night
> dragged down Glovers Alley, raped there,
> battered to a pulp. Still unnamed.
> (Pillow Talk)

The anxieties are real, not mythical, based on stories told first-hand by victims. The politic here is one of deepest female empathy, a circling of those not too well fixed in the city of dread.

An Irish urban landscape emerges from these poems, a landscape that is as well-defined and distinctive as a Bill Brandt streetscape. Like the wet industrial cobbles of Carol Reid's films it is trodden earth, hardened ground, an anti-pastoral, anti-romantic Ireland.

But Paula Meehan's world is not a land without 'nature', not an inorganic world. It is the very opposite, in fact, garlanded with herbs and flowers, with knowledge of husbandry and a sensitized awareness of the changing seasons. Of 'Elder' she writes:

> *I love its fecundity, its left alone*
> *self designing wildness, especially in June,*
> *the tomcat pungency of elderblossom*
> *(reeking in our rooms).*
> (Dharmakaya)

But the garlanded nature of husbandry, that refuge of scented order, had been with Meehan from the beginning. In *Return and No Blame* she had written:

> *In a geranium room*
> *Among your choice*
> *Of books and plants*
> *Carefully tended —*
> *Because none knows better than you*
> *How precious life is in that city . . .*

It is in the garden she receives the epiphany of her father as St Francis, her father in the pandemonium of a frenzied Finglas dawn feeding chorus in *Pillow Talk* (1994): and it is in the garden that herbs, flowers, memories pass judgement upon broken relationships and 'abandoned gardens, abandoned husband' as she named the husbanded spectres that accuse her:

'None of us well fixed'

Not alone the rue in my herb garden
passes judgement, but the eight foot
high white foxgloves among the greys
of wormwood, santolina, lavender,
the crimson rose at our cottage door,
the peas holding for dear life . . .
                                             (Pillow Talk)

The world is intensely personal at all times through two decades of writing. The garden, the kitchen, the cobbled Dublin street: each is a metaphor surely, an image for the sociologist or critic to juggle with; but each is a lived place, an architecture built up around a set of very personal experiences or memories. The poem, the metaphor itself, is fulfilling an almost physically personal function: in Meehan it is the thing itself as well as its set of meanings. The images are organically attached and strenuously lived in. The poems accumulate and blend over decades and seem part of a unified thought, the mosaic of a single, twisting strip of DNA: in terms of poetry, a single meditation or Buddhist insight. Each Meehan book leaves the reader with an aroma of flowers and the memory of a struggle but all tightly controlled by a mind at ease in a vortex of chaos. Not to understand this personal power in Meehan's work is to miss the point completely. There is a great still centre, a sense of ease that comes from having filtered a great personal pain, combined with an impulse toward mediation and empathy.

Meehan came into her voice, also, just at that worldwide political moment when Reagan and Thatcher's cruel view of history was ascending. The era of peace and love, the garden of the *Whole Earth Catalog*, the great experiments in personal life in West Cork or Southern California, were coming to an abrupt end. The war against the working class, the destruction of unions, the defeat of the miners and printers were all at hand. The poor could hope for nothing except their own solidarity and witness. Meehan's is one of the radical voices that sidled away from that 80s picket line; she carries a radical placard, on her own behalf as well as others, into the self-satisfied territory of the agreed agenda. Her empathy with ordinary, unheroic suffering, her contempt for claptrap, her technical skill as a poet, all come together in collection after collection to strike an authentic new note in Irish poetry. The note is one of solidarity, lyrically expressed and painfully earned.

Her Ireland of the early 80s was the beginning of something else in poetry — a powerful creative impulse among women. The condition of possibility, of acceptance, so well described by Jane Cooper in her essay 'Nothing Has Been Used in the Manufacture of This Poetry That Could Have Been Used in the Manufacture of Bread' was being swept away: 'I saw clearly how hard it would be for me to make a lasting relationship, bringing up children and "live a full life as a woman", while being a committed writer. The women poets I read about were generally not known for their rich, stable sexual and family lives' (*Maps and Windows*). In the wake of Doris Lessing and Adrienne Rich came a battalion of strong female voices, from Caitlín Maude to Carolyn Forché, from Nell McCafferty to Eavan Boland. With the enemies of a full life, an interrogated life of the earthly and human spirit, ascending the thrones, Meehan's strong heart and political instinct flourished in that alternative spiritual company:

> *I'm not your muse, not that creature*
> *in the painting, with the beautiful body,*
> *Venus on the half-shell. Can*
> *you not see I'm an ordinary woman*
> *tied to the moon's phases, bloody*
> *six days in twenty-eight?*
> (Pillow Talk)

Empathy, and its political dynamic, began with Meehan as complete self-knowledge that rotated outward, embracing others: mothers, sisters, lovers, neighbours, ghosts and fellow poets. History is her story, but with a thousand parallel stories running concurrently. The work is saturated with the lives of others; the poet meditates at the still centre of a fairly dramatic and rowdy urban milieu: the noise from the poems is the true narrative of that milieu. The poems survive everything, including her work of continuing, practical solidarity.

I emphasize the word 'solidarity'. It is more than merely giving witness; it is certainly beyond the confines and luxuries of a literary project. It doesn't require big words or banal academic interrogations. It is a matter of listening, gauging the tone and volume of the lyrics, and therefore weighing the weight of one human soul. It was the absence of this soul, the weighty application of a soul-filled counterbalance, that skewed the nature of Irish poetic practice from the very beginning. In the Ireland invented and patented by Daniel O'Connell, Douglas Hyde, and W B Yeats, there are certain key elements missing. As late as the 1920s Constance, Countess Markievicz, speaking in the Dáil, had this to say:

> 'The question of votes for women, with the bigger thing, freedom for women and the opening of professions to women, has been one of the things that I have worked for and given my lifelong influence and time to procuring all my life whenever I got an opportunity. I have worked in Ireland, I have even worked in England, to help women to obtain their freedom. I would work for it anywhere, as one of the crying wrongs of the world, that women, because of their sex, should be debarred from any position or any right that their brains entitle them to hold.'
> (Dáil Éireann Debates, 1922)

'That their brains entitle them to hold': is it not extraordinary how difficult it has been to communicate that clear and simple message, a perception at the very core of the European enlightenment and a truth burned into history on the barricades of Paris and the charred buildings of Dublin 1916? Literary practice, the industry of imagining, writing, editing, and publishing, has been dominated by males, many in Holy Orders, since the foundation of the Irish State. A lesser state than had been imagined was brought into being. A black veil was thrown over the serious lives of women, although women's work was everywhere, on the farm and in scholarship.

The best poetry must be allowed to surface: as it surfaces we are exposed to half the story of the world. When one thinks of the poets at work in Ireland now — Máire Mhac an tSaoi, Eavan Boland, Eiléan Ní Chuilleanáin, Paula Meehan, Medbh McGuckian, Kerry Hardie, Sinéad Morrissey, Leontia Flynn and Leanne O'Sullivan — one could make a strong case that at this very moment in Ireland there are more good female poets than male poets. Does it matter? Well, it's interesting; and one would also expect this excellence to be reflected in all the new or renewed anthologies of Irish poetry to be published in the next two decades. I wonder how many female editors will be appointed to oversee these general anthologies? (I mean general anthologies, not anthologies of women's writing.) The intellectual and vocational conditions of intelligent women haven't really changed that much since Nuala O'Faolain wrote down her memories of Irish academe in the 1960s. Men drink together. After closing time men appoint each other to great schemes. Women seemed to sit at another table and wait. But this 'sitting' and 'waiting' may be a male illusion, a male-centred illusion caused by the noise of Irishmen clamouring with male solidarity. Keeping Countess Markievicz's words in mind Irishwomen may claim the attention to which their brains entitle them. Well, the proof of the pudding will be in the next five anthologies of Irish poetry, won't it? Discuss.

In this context it is well to remind ourselves that in Meehan's 'Manulla Junction' that woman, too, can be the photographer as well as the subject:

> *Why assign her victim? Why deduce grief*
> *from her shiny shoes, from the fresh budded leaf?*
> *What drew Father Browne to her radiant face —*
> *the still centre of the photo — draws me too, intense*
>
> *focus for the drama of the shoot,*
> *energy radiating outward from her now bleached face.*
>   *Not*
> *that she's aware of him or his camera*
> *still less posterity's gaze that recruits her to my opera.*
>
> *I want to give her a happy ending.*
>   (Dharmakaya)

Here Meehan is the photographer, the holder of that recording instrument, who connects in high solidarity with the emigrant woman in Father Browne's photograph, as she had connected earlier with women in the sewing factory, with labour robbed of its dignity in 'The Exact Moment I Became a Poet' or as she connected, literally, with 'The Trapped Woman of the Internet':

> *. . . And the only*
> *rescue I can mount is to shift website*
> *from Asiatic Babe Cutie Triple XXX Sexpot.*
>   *Yet much as I want I cannot leave her*
> *rest. She bothers me all the mundane livelong day.*
>   (Dharmakaya)

I am aware that what may be read as profound trauma in politics, national and gender tensions, may actually be 'acrimony of the bowels', as she writes in *Painting Rain* (2009). There is such self-knowledge in Meehan, such a Yeatsian depth, and such humane blood, that one has to allow oneself to be carried with her later work into deeper, psychic, intensely personal regions where the human condition, the discomfort of being

Thomas McCarthy

in the world, is encountered:

> *I pull the door behind me firmly closed.*
> *The past is a lonely country.*
> *There are no charts, no maps.*
> *All you read is hearsay, as remote*
> *as the myths of this Greek island*
> *where one small boat putters out to sea*
> *in a blaze of morning sunlight*
> *dragging my attention in its wake.*
>
> (Painting Rain)

The memory is important because of the great wisdom and authority of the one who remembers. This is the power of Meehan's work: there is life, but there is earned and studied wisdom, a wise ear, and a wise mouth for poetry. In 'Troika' she writes, 'I wonder even then how it all came to this', while in 'Prayer for the Children of Longing' she writes of 'streets that gave them visions and dreams / That promised them everything / That delivered nothing'. It is between the street and the nothing that Meehan has negotiated a unique passage for the craft of her poetry. It is an assembly of memories, yes, a Senate of representations on behalf of mothers, sisters, children, Joanne Breen, the flat in Seán MacDermott Street, the room where someone died, the Greek island, the garden, but this assembly is addressed by a learned Senator of posterity, a poet.

Meehan's constituency is poetry; she was born there, born as a poet before political awareness grew, but nurtured year after year by that growing solidarity. As her books accumulate her talent grows stronger, her imagination finer and more robust, her verse-craft more crafty and elaborate. It is the weather of unbroken solidarity, the temperature reached early upon the 80s barricades, that animates her every poem. She has grown from a gifted lyric poet to a wise woman of swallows, willows, squid and pickled limes.

Meehan's psychology, her emotional weather, her deepest

'None of us well fixed'

political being are an essential part of the success and power of her poems. This is the very core of her achievement to date. It is amazing how deaf some people are to the unassailable, lyrical sounds made by faith and solidarity: 'O somewhere there is a beautiful myth of sorting, / of sifting through a mountain of dross to find the one seed / whose eventual blossom is such would make a god cry.' (*Dharmakaya*) The secret is in the finding of that one, indisputable 'eventual blossom'. A whole series of factors must work together to make that happen. In *Pillow Talk* Meehan has written of the nature of racism, alienation and betrayal, in a prose poem that reveals a great deal about her political instincts and her sense of common humanity. In 'On Being Taken for a Turkish Woman' she is deliberately given incorrect instructions by a Berliner:

> '*I am considering the nature of betrayal and the circumstances in an Izmir bazaar, his eye suddenly caught by the blue luminescence of the stone that now adorns my left ear.* The sign of one who's chosen the path of the warrior rather than the path of the lover, *he said when he gave it to me.*
>
> *I'm trying to work all this out in iambic, trying to find the strong steady pulse of my walkabout in words. But there's too much danger at the edges, and I need all my concentration for reading the street. Visibility is down to a few yards and I've no way of knowing what will come at me next out of the mist.*'

For Meehan liberation is truly a praxis, a transforming reflection and action upon the world. There is no distance between the pen and the stretcher, between the act of personal imagining and the work of literacy among women in the inner city. Everything coheres into a single, rich karma, a grace of being and a zen of Irish street politics that is way beyond the comprehension of poets or critics with a more traditional, reactionary view of the poet's task. As Denise

Thomas McCarthy

Levertov wrote in *The Poet in the World*, 'There was a little song of nonsense words my mother told me [my father] had sung to my sister when she was very young. She repeated it to me as she remembered it, and I understood what she did not understand, that it was a song about a well, and about the wet stones around the wellhead.' Paula Meehan is a wise and pivotal Irish poet, not only because she knows more than her mother but because she had that mother:

> mother wearing a necklace of skulls
> who calls into being
> by uttering the name
> mater logos metric
>   (Dharmakaya)

Both she and her mother, and all of those mothers' meanings, stand before us as we sit and listen and learn. Exiled in our own way, non-nationals in the unheated waiting room of a national poetry, the poet Meehan speaks to us directly and urgently of the ultimate homecoming when words are committed to the page. We learn to read because of the sheer integrity, the solidarity, the power of empathy in her words:

>   Late November, the dark
> chill of the room, Christmas looming and none of us
>   well fixed.
> We bend each evening in scarves and coats to the work
> of mending what is broken in us. Without tricks,
>
> without wiles, with no time to waste now, we plant
> words on these blank fields. It is an unmapped world...
>   'Literacy Class, South Inner City' (*Dharmakaya*)

An Sionnach,
Spring and Fall 2009

The Bears and the Bees
Imaginary Bonnets with Real Bees in Them (*The Poet's Chair: Writings from the Ireland Chair of Poetry*) by Paula Meehan

The Ireland Chair of Poetry, where a poet of national distinction is appointed for three years to a roving Professorship, is one of those absolutely daft good things that the powers that be in Irish life come up with now and again. As with the formation of Aosdána everyone is astonished at the success of what was potentially an embarrassing idea. This Ireland Professorship is as unique as a hedge school, bringing furtive teachers down from the mountains where they'd hidden, and calling all children to the bottom of a barley field, to that shade by the blackthorn bush where two streams always meet in Irish poetry. This innovative, first-mover risky thing has taken hold and has accumulated a splendid new authority from the names of those poets who are willing to take a punt on three years of commitment, from John Montague to Harry Clifton, from Michael Longley to Nuala Ní Dhomhnaill.

Bob Collins in his Foreword to the present book praises 'the energetic and selfless engagement' shown by Paula Meehan during her now closing term as Professor.

Meehan's elevation to the post seemed like a crowning moment for women's poetry in Ireland but it paralleled the simultaneous elevation to posts of influence of both Gillian Clarke and Carol Ann Duffy across the Irish Sea, creating an impression that year of complete female leadership of the poetic worlds of Great Britain and Ireland. Meehan seized the historic moment and in the lectures collected here she has created both a source book and a catechism for new kinds of poetries. These lectures offer a new open architecture for a different kind of person-centred Irish poetry. This is not the usual alternative, the post-doctoral Beckett-Coffey route, but the modernity of a personal presence in the poem, a poetry beyond rhetoric. Utterly outmoded nationalisms and loyalisms are set aside and in their stead a person-centred aesthetic is established, an aesthetic that derives from the direct treatment of all things, including honey bees.

Her first lecture here is a series of nine 'meditations' on poetry, on what she calls the 'always mysterious purposeful flight of bees in my bonnet'. Her journey begins with an irate teacher and a poem about her dead dog, Prince. The teacher tells the child-poet, who has offered a canine elegy rather than a three-page essay, that she has a bee in her bonnet about those compositions. The incident creates a cascade of associations, from *Little Women* to a singing neighbour to Irving Berlin lyrics, to the smell of those intensely blue starflowers, borage, outside her writing window. One can see the poet's method and the poet's intention here — nothing will be offered in instruction that has not been part of a deep interior life, however at odds with the demands of the world this life may be. Our nostrils full of borage, we tumble with our Professor into Marianne Moore's poetry and its drastic revisions, an encounter that ignites 'the quiddity of the world, the thingness of creation' in the author. It is all downhill after that, as Sister Philippa might have predicted, including an early encounter with Dracula himself, the lyrical John Borrowman. After expulsion from school the young poet was sent to the sanctuary of the Marino, away from the dark influences of the Finglas Sudetenland. But a bookshelf in Marino held the non-prescription drug of Emily Dickinson's poems, the Modern Library *Selected* with an Introduction by Conrad Aiken. This is what the fourteen-year-old rebel read: 'I died for beauty, but was scarce / Adjusted in the tomb, / When one who died for truth was lain / In an adjoining room.' The task

The Bears and the Bees

of her life was established and the journey really begun. 'Maybe the truth in poetry is not in the words per se,' she writes. 'The individual words have autonomous force, I would say magic power, in terms of their auditory force on the physical body, and the shadow power too in the ghost life of the word . . . '

It's at this point that the poet-Professor might begin to lose us more fractious, damaged creatures. I mean, we feel we've heard these awkward awful claims before and they make us want to leave the room the way Philip Larkin left the theatre during a performance of Synge. Ordinary chaps, we hate high claims for art. We refute them as merely intuitive, chancy, as not counter-intuitive and sourced in a reliable critique of ordinary living. Yet Meehan here is only mustering an argument that will be grounded in lived experience on the prison island of Ikaria, the subject of the MacNeice poem in *Ten Burnt Offerings*. Her flights of fancy, her bees in a bonnet, are quickly grounded in a reading of MacNeice and Euripides — and in the urgent news that Doris Lessing has died, Lessing of *The Golden Notebook*, 'my handbook of womanhood and the inner city of my body' that so influenced the young poet. After these thoughts, organically part of them, or a continuation of them, there's honey and yoghurt for breakfast and, after that, with such tastes in the mouth, there's Carol Ann Duffy's collection *The Bees*. Meehan eats words, reprocessing words like wild honey and, in the words of Duffy, their 'scent pervades / my shadowed, busy heart, / and honey is art'. Meehan is in a highly personalized creative zone while thinking on these matters, a zone she trusts absolutely as a mother trusts her contractions; in this territory the body is a walled city with its own laws. Her lecture concludes with the memory of a film scenario for which the poet and her producer friend failed to get funding: a bunch of teenagers wanting to steal the Tarot cards of Yeats who become the victims of strange happenings, 'Not supernatural things but ordinary magical things'. As strange things had happened to Yeats after he wrote about bees Meehan's thesis warns us all that the smell of honey comes only where the walls are loosening.

In 'The Solace of Artemis', her second lecture, Meehan is back in her alma mater, Trinity College, Dublin, where she begins with the ancient Irish brown bear, extinct here for ten thousand years but still living in the DNA of every Arctic bear. But bears bring her to 'arktos' and her mythical Bear Mother, Artemis of the Aegean: Artemis protector of children and wild places.

The TCD classicist W B Stanford is remembered with great affection. Meehan admires his *The Enemies of Poetry* with its argument for the sovereignty of poetry. She retells his argument: 'Poetry is not sociology, poetry is not history . . . poetry is a way of telling the truth about what it is to be human.' She sees Artemis as both an alabaster girl in a shop window on Francis Street and as the Roman Diana moving swiftly with a quiver full of arrows through an eternal Arcadia. The poet's bear family, the carers and custodians, include a crucial grandfather, Wattie Meehan, who teaches her to read. One night the young poet propels herself into a red-hot winter fire, burning her hands — the memory itself is launched forward to be enveloped by Adrienne Rich's image of formal poetic training as a pair of asbestos gloves. Out of this bookish Arcady of the inner city, a high-windowed corner of Seán McDermott Street that looked out on Gardiner Street, the poet was eventually propelled into the New World of Eastern Washington University and the care of a great poetic father bear, James J McAuley: 'It was a lucky day that I became his student.' Her stay in the American North West would lead to an encounter with real bears, a she-bear and her cubs raking berries from the bushes with a timeless animal grace. This encounter left its mark, as it should, as did that first New World encounter with wise bears Galway Kinnell and Gary Snyder — Snyder teaching her not the formality of verse but how to breathe: 'To slow the entire cosmos down to the awareness of this one breath, the simplicity of it.' Here was a world of Micmac folklore, of bear brides, and *Stories from the Six Worlds: Micmac Legends*. Back in Dublin, thanks to Catriona Crowe and the National Archives, Meehan would dig deeper, wider, into the ursuline world of the North Inner City, Lower Tyrone Street, Summerhill. All the while through the writing of poems, of lore and bear-lore, a child with burned hands is consoled.

By the time we reach her final lecture Meehan is throwing yarrow sticks and the I Ching. But only to slow the world down a bit, as in the first breaths of Buddhism. She is on the margins of water, on Papa Stour in the Shetland Islands or on the star-fort that commands the view over Kinsale harbour. In the former place she was full of airy lightness, and in the latter full of confident expectation as the speck in the ocean slowly becomes the seventy-footer yacht of her own homeward Sailor Poet: 'When he stepped ashore I asked him what it was like out there. "A vaaaast ocean."' The theme of her lecture is water: 'All my life, as far back as I can remember, I have dreams where I live in water, can breathe in that element . . . ' In her search she goes back to old wells, but also to the well of poetry, that spring of freshness in Gary Snyder's *Regarding Wave* with its crucial poem, 'What You Should Know to Be a Poet'. Snyder's handbook here, his directive myth-kitty, includes knowing everything about animals as persons, the names of trees, flowers and weeds, at least one kind of traditional magic, and 'the illusory demons and illusory shining gods'. Meehan in her life and method has been one of his star pupils. The mornings bring books, which are really packaged dreams — one from a patient in St Patrick's University Hospital, one Kathleen whose mother was a fish. This statement introduces us to a quandary: what is the difference between a statement in therapy and a statement in a poem? The one may be disturbed while the other may be insightful: 'I might direct the workshop participant to Nuala Ní Dhomhnaill's beautiful poem "A Recovered Memory of

Thomas McCarthy

Water" in its translation from the original Irish by Paul Muldoon.' This train of thought, this light skipping, or deep skipping, from one domain to the other, from life to poetry, from one language to another, is typical of Meehan's deeply satisfying intelligence, and her learned sense, or senses. Holy, holy, holy, is what she says before remembering her father walking down Gardiner Street to the river, raising her on his shoulders to save time in the dark. The image is perfect, it is a clear glass of water flung at the audience in UCD on November 26th of a year in the future.

Overall it is difficult to place Meehan's aesthetic, to categorize it or simply place it on a shelf of linear, developing theories or positions in Irish poetry. The cumulative effect of her thinking is one of a disassociated defiance. One could say that she belongs to a broadening and more sophisticated, holistic, Irish feminist vision. Her vision is welcoming, inclusive, embracing categories rather than creating divisive literary politics.

As poets we must live with this one bitter truth — an entire life spent in art couldn't save a single beehive. Meehan would disagree, resolutely: 'I recite my poem now as a spell against the frackers, energy companies who want to extract the natural gas from the carboniferous shale that underlies the whole of our beautiful lake district, Fermanagh and Leitrim . . . ' But to admit the limited political power of art and to still want to write poems, that's also an honourable starting point. The cumulative effect of these lectures is magnificent and inspiring. In a world that has become more hopeless than hopeful these deeply spiritual essays will be an important dressing station in our worldwide, darkening battlefield.

Dublin Review of Books,
October 2016

'We could be in any city'
Eiléan Ní Chuilleanáin and Cork

Cork disagrees, constantly and seriously. Cork, you must understand, is a very particular place, something like Derry in the North, and sharing the same tendentious relationship with Dublin that Derry has with Belfast. It knows best. Cork never feels under any pressure to decentralize into the rest of Ireland — unlike Galway, for example, that has always inserted itself adroitly and affectionately into the national discourse. Cork, far away in the South, will beg to differ. Certainly a mythical 'Dublin' will not determine its agenda: well, not since the Cattle Acts of the 1600s and the rivalry in trade. In the eighteenth century Cork Corporation appointed ambassadors to the Parliament in Dublin, Hugh Dickson and Eman Pigot, to explain its distinctive point of view; indeed it was for this defence of Cork's point of view that Dean Swift was created a Freeman of Cork: 'you are the Idol of the Court of Aldermen. They have sent you your Freedom,' as the Earl of Orrery informed Swift. Orrery wrote from Cork to appease Swift who had just discovered that he was to be given his parchment of Freedom in a Silver rather than a Gold Box. (One can imagine the discussion in Cork: 'Yerra boy, we'll give yer man Silver. We keep Gold for Our Own.')

Such a misfortune of disconnections, that characteristic fractured relationship with the nation's capital, may have cost Cork not only a loss of synchronization during the Easter Rising of 1916, a typical refusal to 'come out' with Dublin, but more mundane things like the Lyric FM studios or financing for its new airport terminal and transatlantic air routes. This prickly relationship matters. These things trickle down, or steam upwards, and penetrate even the thinking behind poems. For eighteenth-century trade read influence. It is all trade: butter, cheese, Clonakilty pudding, Barry's Tea, International Film Festivals, theatre and poetry. The rules of trade apply in each case. It is not only the place, in trade or poetry, but the description of the place that matters. We live and write within that description. We receive new collections of poetry, and welcome or dismiss them, within that description. Cork is the locus of its own unique selling point: we must negotiate our daily traffic through its lanes and waterways. A poet walking the streets of Cork will pick up that intrigue, that nervousness:

> *Geometry of guilt, the windows*
> *broken or always empty:*
> *daylight sucked in and lost, a bird astray:*
>
> *the knife edge of the street, blinded*
> *fronts of houses like a bacon-slicer*
> *dropping to infinity . . .*

One of the distinguishing features of Ní Chuilleanáin's work has been that constant but elliptical evocation of Cork, both as a place and as a description of that place. Even when the place is not named there is a pirouetting, a flickering penmanship of light and shadow, steps and steeples, that might be the North Mall with its swans and the Dominican cloisters, a kind of Italian evening, or the Warden's House at University College Cork. The play of light on walls, brickwork, stones and doors, does create a very real geography: traces of a waiting past, of the poet's remembered moment as a sunlit foyer, a waiting place:

> *The absent girl is*
> *conspicuous by her silence*

sitting at the courtroom window
her cheek against the glass.

Psychologically and socially Ní Chuilleanáin's Cork is a complex and evasive place, made concrete only through the most intense observation. It is a place made whole not by socializing memories as such but by constant participant observations formed in adulthood. Through Cork childhood itself becomes the constant centre of poems, and becomes the poetic place to come to, like the Smyrna of Seferis or the lost sun-drenched Alexandria of Cavafy. Although her Cork is authentic to the core it is more than merely a place to have come from: for Ní Chuilleanáin it is both a cultural richness and a rhetorical advantage in an intellectual life completed by the discourse of elsewhere. Cork, first and foremost, meant a brilliant and bustling mother; Cork meant an image of extraordinarily competent female management systems in her mother's house. Her mother, Eilís Dillon, has written of those Cork days:

> '*I applied the same principle to my own house, where I had to think of a housekeeper and a children's nurse and three children, including a baby who was born after we went to live in the Warden's House. When all this was in order, after a tour of inspection of the hostel, by half-past ten in the morning I was sitting at my desk beginning my other life as a professional writer.*'

She concludes her memoir of the city as follows: 'So much for those who occasionally expressed the view that living in official housing is bad for children. I can't see that it did ours any harm.'

On the contrary such an early-childhood cloistered life presented Ní Chuilleanáin with an entire wordhoard of images and a grammar or worldview that pervade her poetry. Her mother's sheer energy levels and literary professionalism also allowed the poet/daughter to rise above that atmosphere of disempowerment and domestic imprisonment so eloquently described by Margaret MacCurtain in her contribution to *Irish Women: Image and Achievement,* edited by Ní Chuilleanáin:

> 'Irish women retreated into a secondary role with the setting up of the northern State in 1920 and the Free State in the south in 1922. Around Irish women, as in a cage, were set the structures of family life and women were assigned a home-based, full-time role as housewives, whose talents and energies were devoted to looking after husband and children.'

Ní Chuilleanáin had a mother who rose above such restrictions, who soared in imagination and initiated such things as a commission for a design of Honan Chapel vestments for Séamus Murphy and the founding of the Dante Alighieri Society in Cork. Her mother contradicted history, contradicted this convention of lesser being that the Catholic state conferred upon women.

As she herself has written in her Introduction to the above publication, 'We study the history of woman by studying feminine images because, while much orthodox history has simply left women out, the human imagination has never been able to do so.' It is Cork, then, that gives Ní Chuilleanáin's imagination an edge, or even a ledge, where she can participate in the discourses of a state and its capital with the authority of an elsewhere. She has always spoken from a double province: the Dublin poem, the Cork poet. The poem, indeed, is her continuous official housing:

> *The returning minotaur pacing transparent*
> *in the transparent maze cannot*
> *smell out his stall; the angles all move toward him,*

> *no alcove to rest his horns.*
> *At dawn he collapses in the garden where*
> *the delicate wise slug is caressing*
> *ribbed undersides of blue cabbage leaves*
> *while on top of them rain dances.*

She has a provincial's understanding of the wise slug beneath the rain that dances. Cabbage leaves are the refectory tables and the wise slugs, no doubt, the scholarship of girls of Munster who absorb, with pent-up appetites and out of sight, the atmosphere of learning and the compelling truths of history. The novelist Mary Leland in her fine study of literary Cork identifies Ní Chuilleanáin as a 'child of the college', being the daughter of UCC's Professor Cormac Ó Chuilleanáin and the novelist Eilís Dillon. Leland also uses the word 'irradiation' to describe the haunting presences of Seán Ó Riada, Séamus Murphy and Daniel Corkery within the poetry of Seán Ó Tuama, and then continues to describe the inherited energy, 'the light which shines' upon the new generation of poets. Cork is therefore seen by one of its most authoritative commentators as not only a childhood place, a place to come from, but as a locus of particular poetic energy, a Holy Well. Through birth, then, but most essentially through invocation, visit and revisit, Ní Chuilleanáin draws power from that well:

> *We see the rocks about us and their peaks and ruts*
> *until the weeds wave gently back and enclose us.*
>
> *The water is bitter to us*
> *as we wait for their return.*

Even when she seems to be writing about elsewhere there is that constant return to small city landscapes, a reversion to the slow dream of provincial wardenship. A poem as seemingly distant as 'Dreaming in the Ksar Es Souk Motel' is

Thomas McCarthy

reconnected to Cork, — but something else as well, a distinctive geography:

> *Out of sight the rivers persist*
> *they riddle the city, they curve and collect*
> *making straight roads crooked, they flush*
> *in ruined mills*
> *and murdered distilleries.*

That geography is extended through elegy, in this instance one for the iconic Corkman, Séamus Murphy, who died in 1975 when the city was at its most sunlit and southern. Elegies are not just expressions of grief but, as James Joyce or Benedict Kiely taught us, declarations of belonging and community. By inserting our personal grief into the atmosphere of a funeral we make a personal declaration: we declare ourselves as part of the line. Ní Chuilleanáin declares her sense of belonging through description: she has always made her feelings known through precise description. Here in the sculptor's graveyard she creates a powerful rhetoric of belonging:

> *Carrying black clothes*
> *whiskey and ham for the wake*
> *the city revolves*
> *white peaks of churches clockwise lifting and falling.*
>
> *The hill below the barracks*
> *the sprouting sandstone walls go past*
> *and as always you are facing the past*
> *finding below the old clockface*
>
> *the long rambles of the spider*
> *in the narrow bed of a saint . . .*

It is impossible to overemphasize the full meaning of what is happening here, its Cork and Irish nuances. This is a poem

'We could be in any city'

reprinted and revisited from *The Rose Geranium* of 1981. Here are the black clothes of mourning, the proper well-bred response to a funeral; the awareness of a city watching; the old clockface of Shandon; gifts of whiskey and ham (intensely Cork as well as Irish symbols of comfort, relief, and family celebration) and the final, powerful Celtic Christian evocations of both Finbarr and Gobnait. But this brief elegy is typical of Ní Chuilleanáin's unselfconscious loading of the lyric line, a fixing of the Cork hook with live bait. Her elegies especially are always forms of entrapment and charm as well as declarations of family loyalty. A good deal of her rhetoric is singing rhetoric, a lyrical, evasive Cork politics of belonging.

The 1970s were most definitely a young Ní Chuilleanáin's most emphatic Cork period. Cork never leaves her consciousness, that is true: it is always there as a restorative psychic architecture. She is more accepting of the material than most. There is no sense that she was detained too long at this southern port of childhood, that there were any frantic visa delays as she reached the adult territory of teaching and publishing. There is a remarkable lack of revenge, a slowness to attack her provincial childhood place, such as one finds in the troubled remembrances of Frank O'Connor or Seán Ó Faoláin. She carries the dual citizenship of Irish childhood with tremendous grace and kindness. In the Irish context her lack of bitterness is stunning. It has much to do with her immediate family circumstances. Being the child of a patriot family, daughter of a scholar, she must have grown up in an atmosphere that was resolutely national, of the whole nation, and anti-provincial. Her father's illness and the need to find a warmer Italian climate must have made the home itself, the very threatened domestic interior, a kind of nation to protect and save. Her 'Corkness' was declared early and completely, resolutely, in two major publications, *Site of Ambush* in 1975 and *Cork*, with Brian Lalor, in 1977. For those of us who attended University College Cork in the mid-70s they are among the High Books of our youth, along with Michael Hartnett's *A Farewell to English*, Seamus Heaney's *North* and John Montague's *The Great Cloak*.

Site of Ambush, in general, is an essay on war, conflict, and memory. The ambush is not necessarily the ambush of Michael Collins, but mention of an ambush in any Cork context has but one primary meaning within a basket of images: a dead hero, a state funeral, a country in ruins:

> *At ten the soldiers were climbing into lorries,*
> *asthmatic engines drawing breath in even shifts.*
> *The others were fretting over guns*
> *counting up ammunition and money.*
> *At eleven they lay in wait at the cross...*

At the end of this ambush there is a rusting lorry, dead soldiers, and a deaf child in a disturbed stream. Whatever country it is, conflict is disturbing the living stream. In Part 4, 'Time and Place', a survivor of war 'staggers away from the sea' in the very place where the disturbed stream finds 'Dark weedy stones of a harbour' (p.24). Survivors recollect their loss through skeleton days and Ní Chuilleanáin launches into a pure Andalusian/Cork aria, Patrick Galvin-like, a revolutionary remembrance:

> *Now all their lives on the site of the ambush*
> *they see the dead walking ignorant and strong*
> *as on their dying day. The grey shoulders*
> *against a rainbow skyline approach again and stop*
> *approach again and stop. The child's neck medal*
> *grows glitters and breaks away spinning —*
> *the ploughed field gleams against the sky*
> *furrowed over and harrowed*
> *on the ancient graves —*

It is not possible to read these lines and remain unconnected

'We could be in any city'

to a revolutionary history and a territory raked by guerrilla warfare, a terrain like County Cork. This is a universal place of cruelty and insurrection, a territory that Ní Chuilleanáin invokes as Carolyn Forché does El Salvador in *The Country Between Us*. But Ní Chuilleanáin's instincts are fed from the broad myth-kitty of revolutionary Cork. In Part 5 of 'Site of Ambush', 'March in the Garden', she walks the familiar territory of the UCC campus, a leafy place where the attic windows of Cork 'peer like bulrushes':

> *Elsewhere, in the garden where I saw them first*
> *in nineteen-forty-nine, the shrubs bloom out of season,*
> *their roots in New Zealand, their names*
> *rusting on metal tags. The gardener*
> *is Michael Barry, who threw the bowl*
> *and hit the Chetwynd Viaduct. He shakes hands*
> *and asks am I married yet.*

Here, she meets the legendary UCC head gardener, Mick Barry, a great open-road bowler — 'bough-ler' — who took up the challenge of lofting the great railway Viaduct, beyond Bishopstown in Cork. Meeting him is a restoration to everything that is both familiar and familial. Barry with his bowl and Maurice Craig with his book at the Sandymount window are part of a process of restoration and domestication: for Ní Chuilleanáin both men must represent husbandry and learning. They are comforting father figures. But the sequence closes with a child soaked from drowning — more than a child, though, a demon figure, enflamed by memory: 'Your arms will be burnt / as she turns to flame.' This child returns from a nightmare place, a site of dreams, yes, but also of nightmares:

> *the child exhausted*
> *comes back from her sleep*
>
> *— troubling for a minute the patient republic*

Thomas McCarthy

> *of the spider and the fly*
> *on the edge of the aspic stream . . .*

Here is the constant juxtaposition of images and events and a suggestive, tentative anthology of revolution and survival. The shadow of Yeats is apparent in the image of the stream and the adjective 'troubling', but the word 'republic' is there also. We have shrubs blooming out of season, plants with their roots elsewhere, their nametags rusting, a stream, a lorry rusting, a troubled child, even a railway viaduct, the most powerful Cork symbol of the Civil War. The phrase 'aspic stream' is a stroke of genius, for aspic preserves and holds disconnected elements in the moulded form. Aspic is remembrance. In 'Site of Ambush' we have a tentative but highly sophisticated arrangement of mythical incidents. We are given a history lesson through evocation, the elliptical autobiography of a war-torn country. In 1975 every student and Professor in Cork understood this book as an intensely personal Cork text. Intellectually Ní Chuilleanáin's reworking of material from a revolutionary period might seem a regressive movement of imagination, an unnecessarily backward glance, for a poet whose method and lyricism are entirely modern, and whose instincts are entirely modernist. But there are other sites of ambush such as the ongoing battles about liberalism and the rights of women in Irish life since the foundation of the State as Pat O'Connor has explained:

> 'Within the context of the ideological parameters of the state, the Roman Catholic Church and invisible patriarchy, the existence of women's personhood other than at a reproductive level was effectively a non-issue.'

The 'sites of ambush' faced by Irish women were constantly arrived at in the 1980s and the 1990s as issues of contraception, abortion and labour force equality surfaced, generally

'We could be in any city'

dragged to the surface by reactionary forces working against EU rights legislation and any Dáil moves to liberalize laws on the Irish Statute Book. These were the days when there was a ban on any live discussion of the abortion issue on RTÉ, the taking of legal action against the Dublin Well Women Centre and the removal of British telephone directories from public libraries. In the middle of this national maelstrom the poet made poems and poetry continued to emerge from the personal air pocket of a woman-centred life. The female poets endured, organized reading circuits, founded publishing houses. One has to be conscious of the powerful women and female-management figures that Ní Chuilleanáin encountered at UCC through her childhood in 'official housing'.

Ní Chuilleanáin's Gallery Press book, *Cork*, was certainly one of the most beautiful local books of 1977. Written to accompany Brian Lalor's subtle, and sometimes very slight, drawings of Cork, the poems were full of a sunlit magic. The book itself, as an object, was one of The Gallery Press's finest hours. It marked a restoration of dignity to the world of Irish poetry publishing just at the moment when standards of production and presentation had begun to decline everywhere. I remember the display copies of the limited hardback of this book in the old Cork Craftsman's Guild shop in Patrick Street: how fine it looked, how fitting it was that this volume of poems and drawings was displayed with the best ceramics and woodcuts of the day. The opening poem is probably as complete an evocation of Cork as will ever get published:

> *The island, with its hooked*
> *clamps of bridges holding it down,*
> *its internal spirals*
> *packed, is tight as a ship*
> *with a name in Greek or Russian on its tail;*
>
> *as the river, flat and luminous*
> *at its fullest, images the defences:*

Thomas McCarthy

> *ribbed quays and stacked rooves*
> *plain warehouse walls as high as churches*
> *insolent flights of steps.*

It is a perfect description, pencil-like and deftly matched to the delicate drawings of Lalor. The latter give Ní Chuilleanáin free rein; they allow her to soar with that light method, the elusive and evocative, and even retiring, loose line. She is a lover of things described, of blue volumes, cigar boxes, shiny linoleum, doorways, and sunlit arches. In the fifth section she writes:

> *half veiled by a net curtain,*
> *a lined curtain, a lampshade*
> *the wooden back of a looking glass, then blackness.*

> *We could be in any city.*

But we are not. That is the point. We are in Cork and Ní Chuilleanáin is describing her city with the affection of a daughter and the intensity of a 1940s photographer like Bill Brandt. It is a landscape she knows inside out from observation and a highly sensitized, remembered living. She would never again attend so explicitly to the material of Cork, per se, but she had established a firm and deeply rooted starting point, a quay of departure for her own poetic imagination and imagined projects. After 1977 Cork would permeate everything, but elusively and sometimes at a twice-remove. But, even as late as 2001, images from a Cork childhood could be haunting. In a poem like 'Bessboro', the name of a terrifying home for single mothers, she places the very name of the place within a catalogue of Cork locations, a kind of warning book:

> *and a half-drawn lace of mist*
> *hides elements of the known:*
> *gables and high blind windows.*
> *The story has moved away.*

'We could be in any city'

It is interesting that the story, an unhappy truth, does not linger as part of that Cork landscape. It is almost as if those unpleasant elements would not survive in that imagined and reimagined childhood place called Cork.

One of the permanent legacies of her Cork, of her unique cloistered childhood, is the very specific architecture of her imagined world. This architecture permeates everything. It is an archetypal structure retained from childhood and reminds us of Bachelard's great phrase that the roots of the grandeur of the world plunge into a childhood. A deep well of her poetic is the poetic of her described spaces. The house, the kitchen, and the sunlit interiors where women wait together are overwhelmingly important constructs in Ní Chuilleanáin's poetry. Waiting is always a dramatic, incident-rich activity in every poem. Sometimes the act of waiting is almost a rhetorical device, as it is in the empty rooms and attics of another Cork woman, Elizabeth Bowen. Homes, rooms, arches, bridges, doorways all have character. At all times a waiting room or foyer might stand up and address the reader with some urgent revelation.

It would be too bold to claim an exclusive Cork precedent for this symbolic traffic in Ní Chuilleanáin's work, especially in a woman who has spent her adult life in communion with Trinity College and Italy, but the long waiting room of a provincial childhood leaves a deep template on the mind: a childhood way of seeing things and of making them cohere. In her poems there are children sent out to fetch water, children sent on journeys, women with secrets, side doors for slipping through, absent men and hidden books. This does seem to come from a kind of Civil War terror, a war happening elsewhere; in other words, a childhood.

The house, as we know from the work of Elizabeth Bowen, Molly Keane or Kate O'Brien, can be both a symbol and setting; it can be a place of subordination and death. Molly Keane's last heroine, Nicandra (named after a winning horse of her father), met her death as a house collapsed beneath her.

Thomas McCarthy

The house in Freud or Ibsen can be seen as a place of captivity or a symbol of separation and control. But it is a locus, also, of ruination and national suffering. Ní Chuilleanáin's remembered Cork interiors, those archetypes of childhood, a world of steps, steeples and cloisters, are more complex and more fertile. But her imagined women are constantly attending to memory in these spaces; many of them await power that has been distributed in their absence. While her work, in general, may invoke and propagate an accepted menu of feminist and deliberately gender-driven archetypes, her accumulated biography in the poems, especially her remembered Cork childhood, reconfigures the symbol of the house in terms of Irish biography. In a cloistered, highly educated Cork setting Ní Chuilleanáin's house is less a Presentation Parlour and more a Bowen's Court. Just as for Bowen Cork was a summer place, a place of summer arrival and autumn departure, so in Ní Chuilleanáin we have that feeling of temporary waiting, of childhood anticipation. In both writers there is a powerful sense of both nationally historic and personally expectant interiors. In both novelist and poet fear and anticipation have taken the place of squalor; hunger is something else, it is spiritual rather than physical. Interiors are active, and there is a marked absence of rain. Such pervasive sunlight does have a profound meaning: it lights up the future more than anything. Rain drives us indoors; sunlight invites us to take a journey. Bowen and Ní Chuilleanáin are masterful and well-prepared voyagers. A journey away from sunlit Cork is part of the emotional geography of both writers.

The later poems of Ní Chuilleanáin, like the later prose of Elizabeth Bowen, are peppered with journeys. Both live within a duality of spaces, County Cork and Regent's Park; Cork and Oxford; County Cork and Vassar; Cork and Trinity College. For both writers the journey outwards is a form of enlightenment. In Ní Chuilleanáin's *The Girl Who Married the Reindeer* there is a terrific sense of movement, with sparkling, deeply affecting journeys through Continental Europe:

'We could be in any city'

> Remember us, we have travelled as far
> as Lazarus to Autun...

And all these journeys are taken in the direction of some great comfort at the end: 'My father's glass and the bottle of sour stout at hand.' In each journey there is that consolation of delineation, a high, a highly orientating catalogue of precision. When Ní Chuilleanáin comes to rest in any poem it is always upon the soft landing of an exact description:

> Meanwhile the house is empty
> except for the two women on the ground floor.
> The latch of their room will never shut completely.
> They hear the hinges of the big door closing...

As with Bowen every Ní Chuilleanáin journey can be seen as a voyage away from that place of reflected light: cloisters, bridges, windowsills in Ní Chuilleanáin, the glistening windowed façade of a Big House, the rhododendron and Portuguese laurel shimmering after rain in the work of Bowen. Like Elizabeth Bowen Ní Chuilleanáin has also served her estate, her Cork, with practical loyalty and support. The place is not just a childhood place but a continuing social and literary locality that still offers adult meaning. She understands Cork as a continuing, if distant and mostly unheard, creator of literary meanings. It is possible to return always to the steps and steeples, the furtive lanes and 'kenking' waterfowl of Corkery and O'Connor; but also to the contemporary meanings embodied in poets like Theo Dorgan, Louis de Paor, Greg Delanty and William Wall.

Recently Ní Chuilleanáin read to a packed gallery at the Triskel Arts Centre in Tobin Street, Cork. The occasion was a special one, celebrated with generous amounts of good wine and canapés. It was the joint launch of the veteran magazine *Cyphers* and *Southword*, the journal of the Munster Literature Centre. Here were Ní Chuilleanáin and Patrick Cotter,

Thomas McCarthy

Cork poets, making an effort to bridge that great historic divide, that mental chasm, between Dublin and Cork. It was a most unusual evening with Cork and Dublin being praised in the same room on the same winter evening. Ní Chuilleanáin has also participated — with great scholarship and enthusiasm — in the European Translation Series organized by the same Munster Literature Centre in 2005. Her translations of Ileana Mălăncioiu, *After the Raising of Lazarus*, became one of the highlights of a busy literary year in Cork. Ní Chuilleanáin learned Romanian in a characteristic gesture of complete solidarity. She wished to get closer to the material; nothing would be spared in order to create that radical description of a great Romanian poet within the English language. By their supreme efforts ye shall know when, and through this project, Ní Chuilleanáin revealed herself as a complete professional, a poet of extraordinary integrity. The result was a triumph, a brilliant collection that captures a voice from far away, but reminds us, with the unassailable brilliance of art, that through poems the heart speaks, the voice is heard, the stones reflect light:

> *In the world of water a woman astray*
> *Looks like my reflection in the well*
> *The more I bend my head, the higher it rises*
> *Out of the wide quiet dust.*
>
> *And then when my image passes into the water*
> *My pale face holding there still*
> *To my images wet as though in eternal rain*
> *A shadowy figure clings.*
> *Look well on me, beloved, it's evening...*

It is part of the wonderful achievement of Eiléan Ní Chuilleanáin, and only one part, that she can apply all her poetic gifts with such concentration upon a single task. In this case the task was a duty performed for Cork when it found itself

'We could be in any city'

nominated by Europe, a response to a call to work with the poets of her city in its hour of challenge and need. In doing this with many of the other Cork poets, creating a very fine European Capital of Culture Translation Series, thirteen volumes in all, she was following in that long line of strong women from Cork, from Eibhlín Dubh Ní Chonaill to E L Voynich to Elizabeth Bowen. She was participating in that most powerful of forces, management by women. From the Honan Hostel where her novelist-mother arranged concerts by resident and visiting quartets, or conversed with fellow professional, Séamus Murphy, to the editorial board of *Cyphers* where her values impinge upon events within Irish modernism, Ní Chuilleanáin maintains a psychic bridge between two cranky and petulant discourses, Dublin and Cork. Her poems have become that undelivered Golden Box, forever on its way from Cork to the good Dean, a box of poems which, when opened, reveals sunlight, cloisters, avenues, water channels and sites of ambush. At the heart of the metropolis one maintains the Cork connection through an effort of imagination and a habit of reading. As she herself intimates in *Cyphers*, the motherhood of Cork, the sisterhood of the Honan Hostel and a revolutionary family prepared her for such a task:

> *'My own lifelong panic fear of being left without something to read, and the lesson learned in childhood that at some time one must expect to be rounded up and locked away like my father and both my mother's parents and so many of their friends, were not just childhood terrors, they were part of the conspiracy of the forces of boredom that watches still around the edges of our eventful lives.'*

Irish University Review,
Summer 2007

Echoes from the Cistern
The Boys of Bluehill *by Eiléan Ní Chuilleanáin*

Reading Eiléan Ní Chuilleanáin's new collection I am struck by this affecting truth: we will never again have a poetic mind like Ní Chuilleanáin's available to us. Her sensibility is unique; her society, and her place in it, will never be seen again. She is one of the last representatives of that mid-century haut bourgeois Catholic Irish world. Her literary mentors are in Catholic Europe, in Mauriac's fiction and Kate O'Brien's *Presentation Parlour*, in Máire Mhac an tSaoi's diplomatic briefcase and Eilís Dillon's childhood summers. This world, especially as it is mediated here through an Oxford post-doctoral education and a Trinity workplace of Huguenot reticence, has flowed easily and fluently for her whenever she has put pen to paper:

> *which is why it seems so difficult at last to handle and stack*
> *the whole folded history balanced on two bone shoulders*

as she puts it in 'The Burden of Cloth'. This poem captures the moment when a film crew breaks camp after shooting a scene for a costume drama: in describing the moment she is able to recreate an ensemble that includes a cardinal, acolytes, a nun's veiling, painted calico and lace 'all full of holes'. This is familiar territory for Ní Chuilleanáin, but here it is laced with irony (to coin a phrase) and with some pity. Like Seferis in 'The King of Asine' or 'The Return of the Exile' she elicits information from her own constructed scenarios by persistent

Echoes from the Cistern

questioning — she captures atmospheres as mysterious and echo-sounding as any Mediterranean cistern. She persists in 'An Information' in this method of interrogation, only to be answered with a deathly finality, with an admonishing wind:

> *do not look back to see whose hand*
> *finds it, or where it is hidden again when found.*

This ambiguous approach to facts, this duality of being, and of a sensibility created by velvet whispering, is Catholic in a highly educated Irish sense: 'Didn't she remember / a frescoed wall with resurrected limbs?' she asks in 'The Signorelli Moment', and in 'Judgement Day':

> *Is this where they were bound, the robed*
> *processions of my childhood that wound past*
> *open doors with hallstands, area gates,*
> *narrow entries, wisely departing cats?*

That this is all part of a journey, of a pilgrimage towards a place of insight, of this Ní Chuilleanáin's poetry is certain. Whether the wanderer begins with a line drawn in chalk by Máighréad Uí Mhurchú, or in a room where the grandmother sits shelling peas, or climbing the steps of Palmers Green Station, or in that wakeful mill

> *that once consumed the house keys years ago*
> *saved from Córdoba: the tunes, though,*
> The Boys of Bluehill, Miss Canty's Reel,
> *the orchestral variations*
> *with the lewd words added to the symphonies,*
> *will follow me...*

She knows that each poetic journey will end in some kind of Byronic revelation. A secret-keeper, a sort of non-cooperative detective called Dr Proteus, becomes a ghostly objective of the

Thomas McCarthy

poet's searching: 'Dr Proteus hanging holds the perspective glass / but how through all her changes and her daft / excuses, how to tear it from her hand?' In a reality where *'Flesh has fallen away'* there is nothing left to be extracted but unearthly knowledge, disentangled runes. The word 'Proteus' reminds us of the syndrome of excess, linguistic protuberances from which a shepherd-poet might cling; but also of that King of Egypt, the one who protected Helen in Euripides, sending on a phantom Helen to suffer conflict and leaving the beautiful Helen undisturbed. There is that very strong sense, ferried through all of Ní Chulleanáin's collections, of an abandoned otherness. As a poet she has instinctively made common cause with what was left behind, whether it was Oxford or Cork, Old Irish or Dieppe in 1956: 'Fresh, I remember, like bleached cloth, like lemons, / fresh as the ribbons and cherries / printing my white cotton dress . . . ' Her poetry, for all its vibrant sensuality, still yearns for a time before poetic revelation: trying to voyage back to that undisturbed place of repose has been a constant task in her work.

What distinguishes *The Boys of Bluehill* from most other collections is the depth of its texture. There is nothing tentative, or merely suggestive, in this work. Her academic training is outraged by vagueness, so that the poems grab a firm hold of their subject matter; the work is premeditated: it is never a pen shuffling in the hope of inspiration. Again, for all their sensuousness, these are the poems of a scholar and a scholar's daughter. In their texture and deep lode of references they have more in common with the work of Máire Mhac an tSaoi or Liam Ó Muirthile than with any other Irish poet. Her poetry is directed towards a high point of knowledge where the poem/mountain over time becomes a mountain range. In recalling her father she reminds us that 'he believed that foreign words were real, / their declension revealing even what crawled away'; and recalling Pearse Hutchinson she writes:

Echoes from the Cistern

> *the small difference intrigued you,*
> *between a word in Catalan and its Castilian cousin;*
> *the dense closeness, the narrow gap*
> *distancing the genitive plural in Irish*
> *from the nominative singular . . .*

I can imagine the two friends having this deep conversation in Selskar Terrace. I would contrast this with many of my own conversations with an elderly writer I admired, conversations around the correct measures of gin and Cointreau in a White Lady, or some such after-dinner drink. I'm not saying that there's anything wrong with shallowness but a firm and enriched knowledge of language gives a scholar like Ní Chuilleanáin certain advantages, and possibilities of depth, that are not available to literary butterflies. In poem after poem her knowledge shows; it enriches what was from the beginning a God-given talent — but knowledge enriches the text, there's no denying it. Her rendering of 'Song of the Woman of Beare' makes my point eloquently or — should I say? — reticently. In very carefully honed quatrains, short lines, few beats, she mirrors the bleak depth of the original Irish. This is not only instinct, it's learning, respect for how things got made in the first place:

> *Well for islands at sea,*
> *their high tide follows low*
> *water; I do not hope*
> *my tide will turn and flow*

which brings us back to that Mediterranean sense of voyage, to 'a fragrance like spice enticing from the kitchen — / a pulse beating behind the embroidered veil': to that wise, educated impulse to touch in order to be certain that a voyage has not been in vain. In 'Juliette Ryan and the Cement Mixer' Lord Byron himself becomes the exemplary survivor, the restless youth who survives one kind of amputation. In this poem

Thomas McCarthy

she encapsulates the yearning for dangerous knowledge and the eventual impossibility of knowing. It is her certainty that full knowledge is impossible, that we can only know through metaphors and gestures, that makes *The Boys of Bluehill* such a consistent, mysterious and satisfying work:

> *or as Byron*
> *after travelling through four cantos, and eight years,*
> *through four hundred and ninety-five Spenserian stanzas,*
> *and across Europe and Turkey, so at last*
> *he could finish with the pilgrim Harold and meet himself*
> *as a child*
>   *said*
> *that he laid his hand on the mane of the dark blue sea.*

Dublin Review of Books,
May 2015

Saturated with Light
The Mother House *by Eiléan Ní Chuilleanáin*

Former Ireland Professor of Poetry, emeritus professor of English at TCD, scion of the nation's founding families of Dillons and Plunketts, member of Aosdána and founder of *Cyphers*, Eiléan Ní Chuilleanáin hardly needs an introduction in any part of Irish society, literary or political. In poetry she has used her luck and her gifts wisely and well, both as mentor and exemplar. To teach and to advocate poetry is in her bones, as it is in the DNA of Máire Mhac an tSaoi; but, as in Mhac an tSaoi, this tremendously rich, end-of-an-era, haut bourgeois Catholic life comes with the added gold dust of poetry. Like Mhac an tSaoi she has been the immensely dutiful daughter of gifted parents, and the gold traces left on the page from that inheritance of familial and academic national duty form an essential part of the jewelled hoard of her writing career. In every one of her collections of poetry there have been brief resting points but no hours of idleness. This dutiful, purposeful restlessness is one of the most determining characteristics of *The Mother House*:

> *Now that there's nothing I don't understand*
> *why do they come to me with their informations?*
> *They come in my dreams with their highlighting pens,*
> *they tell me the roman numerals*
> *on the shelf-end panels in the cathedral library . . .*
> ('Monsters')

Here is a child reared to absorb information, and still, like all good poets, a child in her mid-70s. Here, all gold flourishes and leaf script capitals, with a protagonist who makes shrouds of words, the poet's mind is sacrificed to a world of monsters ornate with grapes. The medieval is never far from the poet's mind, and that sense of doomed learning is everywhere. Ní Chuilleanáin's instinct, though, has always been to compose poems with camera angles. From the very beginning of her Cork collaborations with Brian Lalor she has been a word-cinematographer and her camerawork has always been that of a woman voyaging, capturing the light, the angles and the briefly glimpsed faces of strangers or fellow voyagers. I've lost count of the number of boats, seas, exiles, elsewheres and remembered Irelands in this present book:

> *Sister Clara, Sister Antony, meeting a niece*
> *in the quiet convent garden in Desvres,*
> *are overheard reminiscing, always in French,*
> *about their first convent on the hill in Cork*
> *and its precious holdings, the Penal Chalice . . .*
> ('To the Mother House')

Exile, sisterhood, history are celebrated here, as well as the wine and brandy, the lace and 'the little medals blessed and certified / in Rome'. And all of this richness in the poem, this litany of faith chaperoned by educated and consecrated women, is dovetailed into a chunk of marble beneath an altar, marble that can show the bones inside the skin. This is the delicate hardness of an earned belief, the plenitude of connections inside Irish Catholic faith. With Ní Chuilleanáin it has always been women voyaging, right from the earliest narratives of her Patrick Kavanagh Award-winning *Acts and Monuments*. There have always been women setting out on a journey, often women setting out alone, and often women beginning some kind of tour of duty. The schedules and rhythms of Catholic boarding schools and colleges are in every Ní Chuilleanáin book. It has often occurred to me that these rhythms would hardly be visible to a non Catholic

Saturated with Light

reader or to any Catholic under the age of fifty. They are the duties and clockwork of my own generation and she is one of the last chroniclers of this circumscribed 1950s/1960s world.

But Ní Chuilleanáin is not merely a representative poet representing just one set of circumstances. Nowadays, because of the increasing politicization of art and poetry into mere representative fragments, representing specific social experiences such as injustice or marginalization, we have forgotten how each poet's work is essentially an affirmation of sovereignty. In the end all poets will declare independence from all the materials that bind him or her to limited or contested themes. However restricted the poet may be socially or politically the poet will always rush towards freedom inwardly; the gold for the reader is in that inner freedom. Yet for this poet the poetry is also in the camerawork and the camerawork, its insights and flashes, is what amazes the Ní Chuilleanáin reader. Certainly poetry does contain honourable and very important political narratives and it can be a forceful witness in politics and a vital rhetorical tool against injustice. But wanting everything to represent something can destroy genius and comfort the second-rate who operate so effectively in the current academic and poetic worlds. In a very real sense we should always meet a poet as if for the first time, even in a ninth or tenth book. Reading *The Mother House* is a sharp reminder of this — Ní Chuilleanáin was a poet of genius long before her work was meant to represent anything. Loneliness has been her great photographer and this cinematography has been a compelling aspect of her voice. It is all there in 'The Blind':

> *One broken slat pulled from the blind*
> *shows only a slice: the marbled clouds,*
> *a world of bright sky stretching.*
> *But she can't look out. The news,*
> *a thread that crawls and winds, drags her*
> *into the dark well . . .*

Thomas McCarthy

And this collection unfolds with such a canny imaginative firmness. Nano Nagle is the subject of the first poem, 'An Imperfect Enclosure', but this serves only as an overture, a tasting, for the great sequence 'A Map of Convents' with its Cove Lane girls and boys, piano lessons and Latin grammar, a man hidden in a kitchen chimney, and that extraordinary phrase 'those who were absent with permission'. The theme — or trope, really — develops further into the superb 'Sister Marina' and 'To the Mother House'. And it continues with several other women who were absent with permission from motherhood and family including, even, Maria Edgeworth in 1847 who was so moved by the porters who loaded India meal for Irish Famine victims that she knitted a woollen comforter for each working man:

> *Like the girl whose brothers were turned into swans,*
> *she does what she knows, the long scarves piling*
> *softly beside her chair, one after the other like the days.*

Edgeworth's days were short indeed. Before the woollens reached the men she herself had died, an irony that Ní Chuilleanáin has turned into something of great poetic beauty here. Geraldine Plunkett is another shade reborn, with her young Dillon husband in 1916. As is belovèd Leland Bardwell, where the sea, the waves, the suntrap seat in her garden, the ladylike tweed, the little polo ponies in Phoenix Park; all of these things are stitched together and left on the page for us, like a black cat on a dry ledge above the foamy ocean. It is no surprise that the Leland Bardwell elegy is saturated with light, Ní Chuilleanáin's element:

> *making one shining surface of rising water*
> *where all the reflected lights floating shine together,*
> *they carry the glint of all the colours...*
>
> ('The Raging Foam')

Echoes from the Cistern

So I give you, then, yet another perfect book from this poet of sunlight and cloisters. This collection is a joy to read and a reminder, yet again, that the poets are sent to amaze us, to bring us all nearer to the light.

*Dublin Review of Books,
February 2020*

The Flower Master and Other Poems by Medbh McGuckian

Those who first read Medbh McGuckian more than a decade ago were surprised and enchanted by her unique and phenomenal poems. The reissue of *The Flower Master* is, therefore, an important event. Reading poems like 'The Seed-Picture', 'Lychees' and 'The Soil-Map' was like being caught in a suntrap. It is wonderful to read this work again, not just for the technical pleasure of her craft, but to re-live the impact her work first had upon us. Only McGuckian — that incredibly bright, self-indulgent young woman — could have written these intoxicating poems. They are like nothing else. In the early 80s they added to our available reality:

> *My going in to find the settlement*
> *Of every floor, the hump of water*
> *Following the moon, and her discolouring,*
> *The saddling derangement of a roof*
> *That might collapse its steepness*
> *Under the sudden strain of clearing its name.*

Her poetry insists that language is a friable material. She juxtaposes phrases like a quilter arranging blocks of cloth. Her assemblage of flowers, trees, gardens in general and interiors in particular, produces a powerfully narcotic reality. One could visit these poems blindfold for the scent alone. But this Gallery edition is not just a reissue. The cover alone gives early warning of a changed viewpoint: gone is the white trumpet flower of Georgia O'Keeffe and in its place is a simple photograph of a gardener. Poems have been dropped, including 'Problem Girl'

The Flower Master and Other Poems by Medbh McGuckian

and 'The Chain-Sleeper'. The original opening poem 'That Year' has been retitled 'Eavesdropper' and is banished to page 15. Its last line has been changed from 'The grass is no bed after dark' to 'The grass is an eavesdropper's bed.'

There are other changes. The poem 'Gentians' has now become an untitled Part 2 of 'The Orchid House' and 'Distance' has become an untitled part of 'Champagne'. There are other minor changes. A half-line has been shorn from 'The Sun-Trap' and 'adam work' has been adjusted to 'Adam work'. These may seem like trivial changes, but for a poet like McGuckian who drops metaphors like a Mick Mulcahy with oils, it is foolish to reduce the number of metaphors. One revised poem, in particular, illustrates my point. It is the poem 'Tulips', now moved from its crucial No. 2 spot in the original collection to the present page 27. More interesting still is the revision of the third stanza, from:

> *Except, like all governesses, easily*
> *Carried away, in sunny*
> *Absences of mirrors they exalt themselves*
> *To ballets of revenge, a kind*
> *Of twinness, an olympic way of earning*
> *And are sacrificed to plot . . .*

to

> *Except, like all governesses, easily*
> *Carried away, they sun themselves*
> *Exaltedly to ballets of revenge,*
> *A kind of twinness, an olympic*
> *Mode of earning: their absent faces*
> *Lifted many times to the artistry of light . . .*

'The artistry of light' is a marvellous expression, but 'mirrors' has been dropped. This is a technical mistake. How can one have an absence of face unless the image of the mirror had

Thomas McCarthy

already been inserted?

I'm glad to report that the integrity of her famous poems 'Lychees' and 'The Seed-Picture' has been retained. These poems have been widely anthologized. Thank God for those anthologists who sometimes insert themselves between poets and their work, offering refugee status to texts that subsequently give offense. *The Flower Master* is the kind of book that doesn't require any revision. McGuckian is a true artist and, like all those who are truly gifted, she has revised our notion of what constitutes art.

Poetry Ireland Review,
Spring 1994

This is Yarrow by Tara Bergin

Right now it is very difficult to begin a published life in Irish poetry: the market is fractured into regional, almost sectarian, groups; and those readerships are sharper than at any time in the last half century at least. One feels that even major publishers are vulnerable to cliquish 'capture', shutting out any unconnected new poets. I may be wrong. I hope I am. Those of us who took flight into poetry in the late 1970s were blessed indeed. The world was wider and kinder; and the undergraduate poetry audience, then surfacing from a ten-year infatuation with *Sgt. Pepper's Lonely Hearts Club Band*, was chilled and nurturing. Nowadays the new poet must become like Lois in Elizabeth Bowen's *The Last September*, guilty of emotional straying and wondering how to begin a valued life. The answer must surely be: make an impact or die. Nowadays a poet is forced to make an impact even before they can settle into that singular personal narrative that's the consolation of a life in poetry. Now you must be toned and impactful from the start:

> *Here is your talisman, I whisper*
> *hold it in your good hand and sing one*
> *of your songs for me.*
> *How does it go? Oh how does it go again?*
> *There is blood on my hand, la, la,*
> *There is blood on my hand, la, la.*
> *Your talisman, I say, a foul flower . . .*

Tara Bergin's *This is Yarrow* really is a masterpiece. The poem quoted above, 'Himalayan Balsam for a Soldier', is clear, clean,

Thomas McCarthy

mystical — not just one part but something emotionally interlocking the parts, something between tone and setting, sets her clockwork turning on the page. 'Once Aoife ceases to argue / about the fact that we have nothing in our mouths, / we can get on with the task of learning' is how she puts it in 'Acting School', and there's this impatient energy everywhere, giving her poetry a special charge, a linguistic propulsion. Her method is sometimes a medieval riddle or an Elizabethan song, the sound of a dulcimer being plucked beneath the surface of life. Hers is a really intriguing, questing technique, both destructive and gifted, seen flashing in 'Portrait of the Artist's Wife as a Younger Woman':

> *Only I speak.*
> *Only I say: Shh, shh.*
> *Only I say: It's so hot, little one,*
> *It's so sour, little thing.*

Roethke in *I am! Says the Lamb* could hardly have done better than these. Her 'Sonnets for Tracey' are also a marvel, the rhythm and tone here are like some of the best lyrics of the late Patrick Galvin, painfully aware that life is staged, dramatic. Her Tracey poems are beautiful, bohemian in the manner of Carolyn Forché's 'Burning the Tomato Worms' or 'Alfansa'. For sure, Tara Bergin's the real thing.

Trumpet (Poetry Ireland),
April 2017

The Poison Glen by Annemarie Ní Churreáin

A poet of the Donegal Gaeltacht Annemarie Ní Churreáin writes a poetic line whose roots are deep and deeply disturbed. Dislocation locates her art. Her first collection was aptly titled *Bloodroot* and this new book, more robust and overwhelming, speaks of dislocation and loss, of pain and attachment, in a poetry of furious energy and stunning versecraft. There are poems in *The Poison Glen* such as 'Creed' and 'The Screaming Room' that are simply masterpieces, the former with those startling opening words 'I believe in the queer, round window; / in the queer white bird — watcher of bar and bolt — ' and the latter poem with its scorching truths: 'I come from women who found themselves / in trouble . . . In their honour / I can never again be silent.' Hers is a poetry that is fire and rage burning, with an intensity of feeling that reminds me of the intensity of a young Máire Mhac an tSaoi's work, such a work of passion and intense longing. The entire collection is anchored, or rooted, in 'The Foundling Crib', a wonderful poem on a long-closed Dublin Foundling Hospital:

> *When you walk through Dublin you walk*
> *　in the land of the suffering. Sometimes*
>
> *I feel the deer of Phoenix Park roam down*
> *　onto the edges of my breath.*
>
> *Shadow gods with shadow lives, coal eyes burning.*
> *　What are they trying to tell? What do they know . . .*

Thomas McCarthy

And thus begins a marvellous, moving historical narrative of troubled, hunted women, souls who knew no lullaby as Eavan Boland wrote in 'Child of Our Time', words that are the epigraph to Ní Churreáin's poem. Here the babies, 'washed and ink-stamped / on the inner arm', are sent from the room of birth to the room of want where nurses present corpses for inspection. She recreates, with deepest empathy, the harrowing reality of a Soviet-like era: Irish motherhood in its Catholic gulag. In ten powerful cantos the poet makes the dead scratch their pain upon the windowpane of each cell:

> *Wages for want and cold.*
> *Wages for fits. Wages for death.*
>
> *Who am I except an eyeless witness treading a cemented*
>   *site?*
> *Who were these sons and daughters left*
>
> *in a flowerless grip to dwindle head-to-toe*
>   *in cradles swarming vermin and bugs...*

The sequence is the lively pulse of the book, its fierce polemical heart. Bells, clocks, hunger, milk hours, a parade of foundlings with pockets turned out to excite charity; Ní Churreáin layers the detail, slams the colours of pain, those historic pigments, onto the waiting page where they will reach every reader's engaged eye. In the afterlight of social history the poet has knelt, in essence, at the lime-hole where ten corpses at a time were dispatched into the earth. With 'The Foundling Crib' this poet has raised a monument.

But there are many other achievements in *The Poison Glen*; it is not in any sense a one-dimensional book. There are elements of a life beyond St Joseph's Industrial School or Carriglea Park Industrial School or Castlepollard Mother and Baby Home. While each of these homes has inspired astonishing texts here, historic and feminist reverberations in

The Poison Glen by Annemarie Ní Churreáin

pearls of work, this is a poet who also chants life, who going closer to the flame at all times still remains the girl who cannot be stolen, a robin of poetry. Conscious of this power within her Ní Churreáin can tackle anything:

> *But the mare's eye is an orb that shines*
> *as whole and undisturbed as any future*
> *she might yet encounter. Perhaps*
> *she sees within that iris a transformed*
> *shadow of the many-chambered heart...*

'The Mare's Eye', above, is simply an amazing lyric, as beautifully written as white sheets against the sun, as a mother braiding a daughter's hair, reassuring her that *'some day you will be beautiful'*. It is a poem of earth, field and nurture. Charms, promises, myths, invocations to the gods, seed and fruit 'more milk-sweet than before', Ní Churreáin has all of this richness in her myth kitty. Her art is a grain store, youthful and lifegiving. Demanding and technically perfect poems like 'The Lamb Who Became a Wolf' and 'Will You Write a Bird for Us?' give us a perfection of technique and voice, the sureness of craft. 'We good-mouth your sailing' as she writes in 'A Blessing of the Boats by the Village Mothers', a poem of good karma on the sea, of keeping the light for safe return. After history, her story, its pain and irrecoverable loss, this Donegal poet is fully conscious of the redemptive nature of poetry, of the saving power that is such a part of its beauty. It is a stunning, central part of her wonderful art that, after pain, she would have us 'make a bowl / spilling yellow corn-light'.

What a gift Annemarie Ní Churreáin is to contemporary Irish poetry, what an absolute gift to this nation from Donegal. She has given us a masterpiece in this, her first Gallery Press book, *The Poison Glen*.

Dublin Review of Books,
December 2022

Life Saving: Why We Need Poetry
Introductions to Great Poets *by Josephine Hart*

If Josephine Hart had tried to be ordinary she would have been, as James Merrill said of Elizabeth Bishop, merely impersonating ordinariness. Like Princess Grace she was beautiful, exceptional and damaged. From the claustrophobia and grief of her Westmeath childhood to the gilded Saatchi stage of the West End she used poetry as a route map through life. Poets can't save themselves, as we all know, but they can save others: that's the great irony of poetic suffering. When Hart crossed the Irish Sea to England she carried a great burden of grief within her, not least of which was the loss of two of her siblings when she was only seventeen.

In a sense her early grief was worked out over a busy career of fiction writing and theatre production that included West End runs of Lorca's *The House of Bernarda Alba*. Her shrewd and knowing novel, *Damage*, was later filmed by Louis Malle with Jeremy Irons and Juliette Binoche. She wrote five other novels, the most poignant of which is *The Truth About Love*. By the time of her premature death in June of last year she had dramatized the place of poetry in her life through 'The Josephine Hart Poetry Hour' at the British Library. Like most beautiful people she knew her name meant something in that perpetually *arriviste* city of London: humility was never one of her attributes.

It is typical of Hart that she would want to stylize and dramatize what is in essence a deeply private act: the reading of poetry. She insisted upon the drama of recitation. It is always a dangerous gamble, even if it is Harold Pinter reading Philip Larkin. Larkin would look back in anger at any fool who tried to recite him — with the possible exception of John

Life Saving: Why We Need Poetry

Betjeman. As Lady Ottoline Morrell said of T S Eliot, poets can be dull, dull, dull. It is not their business to be publicly interesting, to be like actors. The voice that settles upon a poem comes from a much deeper place than performance. Few theatre directors understand that. A poem communicates directions to the reader through rhythm, vocabulary, idiom and verse structure, but its single most insistent direction is always towards silence, a ruminating silence that allows the poem to expand at the reader's breakfast table. The breakfast table, the park bench, the airport gate, the pub snug, the school library — these are the great theatres of poetry. The most important place where I ever read poems, where they communicated most deeply to me, was the old Glandore Café in the Cork Bus Station. A great orchestra of ordinary County Cork life accompanied my first deep reading of Hugh MacDiarmid, Larkin, Rupert Brooke, Eliot and Ezra Pound.

'It is an art of the nerves, this art of Laforgue, and it is what all art would tend towards if we followed our nerves on all their journeys,' Josephine Hart quotes Arthur Symons in her Introduction to a reading of T S Eliot. Her Introduction here is brilliant, illuminating, contextualizing. It is followed by an equally knowing Introduction to Robert Frost whose 'best poems represent the terrible actualities of his life,' as she tellingly quotes the critic Lionel Trilling. While this anthology collects Hart's favourite poets, in the manner of Edith Sitwell's Gollancz anthology of 1940, it is the collating of her own Introductions that makes *Life Saving* a really worthwhile book. She is a deep reader with a tragic sense of life. The dark part of her heart is peeled open for all to see in this gallery of dramatic ceremonies for which dead poetry is both object and pretext. She has accentuated an English poetic timeline by calling certain voices out of the chorus line and presenting them as friends of the theatre management. Kipling, that enemy of Irish nationalism, is her word warrior with his rare insight into the common soldier, Milton fascinates her with his psychological insight into the soul of Satan, Marianne Moore she loves for her Escher-like complexity and 'fresh-washed quality'. That brilliant Smith girl, Sylvia Plath, is admired for having a seven-year marriage 'drenched in passion and pain' as well as for the painfulness of her method, her consulting of thesaurus and dictionary for each word as if accuracy could bring redemption.

It's true that no Irish needed to apply in Josephine Hart's Binkie Beaumont world of poetry, apart from the out-of-copyright Wilde and Yeats. She traded with Mandarins only, the Eliots and Audens, the Byrons and Shelleys. The Irish nineteenth century of ballads meant for recitation, poems by James Clarence Mangan and John Keegan, for example, would have made for terrific entertainment in front of any London audience. No doubt she had moved on from us — the material of Ireland must have seemed desperately provincial. As a London producer, an introducer, a rainmaker, she had bigger things on her mind. She wanted to save the world from drowning; she needed to be sure that the timbers were sound when they hit the rocks of the West End or Westminster Abbey. As Maurice Saatchi writes, quoting her Life Saving Cert she was awarded at the age of thirteen: 'For practical know-ledge of rescue, releasing oneself from the clutch of the drowning, and the ability to render aid in resuscitating the apparently drowned.'

That was her messianic streak: such an impulse of the beautiful and the damaged required public performance. But the privacy of poetry, like an unsalved grief, she must have been aware of too, as in Christina Rossetti's 'Memory', collected in this anthology: 'I have a room where into no one enters / Save I myself alone: / There sits a blessed memory on a throne / There my life centres.'

Irish Examiner,
2012

For the Desert Air
Ethna MacCarthy: Poems *Eoin O'Brien and Gerald Dawe (eds)*

Sometimes the turbulent world of Irish books throws out a real gem. Lilliput has produced a fair few literary gems in its day but this one is an absolute treasure. The Trinity poet (and I call her that most advisedly) Ethna MacCarthy was a vivacious, spirited, brilliant presence in the lives of three very important male figures in Dublin's literary world. She dominates several early pages of Denis Johnston's rollicking life, she is a persistent romantic presence in the life and work of Samuel Beckett, and she fell in love with and eventually married the great theatre chronicler and Beckett companion, Con (A J) Leventhal. This might have been her destiny, to be a beloved, to be a muse, had Eoin O'Brien not come upon her personal album of poetry in the papers of Con Leventhal and had poet Gerald Dawe not gone back to the work published in forgotten Dublin journals and *The Irish Times* of the 1930s and 1940s. Look what can happen to women in the Irish canon; how can poems such as 'Viaticum' be simply forgotten?

> The sluice gates of sleep are open wide
> And through the House its soothing silver tide
> From ward to ward flows grave and deep:
> Now flood, now fretful trickle,
> And some it leaves marooned
> Who cannot sleep.
> The nurses chart its course all night
> And those who drowse and those who tell their beads
> And those who coma vigil keep,
> Sunken beyond the lure of light.

Thomas McCarthy

This work, the poetry of a highly educated and deeply cerebral woman, has finally seen the light of day in this magnificent first edition of her poems. This is a poetry of heightened awareness, intellectual work that is as penetrating and effective as the stare from her brilliant eyes in Seamus O'Sullivan's 1931 pencil portrait. 'We railed against the psychopedantic parlours of our elders and their maidenly consorts, hoping the while with an excess of Picabia and banter, a whiff of Dadaist Europe, to kick Ireland into artistic wakefulness . . . ', wrote Con Leventhal in *The Klaxon* (Winter, 1923-24). The Picabia referred to must be none other than the porno-realistic artist-father of one Francine Picabia who would recruit Beckett into the French Resistance during the Occupation. In this hermetic Paris-TCD world everything is ultimately connected. The cultural and spiritual interconnectedness of everyone is simply uncanny and thrilling.

Granddaughter of the famed Irish-American poet Denis Florence MacCarthy and daughter of a public health specialist, Dr Brendan MacCarthy, Ethna was born in Coleraine, County Derry. The family moved to Dublin in the early nineteen hundreds and lived at Sandymount Avenue. She became a Foundation Scholar and First Class Moderator at Trinity College where she studied French and German, becoming a lecturer in French and Provençal. In her mid-thirties she switched careers, entering TCD's School of Medicine and graduating in 1941 with a BM and BS, followed by the professional MD of Trinity at the age of forty-three. Like her father she became a specialist in paediatric public health, becoming physician to the children's dispensary at Dublin's Royal Hospital. Although she was Beckett's first love, the inspiration for *Dream of Fair to Middling Women* and a presence in *Krapp's Last Tape*, her lifelong love was Con Leventhal whom she married in 1956 after his first wife's death. Theirs was a brief marriage as she died from throat cancer in May 1959 at the age of fifty-six.

In his fascinating Introduction to the work here Eoin

O'Brien recalls his receipt of Leventhal's case of papers, diaries and notebooks from his partner, Marion, in Paris, and how he found therein the typescripts, manuscripts and newspaper cuttings of Ethna MacCarthy's work. It was an important moment of recovery; the recovery not only of a forgotten poetic talent of the 1930s and 1940s but the reclamation of an entire lost atmosphere in Irish writing. Ethna, Leventhal and Beckett were all part of a bustling, outward-looking, cosmopolitan Trinity junta; keepers of a defiant flame of modernism in an Ireland that was becoming determinedly incestuous and backward. What a pity that Ethna MacCarthy didn't live for at least a further ten years, into that decade where she might have met James Liddy or Michael Smith or Gerard Smyth, who would have understood her restless, modernist voice. She would have surely become a poet of New Writers' Press, sitting comfortably with Smyth, Brian Lynch and Durcan, and extending the roots of New Writers' Press back to its modernist 1920s Dublin origins. But, for all her wit and sharpness, her vivacity and brilliance, Ethna suffered from a common MacCarthy trait, indolence. Like Máire Mhac an tSaoi with whom she shares many upper-class Catholic emotional and literary traits, Ethna seems to have had that dubious gift of literary patience. Patience is a catastrophe if you're going to die young. Like Mhac an tSaoi MacCarthy would first test her skills as a translator of Spanish and German poetry before settling into a full acceptance of her own voice. She became a poet who could write like this, creating this cat poem, as good as anything by Louis MacNeice:

> *My silver cat with burning eyes*
> *thinks the wall a paradise*
> *for angling human kind.*
> *She knows the world belongs to her*
> *for her to rend or kill or bless,*
> *the very wind that stirs her fur*
> *she tolerates as a caress*

Thomas McCarthy

> *ruffling a can-can glimpse of white*
> *beneath pale infant loneliness.*

The accomplished technique of MacNeice's 'The Death of a Cat' or a lyric like Máire Mhac an tSaoi's 'Suantraí Ghráinne' or Richard Murphy's 'Coppersmith' comes to mind when you read such work by MacCarthy. The fuller oxygen of book publication, of a public response and a wider audience, would have worked wonders for her in her poetic career. But she hesitated, or she seems to have hesitated. Was she intimidated by the brilliant men in her circle; did she cede too much aesthetic ground to them? Or was she simply too well brought up in an haut bourgeois Catholic atmosphere to place her own literary ambition front and centre in this rollicking tide of Dublin masculinities? At that moment in time, between 1927 and 1947, she was a far better poet than Samuel Beckett: anyone with even the most basic understanding of what constitutes a successful poem would have to admit that. Beckett's lyric technique is garishly derivative and some of his lyric music was Ethna MacCarthy's. There is something furtive and hidden about her own brilliantly demanding personal life, some unstated hesitation or unhappiness, that still needs to be investigated by some literary sleuth like Knowlson. The men in a vivacious woman's life are never a really good starting point. We need to know more about her, and only her. What were her thought processes? Why did she escape back to Medicine from French? Her poems of inner city life, of Dublin hospital wards and clinics, of nurses and Masters, are hypnotic and masterful.

In his section of the Introduction Gerald Dawe creates a terrific introductory map of her work, noting her responses to the Jewish poet Else Lasker-Schüler, as well as her poetic landscape of Grafton Street, the Provost's House and Sandymount. But Dawe is sharp enough, and a good enough poet, to spot 'the conflicting strains of emotional energy ... in the conventional and performative aspects of her life'. Dawe emphasizes the technical power of lyrics like 'Barcelona' and 'The Migrants', noting how MacCarthy gets better and better through an educated web of allusion, inter-text and connection across languages. Indeed, as I've said, he is mapping a poetic talent that would have thrived under *Arena* or New Writers' Press.

For poems like 'Clinic', 'The Charity', 'Viaticum' and 'The Theatre' Ethna MacCarthy deserves to be more widely known and celebrated in her own right. This book certainly is that brilliant starting point, a female voice recovered, a beauty of a book, a precious, important gift to give to any young Dublin poet who is just about to begin a life in literature.

Dublin Review of Books,
June 2020

PART THREE

QUESTIONS FROM AN ASCENDANCY

Snow, Göring's Train, Hofstetter's Serenade

You'd better go down straight away, the housekeeper said. He's not too good. He had a second blackout. He was out for nearly an hour. He's not too good. He was going to phone you before the second blackout. You haven't been down to see him for months. Where have you been? They took him to Ardkeen. Will you go down straight away? He's not too good.

'Is this a field hospital, Thomas? Have I been hit again? Bloody bad luck.'

I stand over the functional gridwork of a hospital gurney. We are in a busy men's ward of Waterford Regional Hospital. He has been hit again, but not in the way he thinks. The war happened over sixty years ago, a war of ferocious tank battles. He survived the bloody armoured breakout of the Falaise Pocket, the crossing of the Rhine, the flooded Dutch battlefields. Now he lies disorientated in a very ordinary place. An affable young nurse has been paying him particular attention: 'You're all right, Denis. You just had a fall. You'll be right as rain. Don't look so worried, Denis.' The familiarity of her tone is shocking. He looks at me with astonishment in his face. 'Do you know her, Thomas?' he asks in that very confidential tone of an Old Etonian. What he means is, do I know her family, is her father one of the prosperous tenant-farmers of his grandfather, the Duke of Leinster? Was she born into a prosperous family that benefitted from the Wyndham Land Acts? In his growing dementia he thinks that the men's ward is his house, now confiscated to set up a field hospital. He raises his arm and gestures sadly, hopelessly, 'I don't mind them putting up these silly curtains everywhere, but the chaos in our sector is frightful. Can you restore order, at least in this area?' They say he may snap out of his dementia but that he may have to go into a nursing home to recover his strength.

It is sad to see him struck down so forcibly: a man who has survived everything, war, dislocation, injury. I begin to tell the nurses about him: his surviving a direct hit from a Stuka bomber, his leadership at the Liberation of Brussels, his crossing the Rhine as the youngest Colonel in the Allied Army, a FitzGerald from Cartan and Kilkea, a direct descendant of Garret Mór, Garret Óg and the patriot, Lord Edward.

Suddenly, he asks, 'Is it snowing? Thomas, is it snowing?'
'No. It's early summer.'

But he has heard a sound, a very particular sound, almost clairvoyantly, a split second before I hear it. It must be coming from a radio in the corridor or out in the car park. It is 'Hofstetter's Serenade', the andante of a string quartet wrongly attributed to Haydn. It is a sound that Denis associates with the War, with Germany in the winter of 1945, with Göring's train that he had commandeered as a Guards Armoured command post. Then he was a victorious young Allied Officer, on top of the world, capable just at that moment of wild gestures and a commanding authority. He had already commandeered a truckload of champagne, stored for the German General Staff and quickly shared among the ranks of the Irish Guards, Third Battalion. Then he had Göring's train fitted out, something monstrous made humane, and over and over again on his wind-up gramophone he played the only unshattered vinyl that he possessed after his eventful journey across northern Europe — that German vinyl with 'Hofstetter's Serenade'.

Laid low in the public ward of Waterford Regional Hospital,

with the paralysis of yet another stroke, he was listening once more; and he was young, younger even than I, as young as the Tipperary nurse who was kind and even ebullient in his presence.

'Look, he's totally alert. He's listening!'

The young nurse smiles approvingly. We all share a rare moment of peace in an Irish hospital. The ghosts of Europe assemble around us. The sunlight of Ardkeen is darkened and in its stead a heavy snow is falling, falling on all the ruined cities, falling on all the misery and starvation that our young Commanding Officer can see from behind his blast-proof carriage windows. How often did he describe this scene to me when he was in his early seventies, in better health, sitting beneath a portrait of his mother by the drawing-room fire, holding up a tiny glass of dry sherry? How lucky I was to be available, between lives just at that moment, suspended in a moment of early manhood, just as he had been. Time is strange. It delivers duties to us that seem to have been sent from heaven or, at least, from places far away.

Once that vinyl 78 was worn and gutted by heavy needles he never replaced the record. I never heard him play it, only the memory of it, like the memory of snow falling on Germany in 1945.

Sunday Miscellany, RTÉ Radio One, December 2021

Mrs Victor Rickard

Who now remembers Mrs Victor Rickard, Jessie Louisa Moore Rickard, of Montenotte Road, Cork, author of over thirty novels published by Constable and Dodd Mead as well as Doubleday, Doran in New York between 1912 and 1960? She is recorded in the catalogue of Cork City Libraries merely as author of *The Story of the Munsters at Etreux, Festubert, Rue Du Bois and Hulloch*. It was her compelling, emotional descriptions of the pre-battle scene in 1915 in this pamphlet that guided the War artist Matania in his painting of the canvas 'The Last Absolution of the Munsters'. In the painting Mrs Rickard's husband, Lt Colonel Rickard, is on horseback to the left of Fr Gleeson, the Munsters' chaplain. The battalion, including its Colonel, was wiped out in the subsequent battle: all part of the slaughtered Irish hordes who answered the call of John Redmond in 1914 and 1915.

During the summer this year local historian Brendan Goggin gave the first account I'd ever heard of this author in his wonderful lecture at the Frank O'Connor Library on authors of Cork's North East Ward. That August, and therefore quiet, morning of his library talk we arranged twelve chairs in a circle in the centre of the lending section. We didn't expect a large crowd: it was, after all, the dog days, the dead days of early August. But a trickle of familiar and new faces began to appear near the Lending Desk. Soon all the chairs were occupied and another dozen were arranged, then another dozen, then another. With five minutes to go we ran out of chairs. More than a hundred middle-aged and elderly readers had assembled to hear about this forgotten local author. The unflappable Brendan Goggin seemed no more surprised by this huge crowd than he might have been had only three persons turned up to hear him. Mrs Rickard's novels have disappeared from the library stock, yet the huge crowd were held spellbound by Brendan as he described her life, her widowhood, her professional life as writer and single parent of two children. She was also a great woman for *soirées* and cocktail parties. One elderly man in the audience remembered helping out as a boy at one of her grand parties in Lower Montenotte Road: it was the first time he'd tasted cucumber sandwiches, 'disgusting things' he thought. Brendan Goggin also informed us that Mrs Rickard had founded the Detection Club with Dorothy L Sayers, G K Chesterton and Father Ronald Knox.

Jessie Louisa Moore was the daughter of Canon Courtney Moore of Castletownroche and Mitchelstown. Her father was an Irish Nationalist, author of two novels, co-founder of the venerable Cork Historical and Archaeological Society and Editor of *The Church of Ireland Gazette*. The daughter became estranged from the family when she divorced her first husband to marry the dashing Colonel Rickard. She was thirty-six when she published her first novel, *Young Mr Gibbs*. A great tumult of novels followed, including the war novels, *The Light Above the Cross Roads* in 1916 and *The House of Courage* in 1919. Her descriptions of people are brilliant: here she is, describing Kennedy Gleeson in *The House of Courage:*

> '*Kennedy was dressed with no eye to creating a sensation, in a grey suit which had seen wear, and a dark tie. He had the easy air of a man who is perfectly sure of himself, and he was interested in his own thoughts. At the age of twenty-eight he had come to realize the value of isolation, and though he liked his fellow-men and was unquestionably popular, he often preferred to be alone. At that very moment he might have been the welcome guest in a dozen different houses, or sitting at*

> his club surrounded by enthusiastic friends. Even in his grey suit he could have gone to any of the most exclusive of the London restaurants without causing a single eye to travel over him with the limitless scorn which would have been meted out to another. His thick hair was brushed straight back from his forehead, and his clean-shaven face was sensitive even in its quiet strength. There was reticence about the lines of his mouth, and though his eyes had a touch of boldness and even challenge in their quality, they were far more humorous than tender. In every line he silently conveyed the impression of passion.'

Here is her description of the young doctor, Monica Henstock, in *Cathy Rossiter* (1920):

> 'In figure, she was slender and rather frail, and her fine, mobile features had an original and almost mystic suggestion. Her mouth drooped at the corners, and she was full of abstract ardours. Since she began to think for herself, which was very early in life, as these things count, she had flung herself into extremes, and fought for a number of causes. Studied closely, it was possible to discover that there was a deep strain of morbidity in her, which induced her to dwell upon the ugly, dangerous side of things, and her training had accentuated her natural tendency. The force with which she was able to express herself was lightened by her attractive smile, showing white, and her small head was crowned with a wealth of thick red hair.'

That novel opens with an epigraph from Tom Kettle, the soldier-poet:

> Had we but coined the vision when it shone
> We too had ruled, and mocked and dispossessed.

Mrs Victor Rickard

*Well, we have the rags, the prudent have the riches —
We have not lived as wisely as the rest.*

Mrs Rickard certainly lived and wrote wisely through a very long widowhood. When she suffered a stroke in the 1950s she taught herself to write with her left hand and continued with her career. In later years she lived with Denis Gwynn and his wife who was a daughter of Lady Lavery. Lady Lavery herself had been the subject of Mrs Rickard's 1927 novel, *A Bird of Strange Plumage*. This entirely forgotten novelist, even forgotten in her own native county of Cork, died at the end of January, 1963. She is buried in Rathcooney Cemetery, outside Cork City, the city where she was now suddenly re-remembered by a huge library crowd of middle-class and upper middle-class readers. They all remembered her company, her physical presence in Henchy's shop in St Lukes, and the effect of *Cathy Rossiter* and *The Light Above the Cross Roads* upon them and their genteel Montenotte mothers. And we must thank the lecturer, scholar and local historian, Brendan Goggin, for bringing her name to light. She lived again, burning brightly and exquisitely, for all the minutes that Mr Goggin was on his feet. The audience was spellbound. A forgotten writer lived again.

*Facebook,
2013*

Monument to Inner Space
The Price of Stone *by Richard Murphy*

It is thirty years since Richard Murphy published his first collection. His career reminds us that poetry is born out of a private and even a familiar conversation, an argument between the poet's background and his nature, between his expectations and his personal destiny. The Anglo-Irish world from which Murphy broke through into poetry must be one of the most exclusive and complex worlds within which a poet can begin. The Act of Union and the abolition of the Irish Parliament robbed them of their political voice. To be left without political expression is to be cut adrift. In the case of the Anglo-Irish it meant that they were forced into a political and cultural neurosis. In the brief pluralist honeymoon of the first Free State administration Protestants of the calibre of Yeats, Sir John Keane and The Mcgillicuddy of the Reeks made some attempt to be politically integrated. But their careers were crushed by the dominant Catholic ethos that emerged in Ireland. In the Senate election of 1943 Sir John Keane didn't receive even one vote.

Why worry about these things now if poetry is essentially a private matter? The young Richard Murphy had become a pacifist, a loner and a poetry-writing intellectual at Wellington College in the same year that the Anglo-Irish Senators ceased to have a voice. Eight years later, in 1951, he was awarded the AE Memorial Prize. Four years later the Dolmen Press published his *The Archaeology of Love*. He arrived as a poet within a decade of that Ascendancy disengagement from Irish politics. There is certainly a connection between the kind of poem Murphy has been writing and the frustrated destiny of his class, a class born to lead. It is through the therapy of poems, through the operation of a classical English idiom upon Irish material, that he has tried to reconcile himself to his country and to its refusal to accept him as its natural son.

His poetic method has always been classical and bold. Even when he moves from the verdant ground of 'The Woman of the House' and 'The God Who Eats Corn' to the anchorite severity of 'Little Hunger' and 'Seals at High Island' his poetry retains that masculine vigour and classical reserve. Always adequately imagined his poems stick in one's memory because of their verbal solidity. In *The Price of Stone*, his first collection in eleven years, Murphy has constructed a mannered and incisive autobiography. There are ancestral figures dealt with affectionately and characteristic images of itinerant children, various poachers and escaped scoundrels, all dealt with through a lover's familiarity and control.

In this new book he has turned the Yeatsian procedure on its head. Yeats rebuilt his Norman tower to vivify and luxuriate within a post-Symbolist metaphor. But Murphy has abandoned his island of stone in order to construct the one real home, the house of poetry:

> *Dismasted and dismissed, without much choice,*
> *Having lost my touch, I'll raise my chiseled voice.*

Murphy's lifelong interest in archaeology, folklore, place lore, genealogy and architecture are woven together brilliantly here. The sonnet form itself is a major component in this imaginative project. Murphy explained to Fintan O'Toole in 1983, 'The form is a discovery made in the Middle Ages of a structure which was particularly appropriate to certain mental processes to do with love and the desire to recover the beloved.' Each sonnet is a structure speaking. Each building is an expression of memory but also, and in a very real sense, a tomb, a monument to that part of the poet's life that cannot be regained.

Thomas McCarthy

The sequence begins with three phallic symbols speaking: Connolly's Folly on the Castletown Estate, 'My form is epicene'; the chimney of a lead mine, 'You'll know I've lost the fury to renew / The furnace at my root'; and Nelson's Pillar, 'I never controlled the verminous / Poor beggars round my plinth'. The sequence closes with two sonnets describing childbirth. In 'Beehive Cell' a seventh-century woman gives birth on her own 'in my spinal cerebellic souterrain', while in 'Natural Son', a celebration of the birth of the poet's son, William, Murphy provides a symbolic palliative for the stone mania that has come between him and companionship:

> *This day you crave so little, we so much*
> *For you to live, who need our merest touch.*

It is at the moment of birth that estrangement is cancelled, the estrangement caused by good manners, social expectation, sexual adventure and the mania for stone. In an earlier sonnet, 'Birth Place', the sun 'transfigured all of us'. In 'A Nest in the Wall' the poet writes, 'Coming together we live in our own time . . . ' Throughout the sequence there is a shifting reference, between buildings and bodies, restoration in stone and reconciliation through remembrance. Throughout, it is the intimate space, stone folly and lakeside cottage that predominates, rather than the Anglo-Irish Big House.

Despite this classical style and the Public School education there is a fisherman, a Corrib poacher, even a singing Irish traveller within Murphy, all screaming to be released. The restored cottage is a womb-place rather like Roethke's greenhouse which the poet invokes in an effort to reset the historical and cultural genes. Murphy's journey has always been familiar to us in this way, and it is always political. We are fortunate that he has always had that Protestant tendency to clarify and interrogate rather than merely whine. His instinct is to investigate rather than mystify: he could no more obfuscate materials of memory than mix bad concrete.

Monument to Inner Space

The twenty-one poems placed here before 'The Price of Stone' will be more immediately satisfying to the non-Irish audience: poems like 'Trouvaille', 'Tony White at Inishbofin' and 'Elixir' ('When all his wealth was told / It filled a vault with bone-dry speculation') are reminiscent of the lesser poetry workshop poems that we mere mortals dream of writing. For those lyrics, as well as 'The Price of Stone', this new Richard Murphy collection is well worth the entrance fee.

The Irish Times,
22 June 1985

The author with Molly Keane in the Mercier Bookshop on French Church Street, Cork, 1992

The Death of a Fox
A note on the early stories of Molly Keane

Molly Keane, the veteran Anglo-Irish writer, was catapulted back into the public eye last year with the success of her novel, *Good Behaviour*. Most people had forgotten about this elegant writer who, from the late 20s to the early 60s, had produced a wide range of novels such as *Mad Puppetstown* and *The Rising Tide*, as well as a body of successful melodramas like *Spring Meeting* (1938) and *Treasure Hunt* (1949); all of them published under the pseudonym 'M J Farrell' (a name that Mrs Keane picked casually from the front of a County Wexford pub). Her world is that of the 'hard-riding country gentlemen', the colonial Anglo-Irish whose world view was profoundly English and upper-class, but whose passion for the Irish countryside was deep, natural and irrevocable. With her books Mrs Keane extended the tradition of Somerville and Ross well into the twentieth century. And Somerville and Ross, with their jovial Masters of Hounds, their conniving horse traders, their inefficient transport and mails, were, after all, picking up where Charles Lever — in Harry Lorrequer and Charles O'Malley — had left off. Lever, it could be argued, was only putting an Irish face on the rogues, gentlemen and commoners, portrayed in the hugely successful rural stories of Surtees, an English humourist of the mid-nineteenth century.

Mrs Keane herself was born into a horse-breeding and hunting family in County Wexford — so that when she began to write in her early twenties she drew on the stereoscopic power of intimate knowledge and assured tradition. The only thing that was unusual was that she was a woman, so she buried herself behind the pseudonym 'M J Farrell', a name with the protective presumption of maleness. She did this in order to hide her talent, particularly from the male Anglo-Irish who might have considered her too clever to be attractive and feminine. In doing this she bowed to the social pressures and expectations of her class and time, thus becoming an instrument of 'good behaviour'. She had already published three works of fiction when she wrote the linked stories of *Conversation Piece* (1932). With these stories in particular she reinforces the world of Somerville and Ross and intensifies the caricatures from hunting life to be found in Lever and Surtees. I believe that these stories are a very important part of Mrs Keane's career, not just because they assure her of an honourable place in the experiences of an Irish R M tradition but because they anticipate certain characters and tensions that appear in *Good Behaviour*.

In *Conversation Piece* Ireland (or Anglo-Ireland) is portrayed as a blessèd place of extended hunts and relaxed evenings. The narrator of the stories is an Englishman who visits his Irish widower cousin Sir Richard Pulleyns and his children, Willow and Dick — 'To be with these Irish cousins, their kindness mine and the quick fire of their interest changes me strangely, I think, so that all safe known values are gone from me . . . ' Eventually all of the narrator's days are spent in anticipation of the hunt, in preparation and training, in looking over yearlings and attending the crushes of point-to-point races. The hunt is the backdrop for all relationships; an ability to manage outdoor sports is in itself an assurance of social, even sexual, success. (Mrs Keane uses this idea brilliantly in *Good Behaviour* where 'Papa's' success with women is restored after he, one-legged, learns to manage horses again.) In the opening story, 'Pullinstown', we are introduced to the English narrator who's led a sedentary life of an artist and who has just arrived at Pullinstown to be met by the frosty indifference of his Irish kinsmen: 'Since my cousins (in a second and third degree) made no demands on my attention,

The Death of a Fox

I looked about me and maintained what I hoped was a becoming silence.' But two stories further on, in 'The Chase', we find the narrator not only participating observantly but immersed in the enthusiasm and brutality of the hunt. The brilliant description of the fox kill is made at a point of deepest empathy with the Irish cousins:

> *'An instant's silence in the heather and gorse — a moment from the evening that belonged to the death of a fox... Fifteen minutes later not one rag of brown fur remained on the hillside to tell of the proud end of a good fox, nothing but his mask hanging down from the Ds of the whipper-in's saddle. Nothing but the warm air which would live for us in our remembrance of that good hunt (sixty-five minutes and six-mile point) — a fox's most fitting immortality.'*

There we have an end to caricature and the beginning of seriousness. In the two stories that follow 'The Chase' — 'The Ladies of Templeshambo' and 'Prime Rogues' — the narrator identifies more closely with his cousins. When introduced to Mr Billy Morgan in 'Prime Rogues' he is immediately aware of the differing accents of Morgan and Pulleyns and the social resonance of that difference: 'their voices cannot be compared. Theirs never lack a certain quality. His never attained that certain quality.' In 'The Ladies of Templeshambo' the narrator becomes drawn into the relationship of Sir Richard with Lady Honour and Lady Eveleen. The characters of these two women, the one acidic but both of them effusive and economical, and fallen on hard times, surely anticipates the characters of the Crowhurst twins of *Good Behaviour* who are visited by the father of Aroon St Charles: 'Well, we made their day,' Papa said. 'I suppose that's something.'

In the final stories of *Conversation Piece*, 'Stranger' and 'I Praise Not', Mrs Keane moves away from the temptations of

Somerville and Ross. She explores the Pulleyns' household under threat from strangers, the equilibrium of outdoor life. The love that binds the whole family, becomes unbalanced. In 'Stranger' the very close brother and sister relationship between Willow and Dick is threatened by Dick's new formidable girlfriend. Here is the jealous Willow's description:

> 'she always does everything with everyone. Fishing with Dick and walking round the horses with Sir Richard — till she must be nearly growing a horse's tail...'

The theme of that story is the fall of the new girlfriend in the eyes of the household and in Dick's eyes. The girl becomes isolated by over-enthusiasm, her lack of skill and final embarrassment. Having boasted about her skill with horses she's thrown from a fresh mount. Later she spends hours, days, by the riverbank determined to catch a salmon to prove herself. When she finally lands a fish, with a stolen fly, it turns out to be old and diseased. Her theft of the low-water fly gets Dick into trouble with his father and, rather than face the music, she bolts from Pullinstown with a fiver borrowed from the narrator. She had tried too hard, she broke conventions and codes of honour, and therefore failed.

In the final story the Pulleyns family comes as close to break-up and disgrace as it ever will. The threat to the unity and social stability comes from Willow's infatuation with Billy Morgan, the puller of horses and shady trader: 'a buckeen of a bounder', in Sir Richard's words. Willow has a long, heated exchange with her father in the study at Pullinstown and while this interchange goes on Dick informs the narrator that if Sir Richard says 'too much' to his daughter she will marry Morgan out of spite. The tone of the narrator's reply shows just how immersed he had become in the welfare and status of the family: 'She can't do it,' I said. 'She can't possibly do it. Why it would be absolute madness, Dick. Hopeless.'

The Death of a Fox

Willow is eventually persuaded to give up her belovèd after hours of discussion and a promise of a new horse and fifty pounds 'into the heel of her fist'. When the narrator asks why she's got fifty pounds and 'not a million or a fiver', Dick replies, 'He hasn't a million to offer her ... and that's not the one to give up a man for a fiver. She has twice too much spirit.'

The spirit of toughness in Willow is reflected, fifty years later, in the character of Aroon St Charles, the narrator of *Good Behaviour*. In fact Miss St Charles might easily be an embittered Willow, bought from youthful passion and unprofitable love with a pay package of good manners. The intensity of Dick and Willow's relationship is also reflected in the love of Aroon and Hubert St Charles. The movement in *Conversation Piece* is a movement away from caricature towards deeper and closer portrayals of mature character. In *Good Behaviour* Mrs Keane still uses the horse-owning and horse-rearing world as a backdrop for her character studies. She again builds a strong father figure like Sir Richard Pulleyns in the character of 'Papa', the witty, flirtatious and one-legged Papa St Charles. The Crowhurst sisters of the later novel are already present in the Ladies Eveleen and Honour of *Conversation Piece*. So also is the shadow of an impossible marriage like that of Mr Kiely and Miss St Charles.

The world of *Conversation Piece* is a self-contained and perpetual place, whereas the Anglo-Irish hinterland of *Good Behaviour* is a besieged, claustrophobic and even a sinister place, very like the sinister mansions of Jean Rhys. In both Jean Rhys and Molly Keane there's a sense of a world gradually drifting away from secure moorings, from central and supportive social meaning. Good manners have a high place in the esteem of Sir Richard Pulleyns, but in the besieged world of Aroon St Charles good manners parade around with unremitting tyranny. Aroon St Charles might easily be a Willow Pulleyns embittered and stifled by convention.

Thomas McCarthy

Even after the death of her brother, Hubert, Aroon says, 'There was to be no sentimentality. It was the worst kind of bad manners to mourn and grovel in grief.' Earlier in the narrative Aroon had missed her chance of love, certainly her chance of sexual experience, by not helping her would-be lover over the threshold of good behaviour: 'I really must *not* touch you,' he said quickly. 'We'd regret it always, wouldn't we, Piglet? Wouldn't we?' And Aroon replies, 'Yes. We'd hate ourselves.' Other things like Papa's infidelities were 'accomplished within a code of manners'. And Papa's good sense even extended to the shooting of Ollie Reilly as he lay mutilated in the trenches of the Great War: 'Tell Rose that he died instantly; he never knew what got him.'

The world of *Good Behaviour* is a superb achievement, a tactile, sinister and distressed community. Aroon St Charles and 'Papa' and Mrs Brock are the finest character studies in Mrs Keane's oeuvre. But in her early stories, in the lighter but no less self-absorbed world of Pullinstown, she had already built a believable world and a set of characters that would have ensured her place on any shelf of Anglo-Irish fiction.

Quarryman, UCC,
1982

Reading Molly Keane's Papers on Christmas Eve

Molly Keane was the last in a great line of Irish Ascendancy female novelists that begins with Maria Edgeworth and deepens imaginatively in Edith Somerville's *The Real Charlotte* and Elizabeth Bowen's *The Last September*. It is not possible for us, now, to fully know that world because the political interests that gave it its fuller architecture have, politically and socially, become dust, leaving behind in the Irish landscape over two thousand beautiful Anglo-Irish mansions and magnificent parklands that seem to wait for some lost son or daughter to come home from War or the Colonies in the late April sunlight. These Anglo-Irish spaces are haunted because they once really did heave with a complex and abundant life. The women of these houses and the lives they lived are at the heart of everything that Molly Keane wrote, whether they are the mysteriously attractive Perilla Mary Fuller of *Taking Chances*, the possessive lesbian Jessica and her partner Jane in *Devoted Ladies*, the beautiful and tragic Cynthia of *The Rising Tide* or the delusional Aroon St Charles of *Good Behaviour*. That world of powerful, passionate and wilful women was very real and the novels are mirrors held up to these female social and domestic lives of the 1920s and 1930s. This is a world also beautifully captured by Molly's daughter Sally Phipps in her crisp and lyrical biography, *Molly Keane, A Life*.

It is now forty years since this great Anglo-Irish novelist burst onto the international literary scene after a thirty-year silence with her late masterpiece, *Good Behaviour* (a novel recently republished by the *New York Times Review of Books*, with an Introduction by Amy Gentry). I will never forget that September evening in 1981 when I heard the BBC broadcast her name on the Six O'Clock News as one of the shortlisted authors for the Booker Prize. I was with her elderly friend Denis, a grandson of the Duke of Leinster, as we listened to her name announced over the airwaves from London. How magical and mysterious that late success of Molly Keane really was. The novel *Good Behaviour* would go on to be dramatized for the BBC by Hugh Leonard, published by Knopf in New York, translated with great success into French, German and Italian, and subsequently reprinted twenty-five times by E P Dutton, Obelisk and Penguin Books. Within ten years perhaps half a million copies would be in print in Europe and the United States and novelist Eudora Welty was moved to write to Ireland from Jackson, Mississippi, to tell Molly of her admiration:

> '*I wish I could tell you how extraordinary and how crowning a piece of work I found it... I felt the kind of admiration for it that's exhilaration, really, something that goes right to the heart of the hope every true lover of fiction feels on opening some longed-for book... I knew I had a masterpiece in my hands.*'
> (letter, 31st August 1981)

Soon after that Molly Keane was the star guest of the *Russell Harty Show* on BBC Television, interviewed by Terry Wogan and a guest on the BBC Radio's *Desert Island Discs*. She was awarded Life Membership of the Royal Dublin Society, membership of Aosdána and was an honoured guest at gala dinners at the Royal Academy and the Garrick Club. Mrs Keane was a supreme writer, a craftswoman for whom the making of a literary sentence was a purposeful act and full of love. The late Keane effect would continue apace with the publication of her *Time After Time* in 1983, prompting an ecstatic Editorial Director Robert Gottlieb to write from his Knopf office in New York:

Reading Molly Keane's Papers on Christmas Eve

'Dear Molly — Reviews are <u>pouring</u> in — here's a first batch. What's interesting is that it comes — the second book — as less of a <u>surprise</u>; that is, they've been overwhelmed by your voice in Good Behaviour *and it's less an Event the second time around. But despite that they're riveted!'*

By the time her third novel in the new series, *Loving and Giving* (*Queen Lear* in the US), was published in 1988 Molly Keane enjoyed a public profile and a wider readership than she had had at the height of her fame as 'M J Farrell' in the 1930s. Her late success became one of the thrilling stories of the contemporary book trade in Ireland and the UK.

Molly Keane's invented characters live in a surviving Anglo-Irish world of great houses and diminished estates, hanging on for dear life to walled gardens and demesne woodlands while coming to terms with the victorious Nationalist Ireland around them. Her two great novels of the Irish War of Independence, *Mad Puppetstown* (1934) and *Two Days in Aragon* (1942), are written from the landowning Protestant viewpoint, yet the narrative is uncannily aware and respectful of the Irish victory and the inevitability of change brought about by sudden revolution. The character of the handsome and brilliantly arrogant Foley O'Neill, son of the servant Nan Foley in *Two Days in Aragon*, is one of the most complex characterizations in all of Irish fiction. Both books are supreme and knowing inventions, yet also marvellous witness documents of an Anglo-Irish woman's survival and integrity during the Independence struggle. Keane fully possessed her imaginative and imagined world of the new Ireland: Molly had no wish to describe elsewhere, and she rarely strayed from the tense atmosphere of that Anglo-Irish world, a people Samuel Beckett-like, marooned in history.

So who was this extraordinary woman, author of fourteen successful novels and several successful plays that had long runs in the West End of London and on Broadway? Her huge 1938 Broadway success, *Spring Meeting*, written with John Perry, was quickly made into a feature film starring Margaret Rutherford. Other plays followed: *Ducks and Drakes* at the Apollo Theatre in 1942, the hugely successful *Treasure Hunt* at the Apollo in 1949 and *Dazzling Prospect* at the Globe Theatre in 1961. As she herself wrote of Elizabeth Bowen (in manuscript in this archive):

> 'For me Elizabeth's writing is in a class apart. There is never a flawed intention. The end is always in her sight though the theme may be as convoluted as some of her sentences . . . What I would like to express, to make live . . . is the immense quality of attraction which Elizabeth possessed in high degree.'

Molly, or Mary Nesta Skrine, was born at Newbridge, County Kildare, in 1904 and reared at Ballyrankin House, Bunclody, County Wexford, by a succession of maids, governesses and tutors. Her father, Walter Clarmont Skrine, who died when Molly was in her mid-twenties, was originally from a gentry family near Bath in Somerset. He had farmed successfully on a ranch in Alberta, Canada, but came to Ireland to farm, and breed and train horses. Molly's mother was an Ulster writer, Agnes Shakespear Higginson, the then famous 'Moira O'Neill' of the bestselling poetry book, *Songs of the Glens of Antrim*, a constant contributor to the conservative *Blackwood's Magazine*. Agnes Higginson's grandfather was James Macaulay Higginson, the colonial Governor of the island of Mauritius, following Colonial Service in India and the Middle East. He and his wife's deep Ulster Protestant sense of religious duty and morality created the prevailing atmosphere of the Skrine household. Duty, right-thinking, loyalty, and brothers who served as officers in the Army and Navy, all formed part of a firm family background against which Molly revolted almost as soon as she could speak. She was a stubborn and certainly an argumentative child, not popular, with strict parents and barely tolerated by the family servants. Molly seemed to detest her mother, believing that she loathed her. She continued to believe this with intense affectation even in her old age, as reported by an interviewer in the *Observer Sunday Magazine* of September, 1983:

> 'The teapot was her mother's and she always adored it. Late in life her mother (with whom she always had difficulties) was once with her brother Godfrey, who became a gentleman solicitor in Dublin, making her will. "Do you remember that teapot — the one that Molly liked?" said her mother. Godfrey did. "That," said her mother, "is to go to dear Susan."'

As a teenager Molly attended the French School at Bray, County Wicklow, a place where she was disliked and where she hated everyone. On a summer's night in July 1921, within days of her seventeenth birthday, her family home, with all her childhood possessions, was burned to the ground by three units of the Wexford Irish Republican Army. In that burning of a Big House every fragment of her young girlhood was lost. It was a trauma from which Molly never fully recovered, though her father built another house, New Ballyrankin, almost immediately, declaring that he would rather 'be shot in Ireland than live in England'. Molly soon began to display symptoms of tuberculosis and was sent to bed for several months. Her symptoms of lassitude and collapse might nowadays be more correctly recognised as adolescent Post-Traumatic Stress Disorder. This trauma may have propelled her into the writing life. In the confinement of her room she wrote with fury and determination, completing the novel that was published as *The Knight of Cheerful Countenance* (1926) when she was twenty-two. Horses, especially full-blooded hunters, were her other great love; she knew the Irish horse world intimately and was a fearless horsewoman, riding out each bleak Irish winter morning with the Island Hounds of Wexford, the Tipperary Hunt and the West Waterford Hunt. When she wasn't on horseback she was at her writing desk — as 'M J Farrell' she would write seven novels in nine years by the age of thirty-one. *The Knight of Cheerful Countenance* was published by Mills and Boon (M&B may seem an odd choice for a serious novelist, but the secretive young Molly, hiding her writing from her mother and not seeking advice, found the Mills and Boon address in a copy of her mother's *Times Literary Supplement*). *Young Entry* (1928) and *Taking Chances* (1929) were subsequently published by Elkin Matthews; and *Mad Puppetstown* (1931), *Conversation Piece* (1932), *Devoted Ladies* (1934) and *Full House* (1935) were all published by William Collins in London and in the United States by either Henry Holt, J B Lippincott, Farrar and Reinhart or Little, Brown. The curious Senior Editor at Little, Brown and Company, C Raymond Everitt, wrote to Molly in February, 1936, combining both of Molly's interests:

> 'This is just a casual note expressing the hope that some time you will be able to sit down and tell me about the season's hunting and when you might be doing another novel.'

Her London publisher, William Collins, on the other hand, was much more interested in business, pinning down the young novelist to another three-book contract following the success of *Full House* that had sold more than 7,000 copies in hardback.

It was through her friendship with the Perrys of Woodruffe in Tipperary that Molly found entry into an entirely new and exciting world, the world of theatre. She had met Willie Perry while out hunting in 1928 and he invited her to stay at Woodruffe where she met a brilliant entourage of horse-loving and theatre-going people — Dolly Perry, wife

Reading Molly Keane's Papers on Christmas Eve

of Willie and mother of the beautiful-looking homosexual John, and John's equally exciting bisexual sister Civvie. Molly's disapproving mother considered Woodruffe a 'fast' house where adults exchanged gifts of scent and got drunk — the very antithesis of the melancholic and serious Ballyrankin. Molly, all her life a lover of glamour, gossip, pearls, diamonds and champagne, had at last found her true soulmates. John Perry was the lover of both Sir John Gielgud and Binkie Beaumont, the powerful owner of H M Tennant Plays of London's West End. Molly was persuaded to write a play and she co-wrote *Spring Meeting* with John Perry, a play that was a huge success in the West End and on Broadway in 1938. With money from this play Molly took her new husband, Robert Lumley Keane of Cappoquin, County Waterford, to New York where *Spring Meeting* was enjoying a terrific run. Her close friendship with Sir John Gielgud deepened at this time and they wrote to each other endlessly — we are lucky that so many of these unknown letters ('Darling Moll') are part of Molly's great archive, as are the wonderful letters and cards from other theatre friends, Dame Peggy Ashcroft, Margaret Rutherford (who took the lead role when *Spring Meeting* became a feature film), Adele and Fred Astaire, even Fred Astaire's mother who embroidered a fire screen as a wedding present for Molly and Bobby Keane. Old and lifelong County Wexford friends are also here in the correspondence files — the aristocratic Daphne Hall-Dare of Newtownbarry House, surely the model for the character of 'Peter' in *Young Entry*, was a terrific, newsy correspondent, Molly's brother Walter, a Lt Colonel in the Royal Artillery and champion jockey, wrote many long and important letters, as did Lady Ursula and Stephen Vernon: the bisexual Stephen had been invalided out of his Guards regiment with polio soon after D-Day and he became second husband of Lady Ursula, sister of the Duke of Westminster. They shared a friendship with Elizabeth Bowen; and the peripatetic Elizabeth, for years after her Bowen Court had been lost, would be ferried by Molly from her home in Ardmore to Fairyfield, the Vernon house in Kinsale, County Cork. Stephen Vernon's letters, just like the many letters from John Perry, are gossipy, brilliant, salacious and witty — these correspondents knew exactly what Molly liked to read. She loved information that had an edge to it. And the great trove of letters goes on . . . from Lady Catherine Dawney, Lady Dobbs, Janey-Lady Donoghmore, Rosemary FitzGerald (daughter of the Duke of Leinster), Mariga Guinness, Lord Glenavy, Derek Hill, Denis Johnston, Anita Leslie, Lady Sibbie Rowley, Walter, Godfrey and Susan Skrine, the Knight of Glin, Lord Waterford, the Duchess of Westminster and, of course, the Turf Club. And all the others, those not related to Molly Keane by blood and society, the editors and theatre producers, bank managers and agents, journalists and old family servants, all such letters accumulating to create the richest possible picture of a long and important Anglo-Irish life.

Among the saddest letters here (in retrospect) must be the correspondence from Willie Collins, her old publisher, who rejected the early draft of *Good Behaviour* — one of the most disastrous business as well as literary decisions the unfortunate Collins ever made. Writing to her in July 1974 he invokes the questionable camouflage of an employee: 'I gave your manuscript to a very good editor here to read who has the same criticisms as I have. She says that the first chapters show us a thoroughly unlikeable character of 65, and the rest of the book tells how she got that way.' (But, I can hear at least a million subsequent readers say, isn't that why the book is so interesting?) Yet this fateful rejection by Collins was to propel Molly into the most exciting decade of her writing life, the glorious years 1980 to 1990. By 1980 the entire world had changed and now both book and magazine publishing contained a cadre of supremely confident and able women — at this moment they all entered the writing career of the elderly Molly Keane: their glorious presence illuminates these correspondence files, creating a joyous realm of strong women. Enter Gina Pollinger, of the Murray Pollinger Agency — it was Dame Peggy Ashcroft who showed her the manuscript of *Good Behaviour*. Through Gina Pollinger the typescript came to the attention of Diana Athill of Andre Deutsch. The letters from Diana Athill, seen together here, constitute one of the most important series of letters on the art of fiction ever written. Here is part of what she wrote to Molly, a year before *Good Behaviour* was actually published:

> *'I'm speaking less as a publisher than as someone seriously interested in writing and with, so I flatter myself, a true feeling for it (which very few people have, and that is why alas alas the question whether writing is really good or not is more or less irrelevant to those who speak purely as publishers). I think the difference between* Full House *and* Good Behaviour *is a fascinating example of what style is — of its almost moral nature, so mysterious and un-pin-downable. The flaw in* Full House *is that the writer was too fond of her subject (the background and the people rather than the plot) in a slightly corrupt way. Intermittently, very, very slightly, she is implying "Look how attractive — or how comic — or how this or how that — we are." It is a class thing, a frequent taint in memoirs of privileged childhoods.'*
>
> (July 18th, 1980)

Two years later, on December 8th, 1982, after the great public success of *Good Behaviour*, Diana could write excitedly to Molly, care of John Perry at Knot's Fosse:

> *'Dearest Moll, so lovely we will soon be meeting. There will be a whole week between your return to London and my departure to Norfolk on the morning of Christmas Eve, so please come to dinner with me . . .'*

Thomas McCarthy

On January 7th, 1986, a letter from 23 West 43rd Street, New York, from a new correspondent, dropped through the letter-box in Ardmore. It was from Mary D Kierstead, a fiction editor at the *New Yorker*:

> *'Dear Mrs Keane, I would very much like to write a piece about you for* The New Yorker. *Your agent has probably informed you of this by now, but I wanted to write and give you some idea of what you'd be letting yourself in for . . . How I go about this will depend largely on your level of tolerance for a stranger (this stranger). Ideally I'd establish a foothold within striking distance of Ardmore, and hang out (as my sons would say) with you at your convenience — preferably in the kitchen . . . '*

This letter led to a new, deep friendship in Molly Keane's life. Her 'Cherished Mary D' became one of her closest late friends, and Molly spoilt this sophisticated and worldly *New Yorker* editor, praised her and fussed over her for the next decade. It helped enormously that 'Mary D' was already a friend of Joan and Bill Roth of Tipperary and San Francisco. Molly loved the wealthy, highly educated Roths, graduates of Barnard and Yale who also owned a third home in Princeton. The complete friendship of Molly and 'Mary Dee' is recorded in many letters here from Mary D Kierstead, but also in the nearly forty letters written by Molly herself. On January 4th, 1990, Molly wrote from the heart:

> *'Dearest Mary Dee, I am so thankful I met you before I became so vulnerable and senile. You are one of the undeserved delights in my life that I can put along with John G and Binkie and Noel and Elizabeth Bowen and many many unknown names that fill my memory and my heart.'*

Reading Molly Keane's Papers on Christmas Eve

But this treasure is only one of the many. This last decade of Molly's life would be full of such new friends and the many letters here are enduring mementos of those friendships — Carmen Callil of Virago who would spend an entire summer and autumn of the mid-80s going through Molly Keane's earlier 'M J Farrell' novels with Polly Devlin who was hard at work on the Virago Introductions. Polly Devlin too would become an essential component in that rediscovery of the lost Molly Keane novels. Other letters in the archive attest to a powerful gathering of female journalists and fiction writers at that moment in Ireland — Maeve Binchy, Elgy Gillespie of *The Irish Times*, Isobel Healy of *The Irish Press*, Clare Boylan of *Image Magazine*, all corresponding and visiting and all delighted to spread the story of this rediscovered novelist. The excitement of those years is in all these letters as well as in all the published reviews and interviews that have been collected here in this magnificent archive.

Then I go through the original manuscripts and typescripts with Virginia Brownlow, the novelist's daughter. How could anyone fail to be astonished and overwhelmed by this largesse of pencil, ink and print? Despite the often distressed and urgent dislocations in Molly Keane's life — particularly in those years after her very young husband, Bobby Keane, died after surgery in a London clinic — somehow, miraculously, almost everything has been rescued and preserved here, right back to the first novel in manuscript. First drafts of almost everything here, the flawless first draft of one of my own favourite novels, *Taking Chances*, the endless scribblings and retypings of *Good Behaviour* — how strange to discover, upon examining the manuscript, that its original title was *Vacant Possession*, just as *Time After Time* was originally titled *Time and Time Again*. And here too, Sir John Gielgud's working copy of *Spring Meeting*, with his handwritten notes and alterations. And the other plays, *Ducks and Drakes, Treasure Hunt*, even the ultimately unfinished project with Micheál Mac Liammóir of the Gate Theatre, *The Bagges of Heaven*.

Thomas McCarthy

Micheál, like Norah McGuinness and Denis Johnston, was so much a part of Molly's 1940s Dublin life.

All of the papers we spent this Christmas season reading, Catherine, Virginia and I, savouring the fruits of a rich and bountiful Anglo-Irish imagination, must constitute one of the most important assemblies of Irish literary materials ever accumulated anywhere at any time. Molly Keane was without dispute one of the greatest novelists of the Anglo-Irish world. I think of her with such possessive pride as I replace her notebooks in their files:

> 'Ballinatray entirely kills the imagination by being too much. Too beautiful, too dilapidated, too stupid in its past. It is as if one looked down into flowing water and saw the house and its surrounding . . . Bobby said there is an affectation about so much dilapidation.'
> (Notebooks 1937-38)

Never again will I be in the company of such material, or hold in my hands the fragments and blessed particulars that led to such great novels as *Good Behaviour, Mad Puppetstown, The Rising Tide, Two Days in Aragon*. I paused so many times, like the servant Rose, or like Nan Foley pausing in the unlit corridors of Aragon, and considered the astringent feel of her real life that had moved me so completely; the scent of her in the air as the December sky darkened around us, closing in upon the house in Ardmore that still holds so much of her personal atmosphere.

*Lecture at Glenville Park, County Cork,
December 2022*

Elizabeth Bowen and Molly Keane

Two great Anglo-Irish novelists, tossed ashore by the receding waves of Anglo-Ireland just as Irish Nationalism achieved its great victory of an independent State: they now seem like beacons of a dissenting light at the edge of the larger Irish history. They are godlike as they stand erect in the desert of history, polished, larger-than-life, yet they were both intensely private women, shy, even, and fired by a common ambition: to write down the social details of all they knew, to make themselves into the last representatives of a lost Anglo-Irish world. If there was a difference between them it was simply this: Molly Keane lived intensely inside Anglo-Irish life while Elizabeth Bowen commented, rather than lived, intensely inside the same complicated life. And they were such friends, friends to the very end. There's a photograph of the two women shopping together in my native Cappoquin, County Waterford, taken by Noreen Butler of Kilkenny; the two were shopping for an attractive wig for Elizabeth who had lost her hair from the chemotherapy for the cancer that would soon kill her in 1973. Molly would live on for another twenty or more years — years of intense writing and crowning success. Sally Keane Phipps in her superbly written memoir of her mother describes the two women together by the fireside at Belleville Park, Cappoquin, drinking wine and discussing the difficulties of fiction. And, no doubt, the difficulties of love. Molly was always intimidated by Elizabeth's intellectualism and cosmopolitanism, while Elizabeth could be equally terrified by Molly's seeming hardness: 'Molly Keane has been staying here since Tuesday. We have been working away like beavers ... Molly Keane is a fascinating little character and I'm fond of her. She's as clever as a bag of monkeys. But her cynicism and pessimism are terrifying. She makes me feel quite a blobby old idealistic sentimental optimist by contrast . . . ' (letter from Bowen's Court, 23 March 1957). Elizabeth Bowen, last of the Bowens of Bowen's Court, County Cork, came back to her Anglo-Irish world imaginatively when she was in her late twenties — up to that point of her ancestral encounter she was a suburban fiction writer, intense, stylish, English, with suburban Harpenden and the Essex coast in her imagination. *Encounters*, her first collection and the wonderful novel, *Death of the Heart*, place her firmly inside that 1920s/30s English generation of Winifred Holtby, Virginia Woolf and Vera Brittain. But with *The Last September* (1929) she uncovered a family territory of fictional experiences that couldn't be claimed by any other young London writer. In creating the world of Sir Richard and Lady Naylor of Danielstown and placing the character of their niece, Lois, at the centre of the story, Bowen offered us the familiar drama of Anglo-Irish ascendancy struggling for relevance in a land at war. She creates a brilliant picture of how tangential native Irish life and its politics could be to occupants of a Big House, tangential yet fatal, as the young Ascendancy woman Lois was to learn to her cost. The personal tension in *The Last September* is paralleled by the political tension that surrounds the doomed Big House of Danielstown, that mansion where a lost Lois tries to create an adult beginning in her life through close observation of her elders and tentative attempts at love. The unsure, observing, semi-detached Lois is one of Elizabeth Bowen's many memorable and finely drawn characters — a great procession of marginalized women that includes Portia of *Death of the Heart* (1938) and Stella of *The Heat of the Day* (1948). Anglo-Irish, never quite at home except when on the ferry between England and Ireland, Bowen was a master of placing lives that were marginalized centre stage. All of her characters suffer in their differing, tentative attempts to form lasting attachments and the perpetual metaphor for that lack of attachment is the solitary Big House in the Irish landscape in contrast to Molly Keane, it must be said.

Keane's characters thrive on excessive love, rage, resentment, attachment. They suffer not because of the weakness of attachment but because of the wickedness of others, the wickedness of rivals. It is the war between personalities that consumed Mrs Keane — she was ferocious in her own loves and enmities, determined and unforgiving, and tigerlike in her protection of friends and family. As far as Molly was concerned history and politics were merely troublesome misunderstandings between men in authority, men who should know better. What mattered for Mrs Keane were personal attachments and the thrill of social interaction. Here is how she describes her heroine of *Two Days in Aragon*, Grania Fox:

> 'Grania had no repose. She flew about doing things all the time . . . Grania was a fat little blonde with pretty bones under her flesh; rather a slut, and inclined to wear party shoes with old tweeds. She would be in her bath, and forget to wash very much, but she was a great hand at curling up her blonde hair, of which she was very vain. Three of the most marriageable men in the County Westcommon had asked her to marry them; but they had no skill for love-making so she refused them all, and returned to Foley O'Neill, who embraced her in the wood and other out-of-the-way places, whereas the eligible young men seldom did more than hold her hand before they proposed . . . '

It is difficult to explain to our children, or to interested readers, just how magical and unexpected the late success of Molly Keane would become. Socially I was not as intimate with Mrs Keane — or Mrs Bobby, as she was familiarly and not uncritically known in Cappoquin and West Waterford generally — as was the Brigadier, the grandson of the Duke of Leinster (a social distinction not lost on Molly). But I knew her even then as a supreme writer, a craftswoman for whom the making of a literary sentence was as purposeful and full of love as an arrangement of flowers or the mixing of a 1920s champagne cocktail. While John McGahern had his Garda barracks, Seamus Heaney had his bogs and Kate O'Brien had her presentation parlours, Molly Keane simply had her horses and stable yards. Her invented characters lived in a world of horses. They were not so much Big House people, in the manner of Yeats's politically-vectored poetic characters, as horse and hunting people. In Ireland, ironically, being on a horse was less exclusive and less excluding, less eighteenth century, than occupying a grand house. For Molly Keane and her circle there were always horses, for riding and petting and buying and selling — even in the middle of wars, the Great War, the Irish War of Independence, the Irish Civil War. Her description of the still Edwardian Dublin Horse Show in *Rising Tide*, published in 1937, is a terrific pen-picture:

> 'That Horse Show was like every other Dublin Horse Show . . . Women in grey flannel coats and skirts, awful hats and brown suede shoes sat on shooting-sticks round the rings and gossiped and criticised and sometimes admired. There were busy men in clean breeches and boots without a moment to spare for anybody, and less-busy men in suits and bowler hats who had lots of time for a drink with anybody who would pay for it. There were Indian princes in Jodhpurs that zipped down their legs in all directions, and everyone in Ireland with a horse to sell coveted their acquaintance . . . There were lovely girls from England who made the lovely girls in Ireland look nothing. They wore their clothes so much less briskly and painted their faces with less-advanced skill and determination . . . And last and first and all the time and through everything there were horses. Horses in

> the rings. Rows and rows and dormitories of stabled horses. Horses led and ridden about wherever anybody wanted to sit and have a chat. Never in any place are horses so thick upon the ground as in Ballsbridge at this time.'

And fifty years later, in her mid-seventies, in *Good Behaviour*, 1981, she could still capture the moment like this:

> 'The Horse Show proceeded on its traditional five-day course, but how differently from earlier martyrdoms of fixed and smiling loneliness. On the last day Richard bought a yearling in the Bloodstock Sales. I sat between him and Hubert on the circular benches, while the yearlings, coming up for auction in the ring below us, were pulling back, kicking, or mincing politely round. I didn't even realize Richard was bidding, his gestures were so quiet and small and knowledgeable. I thank God still that I didn't happen to be talking, just thumbing through the lots in my catalogue.'

It is certainly true that Molly Keane and Elizabeth Bowen's entire careers teach us a key lesson about the life of writing — write only about what you know or what you passionately wish to possess. Everything else will seem vague to the reader. Keane possessed her imaginative and imagined world passionately, in its entirety. She was the last of that great line of novelists that began with Maria Edgeworth and deepened imaginatively with Somerville and Ross. Elizabeth Bowen wrote always with the passion of her desolate self, inventing characters who cling to the edge of society, yearning always to somehow begin an authentic adulthood. It is not possible for us to fully know their world now because the social yearnings and undiminished British Empire that gave it its full architecture have become dust. These Anglo-Irish spaces are haunted because they once really did heave with an abundant life. This world was not ours but it was vital and real.

We are now blessed with the afterglow of this world, in all its glory and decline, its beauty and political hypocrisies, in the key novels of these two great friends. If you haven't read these four novels you must read them straight away. I'll give them not in the order which they were published but in the order in which you should read them: *The Last September, Two Days in Aragon, The Death of the Heart, Good Behaviour.*

The Lowell Review,
2020

Bowen's Court, an Introduction

The Anglo-Irish world has produced many gifted aristocrats but Elizabeth Bowen was one of the most magnetic and attractive of them all. She was a superb novelist and short-story writer, possibly the most gifted of that London group that included such luminaries as Rosamund Lehmann and Cyril Connolly. She was also a brilliant talker, despite her speech impediment, and a faithful friend to many of the disorientated intellectuals of the mid-century. Her dinner parties were as famous as her literary style. Personalities as different as Eddie Sackville-West, Molly Keane, Seán Ó Faoláin and A L Rowse were entertained in her County Cork mansion in its declining years. All felt themselves drawn to her as if they were musicians in an orchestral performance. Charles Ritchie, the Canadian diplomat who was based in London during the War, wrote lovingly in *The Siren Years* about Bowen's personality:

> 'Elizabeth has been going to an Austrian psychoanalyst to be cured of her stammer (which was so much part of her). So far it seems to me that she has told him nothing while he has told her the story of his life. This hardly surprises me... Of what is her magic made? What is the spell she has cast on me?... I have been discovering more and more of her generous nature, her wit and funniness, the stammering flow of her enthralling talk.'

It is unlikely that Elizabeth Bowen could ever trust her memory enough to reveal the full story of her life. Memory, for a writer, is far too ambivalent, far too useful and impersonal, to be sacrificed whole. Writing changes the nature of one's past. The past is not so much a country as a series of countries, a victim of the changing writerly activity: 'Almost no experience, however much simplified by the distance of time, is to be vouched for as being wholly my own — did I live through that or was I told that it happened, or did I read it?'

The reticence of Bowen under psychoanalysis leads us directly to the licence that Bowen allows herself as historian and custodian of memory. Part of the attraction of *Bowen's Court* lies in the subjectivity of its remembrance. This book, now published in her native Cork, is beautiful because it often reads like an historical novel. The history is accurate, the heraldry is correct, but the personalities are fleshed out. Irish history is a room that becomes animated when Elizabeth makes her stylish entrance. She writes about her distant ancestors as if they were relatives who had just been left on the Mallow train. Dealing with Jane Cole, who married the second Henry Bowen in 1716, she writes, 'Perhaps they strolled outdoors in the long white Irish twilights or in steely evenings after rain — Jane holding the hem of her long stiff skirts clear of the damp ... Henry would tell Jane again about the treasure, and she would, vaguely, reply, what a pity it was not found.'

The Anglo-Irish author of *Bowen's Court* was born in Dublin in 1899. She was the only daughter of Henry Cole Bowen, the reluctant heir to a County Cork estate and Big House, and author of *Statutory Land Purchase in Ireland*. She was Dublin-born but her summer place was Cork: 'I used to believe that winter lived always in Dublin, while summer lived always in County Cork. By taking the train from Kingsbridge to Mallow one passed from one season's kingdom into the other's,' she wrote in *Seven Winters*. The idyllic part of childhood did not last long for when she was seven years old her father suffered a nervous breakdown. She moved to Kent with her mother and waited for her brilliant father to recover. Henry did recover by 1911, but a year later her mother died. Elizabeth's childhood and adolescence were therefore disturbed and fractured. She left school in 1917 and began writing fiction a year later. Her first volume of stories, *Encounters*, was published in 1923. These stories were precocious, very clever and stylish, and owing a great deal to E M Forster's style. But she quickly developed her own inimitable, dense and yet crisp, writing method in a further ten novels and nearly one hundred stories. Her most perfect and intoxicating works are *The Last September*, *The House in Paris* and *The Heat of the Day*. The epicurean reader should go straight from *Bowen's Court* to *The Last September* for the sheer pleasure of her sustained narrative and poetic powers.

The Big House, but especially Bowen's Court, became a symbol as well as a setting in the fiction of Elizabeth Bowen. The great houses were a bold social and political gesture built in spite of history; they remain in the Irish landscape as an admirable performance, a pure victory of style over necessity. The irony of Anglo-Irish life is that it seems most beautiful when perceived at some point of decline. Decline was part of its unassailable elegance. The gentry, and Southern Irish Anglicans in general, were born for remembrance. Their children took to autobiography as naturally as they'd taken to horse riding. What characterizes so many of the Anglo-Irish, from Bishop Berkeley to Bowen, is that dramatic self-awareness so conspicuous in poets. Under siege they developed a deep soul.

The political position of the Ascendancy was always untenable. Ironically the Penal Laws may have done as much damage to Protestant interests as to the defeated Catholic Irish. As Elizabeth Bowen has observed in this book the Catholic Irish developed a powerful trading sector, awash with the cash piles developed through trade in cattle and butter. But they were banned from holding bank accounts and excluded from the official lending markets. The bitter

Thomas McCarthy

fact is that the Ascendancy of the small Protestant nation was based on a series of injustices, from the Cromwellian confiscations to the Acts of Settlement. Even if the Land Acts of the nineteenth century had not happened the general development of majority Parliamentary politics would have diminished the power of the class into which Elizabeth was born. Political strength based upon an injustice is always power waiting to be diminished. Yet the Anglo-Irish were in no sense merely a garrison like the English garrisons in India. On the contrary the gentry in Ireland were absolutely rooted in the localities where they were proprietors. They identified with their own Irish valleys and neighbourhoods and were as localized in their enthusiasms as the most stay-at-home Irish farmers. The opening chapter of *Bowen's Court* is as good an example as one could hope for to illustrate that deep sense of geography and location within the Anglo-Irish mind:

> '*In no other direction lies any town or larger village, except Shanballymore, for seven or eight miles. Mallow is thirteen, Fermoy twelve, Mitchelstown eight and Doneraile seven miles from Bowen's Court. Inside and about the house and in the demesne woods you feel transfixed by the surrounding emptiness; it gives depth to the silence, quality to the light . . .* '

Elizabeth begins, then, acutely conscious of location, and conscious of the power of the house within the landscape.

Being a mid-century London intellectual as well as the custodian of an Irish Big House Elizabeth inherited and embodied the friction of Anglo-Irishness. She embraced the dual loyalties and the inherited contradictions. She writes, 'In the decade following 1760 the Anglo-Irish became aware of themselves as a race. The "Protestant Nation" had been born already, it was to be christened at its coming of age. It was growing up with judgement, into the power to place its

Bowen's Court, an Introduction

loyalties where and as it willed. This was the Anglo-Ireland that was to present, for England, an alarming parallel with America.' But the Anglo-Irish were no sooner defined than they were defied. The fifty years between 1798 and 1848 were politically hectic and turbulent. Bowen's Court was attacked in 1798 and Elizabeth focuses upon the (imagined) feelings of fear and siege within the Farahy household. The whole of that era, a truly momentous one that scorched the edges of Ireland with French revolutionary ideas, is distilled by Elizabeth Bowen into one startling image:

> *'There was a pear tree a few yards down from the south-east corner of Bowen's Court — one surviving shoot of it is in bud as I write. The morning after the raid, the tree was found to bear charnel fruit: a dead man, who must have climbed up to fire, stayed jammed in the fork of two boughs.'*

Elizabeth moves quickly past the Act of Union: 'I cannot discuss the Union; it was a bad deal . . . Castlereagh finally engineered it; the vast sums laid out in bribes and in buying out boroughs were charged to Ireland's account . . . Prominent Anglo-Irish were bought, to their lasting dishonour, by peerages, by advancements in the peerage, and by sums down.'

Her political opinions could be remarkably sharp, and sharply expressed. If she sounds like an Irish Republican in some of her comments it is not because she has turned against her class, but that she has an overwhelming sense of fair play. Indeed some of her comments on the collapse of Grattan's Irish dream and the creative enthusiasm of the Patriot Party are rueful. The Bowens may have been too far away from the centre of power to have been offered peerages or sums down: the Bowens did seem to have a talent for remaining on the edge of things. When the original Colonel Bowen, descended from the insular Gower ap Owens, came over to Ireland with Cromwell he took a pair of hawks with him. During a meeting with Cromwell he is reputed to have paid more attention to his hawks than to the Lord Protector. But Colonel Bowen survived the tiff with Cromwell to inherit nearly eight hundred acres of Farahy land 'in Satisfaction of his arrears' from the Cromwellian settlement. His son, John, married the wealthy heiress, Mary Nicholls of Kilbolane Castle. Kilbolane would feature in many Bowen conversations for the next one-hundred-and-fifty years. Bowen cousins would sue and counter-sue over buried treasure.

Litigation was in their blood. For years, right through the eighteenth century, the Bowens would concentrate on another lawsuit, Bowen v. Evans, over Kilbolane Bawn and Brandon Castle. Bowen's Court itself was not built until the late 1700s. 1775 was the date cut in the stone. 'At the same time Henry found himself short of money, and it may have looked, at one heart-sickening moment, as though the roof would never go on at all . . . Henry, unwillingly, cut down the original plan: the north-east corner had to be sacrificed. The Italians from Cork were paid off and went their way . . .' Elizabeth reports humorously on the whole episode.

But not before she reports with pride the classical austerity of her family home: 'The great bare block — not a creeper touches it — is broken regularly by windows: in the south façade there are twenty (the hall door takes the place of one of them), in the west side eighteen, in the shorter east side six, in the north back six. All of this expanse of glass, with its different reflections, does much to give Bowen's Court character. When the sun is low, in the early mornings or evenings, the house seems, from the outside, to be riddled with light.'

The Bowens lived on in their Big House for generations, until the fateful marriage of Elizabeth's urbane and very urban parents. With her parents' marriage, and her father's legal obligations in Dublin, 'a break came in the house's continuous human life'. Bowen's Court lay empty for long stretches: 'Fires were lit, but to warm nothing but air.' Elizabeth's father lived

Bowen's Court, an Introduction

the obligatory social life of a barrister among Dublin friends, many of them companions from St Columba's and Trinity College. Henry Cole Bowen loved Dublin life, the theatres, the Law Library and the new cinemas. But it was not only the Big House that was drained of its will to survive. Misfortune stalked the Bowens. Elizabeth lost her aunt to consumption and her younger uncle went down with the *Titanic*. 'He had spent the last Sunday with us before he sailed ... So, the *Titanic* disaster was the first black crack across the surface of exterior things.'

After her own husband's death in 1952 Elizabeth Bowen returned to County Cork. She stayed on in Bowen's Court for seven years. In the end lack of money (that great organizer of our lives) forced her to sell out. The house was bought by a local farmer and, in 1960, was demolished. It was as simple as that. Elizabeth spent the last twelve years of her life as she had spent her childhood, uprooted, wandering, reading and learning. She died in February 1973.

Bowen's Court, the book, is truly the house that has survived. As Hermione Lee pointed out in her 1984 Virago Introduction Elizabeth drew upon many sources for this book, quite apart from the Bowen family papers: Jonah Barrington's *Personal Sketches of His Own Times* (1827), Dorothea Herbert's *Retrospections 1770-1806* and Maurice Healy's *The Old Munster Circuit* (1939). But it is important to read this book as a filial act of memory, a truly excellent and unparalleled memorial to Anglo-Irish life. It could be seen also as a partial rebuttal of the politics presented in *The Last September*, that extremely clever, Bloomsbury-like treatment of Irish history. Big House contradictions are exposed mercilessly in that early novel.

Writing *Bowen's Court* during the Second World War when 'either everything mattered or nothing mattered' Elizabeth was more loyal and faithful to her people. Even her treatment of Lord Orrery, who was a merciless confiscator of Catholic land and a persecutor of Cork Quakers like Exham, Lowe and William Penn, is far too gentle. 'He had not much with which to reproach himself,' she says blandly. But she was writing this family history at a time when generosity was called for. At a time when England faced the might of European Fascism on its own, and when many Anglo-Irish had once more joined in battle against a Continental evil, the Irish Ascendancy recovered a great deal of its moral strength and noble character.

Bowen's Court is one of the most complex and beautiful books produced by Irish memory. Its author was a truly modern woman, displaced and yet deeply rooted. I'll always remember how Molly Keane spoke about Elizabeth Bowen; with reverence and love and a kind of fearful admiration. Many have fallen under her spell, even in recent years: Hermione Lee, Victoria Glendinning, and the broadcaster and pilgrim Donncha Ó Dúlaing who wrote his MA thesis on Elizabeth Bowen.

Through this book one enters the hall door of Anglo-Irish life, to wander across that prodigious gallery of gestures and misunderstandings, ghosts and litigation. It is part of the triumph of imaginative life that this book now endures. It is Elizabeth Bowen's third Bowen mansion, after old Kilbolane and Bowen's Court. It endures as an act of remembrance, long after the battles and repossessions. Here the written word has outlasted all the mortar and cut stone.

The Collins Press,
1998

PART FOUR
THAT ULSTER QUESTION

The Outsider of Irish Poetry
Selected Poems of Louis MacNeice *Michael Longley (ed)*
Louis MacNeice: A Study *by Edna Longley*

Louis MacNeice and Michael Longley are probably Ulster's most devout Connemara men. That Longley should have chosen to make this new selection of MacNeice poems is a happy conjunction of like-minded talents. Both poets are Anglican in outlook yet happy to succumb to life's sensations.

As Derek Mahon noted in *The Irish Times* MacNeice is having a comeback. About time too — it is twenty-one years since Austin Clarke had his comeback and Patrick Kavanagh has been coming back ever since the publication of *Come Dance with Kitty Stobling*. So why has it taken so long for us to rediscover MacNeice? The answers are simple: he was an Ulster poet marginalized by Dublin conversation; in England he was marginalized by association with the Birmingham group; and he was a left-wing poet marginalized by his own scepticism. Most of all he was crippled by that patronizing and inadequate edition of his poems edited by Auden.

For the last fifteen years the axis of Irish poetry has shifted north. The new Kavanaghs and Flann O'Briens need no longer become bogus Dubliners in order to be at the centre of things. These two new MacNeice books are part of the Ulster repossession. 'The rugby tradition makes two virtues supreme — individual endurance and the open game,' MacNeice wrote in *The Strings are False*. He was describing a game between Cornell and Syracuse and was not impressed. He felt that American footballers were too pampered. His attitude to poetry was the same; he admired bravery, honesty and scepticism in politics and religion, endurance in human adventures. In this new *Selected Poems* Michael Longley gives us a much clearer view of MacNeice's breadth. We see the poet up and running, clearer than in Auden's wet field glasses, his obviously lyrical talent made more durable by an epic political intelligence:

> *So reading the memoirs of Maud Gonne,*
> *Daughter of an English mother and a soldier father,*
> *I note how a single purpose can be founded on*
> *A jumble of opposites:*
> *Dublin Castle, the vice-regal ball,*
> *The embassies of Europe,*
> *Hatred scribbled on a wall...*

Autumn Journal and the terrifying, exhilarating years 1938-44 provide the fulcrum of MacNeice's work. When he wrote *Autumn Journal* Kavanagh was working on *The Great Hunger*: two Ulster epics, both published in London, yet worlds apart. Now the psychosexual problems of Paddy Maguire seem dated while MacNeice's 'Conferences, adjournments, ultimatums' or 'Give me a houri but houris are too easy, / give me a nun' or 'Sleep quietly, Marx and Freud, / The figureheads of our transition' are still relevant and influential in tone and theme.

So much of what MacNeice wrote seems a prequel to the work of Longley, Mahon and Muldoon — one reads this selection with a sense of déjà vu. Was it the MacNeice of 'The Closing Album' who allowed Longley to write his Mayo poems? Was it the MacNeice of 'The Sunlight on the Garden' and 'Carrick Revisited' who taught Mahon to write the perfect lyrics of *The Hunt by Night*? And wasn't it the MacNeice of revitalized cliché and wisecrack who taught Muldoon everything? Even minor poems like 'Selva Obscura' and 'Flower Show' have made a hundred minor poets blossom. This selection may reveal what is implicit in all of us, the modern lyric tone of MacNeice. And yet it will inoculate us all against what Longley calls 'political certainties and false optimism'.

Edna Longley has already dealt with Louis MacNeice in two chapters of *Poetry in the Wars* (1986). She is a very thorough critic, great nervous energy pushing her structuralist methods to the limit. She is at the height of her powers with the moral audacity of a Daniel Corkery and the finesse of Ernest Dowden. Her one belief, and her only religious one, is that aesthetic achievements complete and clarify reality — especially Anglo-Irish reality:

> *'MacNeice's efforts to reconcile 'solitude' and 'communion' (the 'union of solitude' of 'Round the Corner'), whether socially or spiritually directed, derive in part from his loss of the fixed cultural-religious co-ordinates which still place a majority of his countrymen.'*

She pursues the dialectical tensions in MacNeice with all the energy of a young terrier.

Longley divides her study into six essays: on MacNeice's Ireland, his urban and English world, *Autumn Journal* (this is quite different from her 1986 book) and his critical heritage. MacNeice enjoyed exploiting the contradictions in his background. His father was a Protestant clergyman, later Bishop of Down, Connor and Dromore, who refused to sign the Ulster Covenant of 1912. The poet was educated at Sherbourne, Marlborough and Merton College, thus acquiring a perfect English veneer. All the explosive natal Irish experience was held inside this cool classical sack. But Longley proves that he was no mere tourist in Ireland: he had 'a stake in the country and the country a stake in his poetry'. Sure, he was a 30s poet but Ireland was the Berlin he had to say goodbye to and, like any faithful son, he came back constantly to say goodbye. To the practising poet Longley's chapter, 'Colour and Meaning', may prove the most valuable. She traces the development of MacNeice's theories through the prose works and, in parallel, the development of his craft through *Autumn Journal* and *The Burning Perch*. Her reading of the long poem is gifted, as always:

> '*The protean quatrain of* Autumn Journal *accommodates every change of tone and angle. It is a precision instrument for establishing all the poem's other alterations: between pictures and generalisations, optimism and irony, necessity and possibility, historical flux and artistic poise.*'

Like all good poets in western culture MacNeice began and ended in ambiguity. 'Coda', his closing poem, is as mysterious as it is beautiful:

> *Maybe we knew each other better*
> *When the night was young and unrepeated*
> *And the moon stood still over Jericho.*
>
> *So much for the past . . .*

'That poem,' Longley writes, 'says everything: an Everyman parable uniting long-term and short-term human history, scepticism and belief.' Louis MacNeice is one Irish poet we all share equally. Like Portora Royal's gifted young Beckett he is our constant outsider. This tightly written study and the new *Selected* should rehabilitate the stature of Ireland's first really twentieth-century poet.

Fortnight,
1988

Documents of Exclusion
The Selected Prose of Louis MacNeice *Alan Heuser (ed)*
Grandmother and Wolfe Tone *by Hubert Butler*

> *'Our island is dangerously tilted towards England and towards Rome, good places themselves but best seen on the level. Everybody is rolling off it and those that remain, struggling hard for a foothold, drag each other down. But it is not necessary to argue, it is only necessary to look.'*

The words are Hubert Butler's from 'The Auction', a personal record of one of his spiritual mentors, Otway Cuffe, whose Southern Protestant Nationalist life, like the life of Lord Midleton's sister, was 'a labyrinthine story of idealism, obstinacy, perversity, social conscience, medicine, family ...' Butler, of the once powerful and still influential Kilkenny Ormonde family, is one of the tiny articulate band of aristocratic Southern Protestants. Most of those families chose silence and disengaged from the machinery of Southern politics. It is part of the irony of history that their properties were, for the most part, burned by people who considered their Big Houses as part of the fabric of the New Free State, Liam Lynch and his gang of Irregulars who were hostile to the Dáil. But even the Dáil and its political culture excluded these people: the scrupulous policy of Irish neutrality put a seal on the irrelevance of the Anglo-Irish. One could say that up to the defeat of Lord O'Neill they lived with the possibility of political expression, but that was based more on the ambiguity of Stormont's relationship to Westminster. Nowadays the democratic Presbyterian interest is as clearly defined as the Catholic national interest between 1922 and 1932.

Louis MacNeice is another Irish Protestant, poet son of an Ulster clergyman: bosom companion of Hubert Butler . . . Ah, but here we run into the first danger of simplistic categories and wide definitions. Here is MacNeice, writing in 1938, 'As for the gentry I did not like them. They were patronising and snobbish, and it seemed to me, hostile.' He was referring to the Ulster gentry. There are now so many varieties of Irish Protestant that the category itself has collapsed. What is left is the vast network of autobiographies, lives as different from each other as George Buchanan's from Hubert Butler's, Olga Pyne Clarke's from Elizabeth Bowen's. The Public Library shelves are full of individual and individualistic Protestant childhoods. The rush to write autobiography — as Anita Brookner noted in a recent *Observer* review — is peculiar to the socially mobile or to those who seek to position themselves in a new context. MacNeice again: 'When I was older and went to school in England my dislike of the North was maintained. At school I felt among my equals, but when I came home I belonged nowhere.'

Both these books, the second volume of the prose of Louis MacNeice and the third volume in the Lilliput rediscovery of Hubert Butler, form part of that great documentary of exclusion. Most intellectuals, and certainly all artists, feel excluded by the societies that prick them into consciousness. But these highly gifted authors are excluded from their host societies for reasons that are less than artistic. Thomas MacDonagh's 'Irish Mode' and Daniel Corkery's Introduction to *Synge and Anglo-Irish Literature* would exclude both from the mire of Irish literature. Even as late as the mid-70s, the presence of MacNeice was marginal on the Irish literary scene. Another Ulsterman, Patrick Kavanagh, dominated the scene, the examination papers and the gossip. In Ireland there is always that interplay of literature and politics, the influence of one upon the other, creating low cloud, a twilight zone where literary judgements cannot be made. Irish politics constantly demands an all-embracing anthology, a single canon, whereas every artistic life rebuffs that demand. I can see now how excluded from the Ireland of my childhood the poet MacNeice was. His admirable reports from London during the War printed in the New York periodical, *Common Sense*, would have made him suspect. The reports, collected here by Alan Heuser, make wonderful reading:

> *'It was a night of a full moon which half the time was lost in fire clouds, and from midnight till dawn HE bombs and incendiaries fell all over the City... I had not realized that there was so much left to burn in our immediate neighbourhood but there was; a building next door sent up an enormous fountain of sparks like a genie, sparks which circled and sidled with the gentle inconsequence of snowflakes and fell down on our heads. In a little time great tawny clouds of smoke, rolling in a sumptuous Baroque exuberance, had hidden the river completely and there we were on the dome, a Classical island in a more than romantic Inferno.'*

Around the same Blitz-time Hubert Butler articulated his war, or lack of a war: 'Just as our island is physically protected by the sea, there is an ocean of indifference and xenophobia to guard our insularity and so save us from foreign entanglements. Whatever its political value, culturally this self-sufficiency has been and will be a disaster to Ireland . . . ' ('The Barriers', 1941). His words were prophetic. He would spend the next four decades writing for or against all causes that make us great — Censorship, Abortion, the National Identity, Religion and Partition. The first 150 pages of *Grandmother and Wolfe Tone* are taken up with these themes; the autobiographical fragments are also intimately connected with theme. As Dervla Murphy says in her stylish Introduction, Butler is 'a resolute crusader for honesty in every area of life'. Between Parts One and Two of the book there is an eerie and disturbing tension. Having discussed all those local causes, our peculiarly provincial obsessions, Butler moves into more grandly evil territory: 'We read in *St Anthony's Messenger*, June 1941, the calm announcement that: "There are too many Jews in Zagreb with their aims of world domination and their perfidy and destructiveness".' The author's travels in post-War Eastern Europe, along with his account of the Eichmann trial, makes compulsive, depressing reading:

> 'What was most terrifying about Eichmann was that he was not terrifying at all . . . He was immensely ordinary . . . by exaggerating the blackness of Eichmann the Jerusalem court managed to bleach the dirty grey background against which he worked . . . Every social institution was implicated in crime. One instance of this should suffice. Like Krupps and I G Farben and many other large firms, Siemens Schuckert, the engineers of the Shannon Scheme, set up factories at Auschwitz and Lublin for the employment of slave labour. The intention of the camp authorities was to kill by toil.'

Nothing could be more valuable or timely than these European essays. Butler chronicles evil on a grand scale: one is left with the impression of mid-century Europe as a daemonic opera: the vicious forced conversion of Serbian Orthodox communities to Roman Catholicism, the implication of almost every European country in Hitler's 'Final Solution'. Only Denmark, beautiful, sane Denmark, stands out as a shining light in all that terrorized darkness. One is ennobled, ultimately, by the things one chooses to record. The selection of subject matter is almost a mythical thing, more so in an essayist than a poet. Butler has that fine-tempered steel of a certain kind of Anglo-Irishman. Like Horace Plunkett and Arland Ussher his mind is fixed on the improvement of his local community yet is capable of seeing well beyond Ireland. If these essays prove anything it is that one can love even a political culture from which one is excluded.

It is also clear from the essays of Louis MacNeice that the mid-century fight against Fascism stimulated him to grow beyond Ireland, to grow mentally and spiritually. Those attractive aspects of Ulster character, tenacity, honesty, sharp wit and a sense of duty all shine through in MacNeice's War journalism. Even his childhood sense of exclusion is mitigated when he writes about Ulster people:

> '... for the great majority of Orangemen their idea of goodness is summed up in the common phrase "a decent wee man". The Decent Wee Man is unostentatious, sober, industrious, scrupulously honest, and genuinely charitable. It is thanks to his predominance in Ulster that foreign visitors — such as Czechs and Hungarians — have been known to declare the Ulsterman far more "human" and easy to get on with than the Englishman.'

One of the characteristics of MacNeice, a characteristic that separates him from many an Irish poet, is that during his waking hours he was really awake. He had the ears and eyes of a good journalist, a gift for detail like Bowen or Greene. His War journalism proves this; so does the report 'Wedding of Simon Karas', reprinted here from the *Radio Times* and, most splendid of all, his rugby reports reprinted from *The Observer*: 'The new centre, 18-year-old Hewitt, made a promising first appearance in spite of a few lapses in defence. Mulligan, brought in at the last moment for O'Meara, showed great intelligence and agility. So did Kyle, who was as cool as ever and brought off innumerable, and very welcome, relieving kicks.' It is against the heavy ruck of all those reports and book reviews that Alan Heuser's scholarship comes into its own. His footnotes are detailed enough to satisfy a glancing curiosity and contain enough source-references to encourage the real postgraduate enthusiast.

Thomas McCarthy

Part of MacNeice's wakefulness was his keen awareness of style. He was so well read he might easily have written in a pastiche of styles. But his style is his own. Now that the cadences of Auden have receded from our ears we can hear that MacNeice really was speaking in his own voice. His prose reveals an immensely attractive mindset, erudite and mischievous. His send-ups of various prose styles (Lawrence, Pater, Yeats, the penny-detective, Hemingway) are brilliant. They show us how little the professional writer need be the victim of his material. His send-up of Hemingway made me laugh out loud:

> *'The cat came and looked at the saucer. Then it dipped its head and began drinking. It drank as if it was thirsty.*
> *The man who had come in got up.*
> *"I must go now," he said.*
> *He put his hands in his pockets and opened the door with his knees. He went out into the rain. The rain was raining.*
> *"What the hell," he said. "What the hell."'*

The kind of music that certain authors create seems to make literal truth unimportant. MacNeice's scepticism always forced him to resist being taken in by music. The prosiness, or lack of tight music, in his lyrics, that some complain about is consistent with his educated scepticism. He does not try to convince by intoxication. He does not try to mystify. To clarify is his great gift. This is the difference between his clear cerebral effects and the more subtle soporific music of Kavanagh.

This general principle is applied in his essays and reviews. He warns constantly against first impressions, hasty poetry. In *Horizon* he writes: 'America, however, is always being generalised about, even by people who have never been there.' Reviewing in the *New Statesman* and *The Nation* he warns that potential reader: 'India is not only a land of para-

Documents of Exclusion

doxes but causes paradoxical behaviour in her visitors: it does something to you, you know.' And reviewing Kevin Andrews' book *Flight of Ikaros* in *The Observer* he wrote 'Many Europeans and Americans visiting Greece fall so in love with it that they gush into print and give a very one-sided picture.'

He is very much the 30s man, motivated by the intellectual's unease, the feeling that there must be another point of view. His review of Brian Inglis's *West Briton* (1962) makes interesting reading:

> 'This feeling of political impotence was probably one reason why the book ends with Brian Inglis leaving Ireland. Another was the fact that the Irish Times never paid him a salary. Yet he remembers that peculiar paper with nostalgia and paints a warm portrait of its eccentric editor, the late Robert Smyllie who, he says "has done more, probably, than anybody else to persuade the Irish Unionists ... to come to terms with the Irish Free State".'

There are hundreds of short prose pieces listed in the bibliography. Heuser has been a good detective. MacNeice was a constant reviewer. I estimate that he must have produced a review every two weeks. When one thinks of the other prose commitments, the autobiography, the book on Yeats, radio plays etc, one can gauge just how indefatigable and professional he was. It is against the weekly tasks of reviewing and the daily task of making poems that a writer's worth may be assessed. The daily and weekly task becomes the writer's native country. When I was a youth, learning my first 'Anglo-Irish' poems in the disturbed Arms Trial atmosphere of the Party, I was left in no doubt that there were sound reasons why one should reject the work of Louis MacNeice. None of the reasons were literary, but had to do with his lack of Irishness, his apparent Britishness, his general lack of engagement with 'the Irish thing'. What a stupid set of reasons not to read a poet. Recently I myself have been subjected to criticisms of my poetry that are entirely political. It amazes me that there are still people around who would censor poets for their choice of subject matter. There is no such thing as 'correct' subject matter. No poet can choose his parents or the social milieu out of which he arose. But it is the country of imagination that demands a writer's loyalty. The ambiguity of MacNeice's background is an enriching thing. He spent a lifetime trying to articulate a few basic beliefs; he tried to find some clear patterns. But as he himself wrote, 'I find it easier to work in a room which is definitely over-decorated.'

The Irish Review,
1990

Incorrigibly Plural
Louis MacNeice and his Legacy. *Fran Brearton and Edna Longley (eds)*

When I was an English student at UCC in the mid-70s there was little enough evidence of Louis MacNeice. I remember conversations between John Montague and Seán Lucy about MacNeice and Irish rugby, or about Hedli MacNeice and the first aromas of great food from Kinsale. That MacNeice had died as a result of pneumonia caught while recording underground sound effects for the BBC was certainly a heroic end as far as young poets were concerned; after all a few of us hoped that we'd find a career, and early death, working on some such memorable broadcast. But at that time in UCC it was overwhelmingly W B Yeats, Patrick Kavanagh and Austin Clarke. There is no doubt but that we all read writers who speak directly to our mental condition and the poets in Gus Martin's interim anthology, *Soundings,* formed an uninterrupted line of succession: Kavanagh and Clarke shared all of our hermetic neuroses as far back as our father's generation and a Christian Brother's anthology *Flowers from many Gardens.*

The Protestant Ulsterman MacNeice was too detached from our lives, both socially and culturally. It wasn't until this weekend when I read this book more carefully that I discovered MacNeice carried an Irish as well as a British passport. But like Elizabeth Bowen he was most completely at home while in transit. Anglo-Ireland is a disturbed nest; those hatched in its drawing rooms must learn early how to balance a life upon stormy branches. Politically Protestant Ireland has its firmest anchorage and its least disturbed sense of self in Belfast, south Antrim and north Down, but for over four hundred years every county in Ireland has been blessed with Protestant childhoods. For each such Protestant child coming home always meant coming home to Ireland.

As in all authors of mixed blood or heritage an interrogation of just one life opens up a Pandora's box of contended issues and disputed territories. It is a question of ownership. Who owns MacNeice? In *Incorrigibly Plural*, this collection of essays and brief viewpoints collected by Fran Brearton and Edna Longley to mark the centenary of MacNeice's birth, the disputed territory of the poet is mapped with all the gusto and knowledge of those implicated in the matter of Ulster and the matter of poetry. There are extraordinary jewels here as well as literary trinkets, but the book glistens with pure gold. Much of the gold is from MacNeice himself: 'As far as I can make out, I not only have many different selves, but I am often, as they say, not myself at all. Maybe it is just when I am not myself — when I am thrown out of gear by circumstances and emotion — that I feel like writing poetry.' In MacNeice the certainty of technique was offset by other massive uncertainties of childhood, philosophy and politics. His book-length study of Yeats rests against the late-1930s like an anchorage and launch pad. From Yeats MacNeice learned the power of rhetoric; his voice has the gusto of Yeats, yet it is sharpened, or made more tragically personal, by his capacity to be modern. His poetry is cinema rather than séance. He parts from each love on trains rather than on horseback. Hugh Haughton's essay, 'MacNeice's Vehicles', reveals the poet's 'instinctive appetite for mobility, his dependence on travel in his daily life', thus amplifying Leontia Flynn's brief essay on MacNeice on trains: 'I can no more gather my mind up in my fist / Than the shadow of the smoke of this train upon the grass.' Terence Brown's characteristically shrewd essay on travel gives a less brief encounter with the subject, noting that MacNeice's poetry not only instinctively employs an imagery drawn from a world of cars, buses, trains, but contains immediate descriptions of the thing itself, the very sensation of travel.

For someone of MacNeice's background and education Ireland must have remained as static material in the public whirlwind of the British 1930s. 'The one constant, in this post-Darwinian, post-Einsteinian universe, is change,' as John Goodby observes in his superb essay on the relationship between MacNeice and Dylan Thomas. Goodby, the Welsh modernist, is painfully aware how Thomas still languishes in metropolitan condescension while our Ulster poet has moved centre stage in the post-Yeats world. In a sense MacNeice has been reconsecrated by our famous contemporaries, Mahon, Longley, Heaney, while Thomas remains unheralded. It was at MacNeice's London home that Thomas's friends assembled after hearing of his death in New York and MacNeice wrote in *Encounter* of Thomas as 'not just a poet among poets; he was, as has often been remarked, a bard, with the three great bardic virtues of faith, joy and craftsmanship.' What moves Goodby most of all is the lost generous impulse — how poets who were so different in technique and taste could equally accept each other. Goodby laments the academic intellectualization of poetry, the 'rigidly enforced cartels of taste and publishing' that make young poets and academics hate the things they haven't even cared to explore.

There are so many important insights in this book, not just about Louis MacNeice but about poetry in general, that it is impossible to do justice to Brearton's and Longley's achievement here. Peter McDonald's 'The Pity of it All', Paul Muldoon's 'The Perning Birch' or Longley's own demanding and challenging essay on 'MacNeice, Graves and the Lyric of Classical Myth' would be sufficient reading for any scholar of Irish poetry. Like the young Derek Mahon who braved an unsatisfactory visit to MacNeice in Regent's Park the undergraduate MacNeice planned a visit to Robert Graves' house in Islip. All three poets, it could be argued, share a common classical heritage, a minimum standard of learning, that

Thomas McCarthy

separates them from that Poundian 'scrap-albums of ornament torn eclectically from history'. This book successfully establishes two distinct facts of Irish poetry in our time, the growing centrality of Louis MacNeice and the intellectual vigour of Belfast academic life.

Irish Examiner,
2012

Northman
John Hewitt 1907-1987 *by* W J McCormack

I wish I'd known in November, 1982, what I know now of John Hewitt, having read this extraordinary biographical study of the Ulster poet by W J McCormack (more widely known as the poet, Hugh Maxton). All those years ago, having listened to my poems at the Belfast launch of Gerald Dawe's *Younger Irish Poets*, Hewitt put his hands on my shoulders and said: 'McCarthy, you are too soft-hearted!'

Ulster encourages the direct and uninvited word of censure.

In the pub later that evening I told Hewitt about the young British soldier I'd seen from the train at Portadown playing with his bomb-disposal Labrador, soldier and dog rolling down a grassy embankment that was peppered with fallen sycamore leaves, the leaves like paprika scattered over soldier and dog. 'Only in Ulster,' said Hewitt sadly, thoughtfully. 'Only in Ulster.'

Why, in Belfast, did the 1970s become the 1920s all over again, reaching an average of ten murders a week by the middle of that decade? It was a question that Hewitt, an active socialist and lifelong Labour Party supporter, spent a great deal of his waking hours trying to explain. He belonged to Ulster, first and foremost, to the artisan, linen-weaving radicals of the North: he loved art and despised grandeur. His left-wing views and associations certainly cost him a job in arts administration in 1957 so that he had to make a career in Coventry, a distinguished and fruitful career as director of Coventry's Herbert Art Gallery where he championed contemporary British artists like Barbara Hepworth. Battles he had lost in Belfast he won in the regenerated and rising Labour-controlled Coventry of the 1960s. In 'An Irishman in Coventry' he wrote: 'A full year since, I took this eager city, / the tolerance that laced its blatant roar, / its famous steeples and its web of girders, / as image of the state hope argued for.'

McCormack paints a full picture of the poet's life here, Hewitt's intense attachment to the art of the Soviet satellite states, his Socialist Internationalism, along with his Belfast and his 'industrial North' regionalism. A great deal of the biographical detail here is gleaned from a private diary kept by Hewitt's wife, Roberta Black, and therein lies a great danger for a literary biographer, a danger that McCormack is aware of, for the determined keeping of a diary by a literary spouse is an aggressive act or — at best — an act of self-preservation. The real biography of a writer is the work itself. All personal evidence is merely hearsay and diarists especially are treacherous companions even in an ordinary life.

Hewitt might have allowed himself to be forgotten were it not for the younger, and more famous, John Montague. Montague negotiated a *Collected Poems* with McGibbon and Kee in the late 1960s and organized a crucial reading tour of Northern Ireland that may have reattached Hewitt to the Belfast that had rejected him. Blackstaff Press took control of his publishing life and while Belfast disintegrated the poet gathered strength. Hewitt's final Belfast years were very good, personally, although he retained that sense of a fading 'empire-Commonwealth' — 'Those happier decades we were dominant / but now that mastery has flaked away.'

McCormack, with his dense, discursive style acting as a counterbalance to Roberta's diaries, has produced an important Ulster book, one that every Southern politician might usefully read.

The Irish Examiner,
2015

Derek Mahon's 'Ophelia'

'The wind that blows these words to you / bangs nightly off the black-and-blue / Atlantic' wrote Derek Mahon in one of his earliest poems, 'Beyond Howth Head', published as a Poetry Ireland Edition by the Dolmen Press in 1970. The ocean wind is always blowing in Mahon's poetry, whining under the door at Achill, the gale-force wind of Portstewart or the shore beneath the Mournes, bringing everything in its air that might threaten 'the plain Protestant fatalism of home', as he wrote in 'A Bangor Requiem'. Mahon always comes to poetry at 'the far west of human life' as he put it in his version of a Houellebecq poem, 'The Clifden Road'. Wind is at its most powerful and dangerous at the edge of things, the hinterland of sea and seashore, the places where shutters are rattled and safety is challenged. Ocean wind, especially, seems more violent and desperate than any other wind; wind raids the shore of poetry at night, but then offers many poetic clearances after the break of day, opportunities of light, or, as Terence Brown once wrote in addressing Mahon's poetry: 'Light breaking through on desolate shores and bleak places'.

The storm 'Ophelia' of Derek Mahon's poem, published in *Against the Clock* (2018), was no ordinary old storm. It was an extra-tropical hurricane, the most easterly of its kind, that hit the Irish coast on October 16th, 2017, with storm winds of up to 156km/h recorded by the Cork Harbour weather station at Roche's Point. It took human life and flooded coastal towns in the South:

> *It started at nine in the morning as things do.*
> *The eye of the cyclone remained out at sea*

Thomas McCarthy

> *but we got the hard edge as it hit the coast*
> *and, anti-clockwise, strove to devastate*
> *a province; the lights failed and slates flew*
> *while I sat it out here in 'excited reverie'*
> *listening to climate change doing its work . . .*

The poet sheltered in his tower, that Yeatsian moment, is captured deftly and ironically. And not just Yeats, but the very modern awareness of climate change, is included in the poet's first view of what is happening. This fierce 'Ophelia' of a storm makes him wonder who names storms, who named this one so inappropriately. The poem goes on to track the storm, 'the roaring blitz of it', and then compares the aftermath, the scene ashore, to that of Key West after a tropical hurricane. But then, after the storm's departure at Donegal, the poet returns to a quieter ending, the suicide of the other, the literary, Ophelia who 'chose a flowing stream and willow shade'. This was a quiet ending 'she'd have refused in her right mind'. The poem becomes a meditation on the wider meaning of that name 'Ophelia'. It yearns for answers now, like the 'royal girlfriend' who sought sanctuary 'from the clamour of crazed voices'. The poet wonders about the hubris of those 'fatal industries' that drive these violent Ophelias ashore, violent endings that may be 'one of many before the real thing began'. This is a perfect storm, then, one of Mahon's best, combining as it does all of those characteristic Mahon preoccupations of shelter, of survival, of intimately human and widely circadian rhythms.

Autumn Skies: Writers on Poems by Derek Mahon,
2021

A Shell Case Full of Flowers

There are many elements in the poetry of Michael Longley that deserve both attention and praise. His is a unique talent, distinctly an Ulster talent in many ways, with markings of both England and Ireland left upon each of his lyrics like the antiquarian pencil tracings of a nineteenth-century Anglican clergyman. He has worn his poetry discreetly but firmly, like a calling to the Church of Ireland, a lucrative but unexpected living in a faraway parish in Mayo or Donegal. Trinity-educated, his foothold in this parish is firm and learned: he knows more about the flora and fauna than any fisherman or *spailpín fánach*; he probably knows more about fishing and he certainly knows much more about the stress levels of the biosphere that surrounds his stone-built presbytery. Like a forgotten clergyman of pre-Famine Ireland he has decided to keep a record from the beginning, to be both a Rev Kilvert and a Dr Douglas Hyde. Educated, unerring, he has recorded these Irish years in musical notation, not just the songs of the people but the chatter of birdlife, the scrambling of mice, and something utterly new, the names of all the flowers.

In 'Alibis' he has written, 'My botanical studies took me among / Those whom I now consider my ancestors' and this poem he completes brilliantly, aptly, with 'a simple question / Of being in two places at the one time'. It is a question of being both a maker and an anthologist, of being both gardener and botanist; but more than that, it is about becoming implicated completely in the fraught material of Ireland. The flower that implicates Longley is the one that grew in abundance over the mass graves of the Great War: it is the flower that follows him, haunts him, carried across the Mayo night, carried by the ghosts up the Malone Road, filling the brass shell cases on a thousand loyal mantelpieces: the poppy. It is the 'wound', as Ted Hughes called it, that shattered a million paybooks and grew out of the decomposing chests of a million English and Irish fathers. Longley returns to it again and again. The poppy is the key botanical detail in his landscapes: 'And the poppy that sheds its flower-heads in a day / Grows in one summer four hundred more . . . ' or 'Around the shell holes not one poppy has appeared / No symbolic flora.' The poppy is more than a flower, therefore; it is community, communion, church and childhood. It is not the Easter lily. It's the other one, more dearly bought, more drenched in blood yet more universally loved.

But the poppy is only one of the pressings in the huge Longley florilegium. In 'Flora' we have 'Blue periwinkles, / Meadowsweet, tansy', in 'Bog Cotton' he writes. 'Let me make a room for bog cotton, a desert flower' while in 'Mayo Monologues' we have:

> *I wanted to teach him the names of flowers,*
> *Self-heal and centaury; on the long acre*
> *Where cattle never graze, bog asphodel.*

Flower after flower is pressed into the glittering shell case of the poem; but all of these other flowers are pressed against the one unassailable flower of communal memory, the poppy. Though the ordinary flora, too, can create a wreath of its own; in 'Marsh Marigolds' he remembers Penny Cabot, 'Decades ago you showed me marsh marigolds / At Carrigskeewaun', and in 'Petalwort' he addresses the great naturalist and *Irish Times* writer, Michael Viney:

> *Let us choose for the wreath a flower so small*
> *Even you haven't spotted on the dune-slack*
> *Between Claggan and Lackakeely . . .*

More than birdlife, more than history, glows in what Longley calls the parish indoors. Flowers are emblems of the saved, they are bouquets pressed only against the lives of the truly faithful and reborn. Surrounded by flowers Longley is more truly, more confidently, the poetic child of Bishop MacNeice than the troubled child, Louis. Through flowers he has skipped a generation and returned to the grandfathers of Ulster, 'Northern Bohemia's flax fields and the flax fields / Of Northern Ireland'. Flax now has a country (NI), we notice, and not a province (Ulster). Like the poppy flax speaks directly to the church elders; it forms the signature of a new little nation gathered around Belfast Lough.

Memory, remembrance, politics, the community, memoranda to posterity, the regiment, the parish, all are invoked by the shell cases filled with flowers. But flowers in Longley, because he knows the names and scrutinized the almanacs, have a firm reality based on observation as well as that wider symbolic weight. Flowers exist, for him, in myth and memory, in Homer and grandfather and father. But they exist mainly as familiar friends, members of a parish, as a choir that sings permanently while their scholar-curate moves from Connaught living to Connaught living — as in 'Gorse Fires':

> *It is the same train between the same embankments.*
> *Gorse fires are smoking, but primroses burn*
> *And celandines and white may and gorse flowers.*

Love Poet, Carpenter: Michael Longley at Seventy,
2009

Your Beautiful Life
The Stairwell *by Michael Longley*
Listening to Bach *by Pearse Hutchinson*

Bells toll for the passing greatness in the neighbourhood of these books. Michael Longley's exquisite volume is dominated by memories of his recently deceased twin brother, Peter, while Pearse Hutchinson, that deeply embedded angel of a serious and literary Dublin, has gone to his eternal reward. They have left us these last collections as final kisses upon our worried foreheads. Certainly Pearse loved his kisses, especially from the mouth of any handsome boyfriend. The evidence of kisses is everywhere in his work. There is a very strong sense from these books that very important friends have left the house late at night, never to return after their final comradely embrace: though, one must hasten to add, Michael Longley is still very much in the wide, vestibule of living poetry; very much alive and not at all a shade. But there is such a strong, uncanny sense of wanting to follow the dead that his collection works as a grand farewell not to the dead but to us, the living. The sense, this effect, is deceptive, for Longley is still the great living note taker of bird life and bog life, regretting only:

> *Why did I never keep a notebook*
> *That filled up with reed buntings*
> *And blackcaps and chiffchaffs, their*
> *Songs a subsong between the lines?*
> ('Notebook')

To which our only reply is: you did; you kept a brilliant note-

Your Beautiful Life

book, in collection after collection, of all the phenomena around you, from the rare helleborines of Passchendaele to the plovers' eggs near Carrigskeewaun. Out of the twin palettes of County Mayo and the Great War Longley has made exquisite pictures for a Protestant gallery of imagination, of a sensibility more complex than the average Irish imagination, yet manufactured from the common dyes, colours and yearnings that are exclusive to Ireland. His work is a confounding achievement of self-restraint and calculated isolation from forces that don't belong to him, national forces that have made other poets giddy and useless as artists. His work is precise and intense, verbally and visually, in the manner of painters like Edward McGuire or Avigdor Arikha. Like the wounded Arikha he has been painting himself all his life, except the pictures have been bog flowers and scraps of ancient Greek. His first butterflies of language were caught in the company of W B Stanford and this he has never forgotten. Stanford's ghost haunts his method as a poet and seeps through his poetry like a preliminary wash in watercolour. To read his work is to touch a deliberately made beauty:

> *When I die I shall give them all their names.*
> *There will be many robin generations*
> *Coming into the house, and wrens and blackbirds*
> *And long-tailed tits will learn from the robins*
> *About the cheese-dish and saucer of water.*
> *I'll leave the window open for my soul-birds.*
>
> ('Deathbed')

The second part of *The Stairwell* has been well flagged. By the time we come to poems like 'The Stray' or 'The Birthday' with their painful and intense grief we have been well armed. These lyrics are heartrending and technically perfect; their perfection works as an antidote to sentimentality or easiness of feeling. They are not comfortable poems, however comforting they may have been to write. The tone is still held, reticent as rural

Down, while Peter Longley is made to live again through boyhood memory and the memory of war. The feeling in the entire book is simply as perfect as this (from 'The Birthday'):

> ... *Oh,*
> *The infinite gradations of sunset here.*
> *Thank you for visiting Carrigskeewaun.*
> *Don't twist your ankle in a rabbit hole.*
> *I'll carry the torch across the duach.*

A brother was never so beautifully remembered.

The astonishing Edward McGuire owl that graces the cover of Pearse Hutchinson's last book is a brilliant and uncanny design choice. Hutchinson was something like that owl, or something like a creature invested with McGuire's luscious plumage. Forceful, domineering, opinionated, learned. Pearse Hutchinson was the multilingual guru of educated Selskar Terrace and environs. His view of life was studied and exotic, his critical faculty was sharp and knowledgeable. People responded not only to his sense of style but to his deep knowledge. He was a wonder, really, and seminal works from *Watching the Morning Grow* to *Le Cead na Gréine* burst forth from this fertile and prodigious mind. His being gay was only part of the loveliness of his work: "'Mrs Hutchinson, one kiss from Pearse's mouth means more to me than all the women in the world,'" the lover Maurice tells his Mass-going mother ('What a Young Man Said to My Mother'). The mother's path and Maurice's path were never to cross again, but a tryst with this spirit of poetry had occurred, a mythical Maurice such as one finds in E M Forster's fiction or Roger Casement's diaries: it is the memory that remains real and becomes poetry. Yet lovers have flaws, as Deesh the Indian medical student would demonstrate dramatically, crunching a glass eye between snow-white teeth ('Merrion Square, 1948'). In his memory of Bert Achong ('All Four Letters of It'),

Your Beautiful Life

Hutchinson would get to the deep core of it all:

> *I wrote your name*
> *on a high hill*
>
> *remembering long*
> *delight new-lost*
>
> *I wrote your name in snow.*

An image of the handwritten 'Near the Grand Canal' (for Patrick Galvin) has been placed as an epilogue to this book. It is a revealing image, the blocked handwriting full of art and discipline — one can see the boy in the writing, the poet with a parenting among printers and others conscious of graphic style. Placing it there for the reader is a stroke of genius, like the owl on the cover, but it does remind us that Pearse Hutchinson would have demanded that kind of finish, or flourish, of design. His was a demanding talent that called each reader to attention. One doesn't approach a Hutchinson poem badly dressed, better to be prepared and attuned. Dense and formal poems like 'The Abbot of Piro' and 'Sleepwalking 2' are interspersed with spare etchings like 'Milarepa' and 'Listening to Bach', but this poet's masterful command of the material is the single most powerful message sent forth by his last book. The way he circles around the theme of 'Near the Grand Canal', pencilling around material as the meaning of Patrick Galvin's life presses in upon him, thinking of James Connolly and all the lost causes, and then, this — a perfect evocation of the beauties of socialism: 'And then again I thought of the great beauty of Lily Connolly, his wife, when, not long before they killed him — and *he* was trying to console *her* — she cried out to him: "But your beautiful life, James, your beautiful life!"'

Poetry Ireland Review,
2015

Heroes and Nasties
The Faber Book of Political Verse *Tom Paulin (ed)*

Editing an anthology of poetry is a thankless task because the act of selection implies many acts of exclusion. Lucky for Tom Paulin most poets don't have access to poisonous umbrellas and those bards with a Jesuitical skill in poisons have long since passed away. There is a double exclusiveness in a book such as the one under review: the poems must qualify as both political and good. What is political poetry then? Is it the poetry of ideology, of propaganda? Or is it the poetry of an author who has had a political past, who has been affected by the machinery of totalitarian regimes? Does it imply political commitment? And what about the private poets (Wallace Stevens, Aleixandre, Ó Riordáin, John Ashbury)?

Paulin tackles many of these questions in his excellent Introduction. He outlines a number of traditions in Anglophone poetry — The Popular Tradition, The Monarchist Tradition (Paulin's nasties), The Puritan-Republican Tradition (Paulin's heroes), The Irish Tradition, The Scottish Tradition, The American Tradition — and he places those traditions within the context of his own Republican Socialist world view. The Introduction is a brilliant reading of English poetry in particular: Paulin is lucid, subtle but stimulating, and he has a very gifted critic's ability to see how themes are delineated and orchestrated by different generations. With this Introduction alone Paulin has done for English poetry what Raymond Williams did for the novel in *The Country and the City*. But there are gaps. He seems to have no interest in those poets who've been citizens of the Irish Free State: Clarke, Kinsella, Eavan Boland etc. This lack of interest creates the illusion that Irish political poetry went straight from Thoor Ballylee to Ballymurphy. He also ignores Australia and the Indian subcontinent: he has given us none of the political poems of Vincent Buckley, A D Hope, Faiz Ahmad Faiz, Shrikant Verma, R Parthasarathy. And, returning to his native Ulster, I am shocked by the exclusion of John Montague. Montague's *The Rough Field* is the most ambitious of all Ulster poems and his *Poisoned Lands* was the opening solo in the great symphony of contemporary Ulster poetry.

As a fervent Socialist Paulin believes in the 'pure republic' of reason: the deadliest enemies of this republic are the monarchists, Arnold and Eliot. He accuses Eliot of ensuring 'that the magic of monarchy and superstition permeated English literary criticism and education like a syrupy drug'. Milton is the vital hero in Paulin's world. Milton, like Cromwell, was imbued with libertarian ideas and committed to 'the free individual conscience'. In generous selections from *Paradise Lost*, as well as in the Introduction, Paulin attempts to integrate the theological and political layers of Milton's imagination. From Milton we move to the more sceptical and dubious politics of Marvell's 'Upon Appleton House'. There is a brief sojourn in the monarchy of Shakespeare, but from Shakespeare we are hurried along to meet the nineteenth-century poet, Arthur Hugh Clough, the second hero of the editor. (Where is that great anti-imperialist poem, 'The Deserted Village'?)

Clough, like Wordsworth and Auden, became a reactionary in his late years. Yet 'It is an ambition of this anthology,' Paulin writes, 'to redeem Clough from the neglect which his work has suffered and to suggest links with Auden':

> *I sit at my table* en grand seigneur,
> *And when I have done, throw a crust to the poor;*
>
> *Not only the pleasure, one's self, of good living,*
> *But also the pleasure of now and then giving.*
> (from 'Dipsychus')

Thomas McCarthy

Between the twin pillars of Clough and Auden Paulin has inserted Kipling (the Enoch Powell of poetry), a modest selection of Yeats, as well as poems by Tsvetaeva, Mandelstam, Akhmatova and Mayakovsky. Three-and-a-half pages of poetry by Hugh MacDiarmid precede twenty-one pages by Auden. This unfair relationship between MacDiarmid and Auden merely emphasizes the difficulty of editing an anthology of political verse. Auden may be a better poet technically, but there is no way — no way — that Auden can be a superior political poet. Auden's boy-scout politics fall to pieces when compared to MacDiarmid's great works like the Hymns to Lenin, 'Island Funeral', 'To Circumjack Cencrastus', 'On a Raised Beach' or even minor poems like 'Reflections in a Slum' or 'British Leftist Poetry 1930-40'. I cannot understand what happened here. Perhaps there were difficulties with copyright.

'The conservative poet is naturally a pessimist,' says Paulin in his discussion on the Monarchist Tradition. Part of his admiration for Seamus Heaney arises from Heaney's positive character, a refusal to flog the 'subject people stuff' and Heaney's admission of the complexity of his own tribe:

> 'Now you're supposed to be
> An educated man,'
> I hear him say. 'Puzzle me
> The right answer to that one.'

From Heaney one moves easily to Scotland's current genius, Douglas Dunn. Dunn's poem, 'Washing the Coins' from *St Kilda's Parliament,* is one of the political gems of this anthology. The concluding poets of the selection, John Cooper Clarke and Linton Kwesi Johnson form a cheeky closure to such a cerebral exercise. Yet, advertising their folksy lyrics is consistent with Paulin's belief in the suppressed English folk tradition that produced such fragments as 'The Peasant's Song' and 'Gunpowder Plot Day':

Heroes and Nasties

I see no reason
Why gunpowder treason
Should ever be forgot.

Many people will be annoyed with this book. By all accounts even the Faber Poetry Editor is not pleased (new critical expressions like 'I'll nail him to the floor' have been reported in *The Observer*). The exclusions of Austin Clarke and John Montague by an Irishman are inexplicable. But it is essential to understand the political nature of Paulin's mind. He may be a fine poet and scholar but, like the aisling poets of seventeenth-century Ireland, he is committed to a particular political world view. He is a Republican Socialist. He couldn't have chosen the easy way, a mild anthology that would have given us the good order of poetry in England at this time. He has given us a selection that is as uncompromising and eclectic as Yeats's Oxford book. What he has produced is nothing less than a political act, a version of history. As he says in the Introduction: 'The idea of balanced judgement is a reflection of consensus politics, and in a polarized society with high unemployment such a concept is bound to appear comically irrelevant.'

The Irish Review,
1986

Tides Revisited
Tides *by John Montague*

What I remember about the original *Tides* is the shock of reading one of the Montague's best poems 'Life Class' for the first time. His easeful poeticizing of the love act was light years ahead of the anguished brooding of Clarke or Kavanagh:

> *odorous nooks*
> *& crannies of love,*
> *awaiting the impress*
> *of desire*

And we had been brought up to see the poetry of love as a kind of poetry of protest: in Clarke or Kavanagh there was the anger of not having given or taken completely, or without struggle, of simply not having been allowed to love. The force of physical love was suggested only through its continuous absence. Montague seemed to sidestep these old boys' hang-ups. What was pleasant for an eighteen-year-old reader at that time was the gradual unfolding of the impact of love, and Montague's agnostic descriptions:

> *What homage*
> *is worthy for such*
>
> *a gentle unveiling?*
> *to nibble her ten*
> *toes, in an ecstasy*

> *of love, to drink*
> *hair, like water?*

I still appreciate that lack of intrusion of any external, moralizing code. The act of love and the process of loving is allowed to write its own laws out of its own experience. The third section of this book deals specifically with that energy, the mental lightning of sex. Montague himself says that the section is ruled by 'the muse as energy, love, the full moon':

> *. . . a secret room*
> *of golden light where*
> *everything — love, violence,*
> *hatred is possible;*
> *and, again, love.*

Other sections put the 'secret room' of human relationships into perspective, the strength of such relationships being continually threatened by time and change, pain and loss. When Eavan Boland reviewed *Tides* in 1971 she recognized the vulnerability of 'the moment of love' as one of the three 'fierce obsessions' of the book. And 'obsession' is the perfect word. Montague has said that this book is 'a temporary exhaustion of an obsession'.

There's hardly a good love poem around that doesn't stare sideways at death. The poems of *Tides* are no exception. But those weeds of death and violence are manageable, somehow, within the garden of love:

> *To become*
> *an object, honoured*
> *or not, as the occasion demands:*
> *while time bends you slowly*
> *back to the ground.*

Such images of death and decay are strongest in two character-

Thomas McCarthy

istically Montague poems, 'The Hag of Beare' and 'The Wild Dog Rose'. In these he uses a favourite persona, the decrepid old woman remembering past glories, the skilled lover who has passed on:

> *Ebb tide has come for me:*
> *My life drifts downwards*
> *Like a retreating sea*
> *With no tidal turn.*

The final section of *Tides* is a poem sequence based on William Hayter's engravings. The poet was asked by the artist to provide these poems. It's quite probable that Montague would have written on Hayter's work without the specific request — his nervous skill and Piscean fluidity is matched perfectly by the wavering lines of the artist.

I've had the original *Tides* on my bedside bookshelf for six years. What amazes me now is the realization that I never tried to mimic the technique or the voice — at various stages in writing our own first poems we used other writers' methods to bounce into our own work. But never this poet of *Tides*. I suspect that Montague's voice is so unique and inimitable that at times it must have seemed eccentric to the narrower needs of a young poet. There's such a varied acculturation process going on in each of Montague's books that to use him as a standard Anglo-Irish mentor would be to dive headlong into the deeper end of the pool. Yet, surely to deny something because of its very richness is to weaken the scope of the narrower Irish tradition. Every time he publishes a book I have to scratch my head for a definition of Anglo-Irish poetry. In his case nothing in Daniel Corkery can help us.

The Irish Times,
1978

Poet of Exile and Return

There was Doris Lessing, just four years ago, walking briskly through the English Market in Cork, surrounded by a phalanx of minders. When the poet Theo Dorgan pointed out a young woman at the olive stall and remarked that she was a daughter of the poet Montague Doris Lessing immediately stopped and addressed her: 'Please tell your father I was asking after him,' and, again, she commanded: 'You will not forget. I wish to be remembered to your father!' Just the other day I fell into conversation with an elderly woman in a local café, a woman who was reading *The Pear is Ripe*, the Montague memoir from Liberties Press. This midday gourmand, who had recently enjoyed the *Collected Poems* from The Gallery Press and *Company*, Montague's earlier autobiography, was a devoted fan, a 70-year-old cheerleader. For her, who went on to quote extensively from 'All Legendary Obstacles', 'The New Siege' and 'Border Sick-Call', this Ulster poet is bigger than rock star Bono. 'Isn't he a mighty man,' she quipped, 'and a mighty poet!'

It is always difficult to estimate the impact a writer makes. A poet's reputation is not fame. It is more subterranean, more the slow application of the red-hot searing brand. It lives in a circle of admirers. With Montague the smell of that burning brand is unmistakable; a poet of love and politics, of exile and patria, his books remain in print, bought and borrowed and argued over. His life is very much like that of Elytis, the Greek poet. His greatest work, *The Rough Field*, has been constantly reprinted, rather like Elytis' national book of poetry, *The Axion Esti*. Since *Poisoned Lands* (1961), where Montague found his stride — a personal angle and rhythmic

Thomas McCarthy

signature — his work has had an expansive fluency and national grandeur. Many critics have argued against his definition of the national range, his assumption that Ireland and Irishness are accomplished and completed facts. In recent years a number of young scholars have attempted an assault on Montague's Tyrone Gaelic towers only to come away diminished and covered in a greenish froth. His work has a splendid, exceptional integrity. It ebbs and flows and shimmers like the tide but contains beneath the surface many crystals of postmodernism and awkward splinters of ancient magic:

> *They sparkle beneath our wings;*
> *spilt jewel caskets, lights strewn*
> *in rich darkness, lampstrings of pearls.*
>
> *And then the plane tilts, a warm*
> *intimate thrumming, like travelling within*
> *the ambergris-heavy belly of a whale.*
>
> *The abstract beauty of our world;*
> *gleams anvilled to a glowing grid,*
> how the floor of *earth* is thick inlaid!
>
> ('Landing')

Montague's is never a poetry for the innocent. He is always much more than the nostalgic Irish child born in Brooklyn and reared by spinster aunts. Always mischievous at readings and in company Montague likes to play down the brilliant Roger McHugh circle of UCD English scholars from which he emerged, that circle who were trained in late 1940s Ireland to be patrician Catholic editors and teachers, or taciturn diplomats of a neutral country represented by lugubrious government Ministers.

His mother's milk was indeed Ulster milk, but he trained in the Dublin playgrounds and his work resonates with the authority of that Dublin viewpoint. It is the Dublin of

Anthony Cronin and Con Leventhal, of Liam Miller and Garech de Brún. His early theatre criticism, knowing and firm as Leventhal's theatre work for *Ireland Today*, was written for Peadar O'Donnell at *The Bell*. It has a confidence born of many seminars: 'I don't think we adequately realize the extent to which the influence of the cinema and newspaper has corrupted drama proper; there is not merely the loose ploys with a hint of social comment . . . but also the unconscious attempt at nonchalant acting, the swallowing of lines as though they were sawdust in the mouth . . . None of the plays at present running commercially in Dublin have any resemblance to the real thing'. (May 1952) Yet an early poem, published in *The Dublin Magazine* in 1949, when he was twenty, already contains a rhythm and a locale that would blossom into his mature Ulster voice: 'I sat in a staid country bus / Soft moving through road-cut fields.' His was a poetry of movement and journeys, of arrivals and brief encounters. From 'Bus Stop in Nevada', published in *Threshold* in 1957, to 'Like Dolmens Round My Childhood', winner of the Morton Prize and published in *Threshold* in 1960, he established a pattern of exile and return that persists in his work to the present day. For *The Bell* he also wrote 'Fellow-travelling with America', an account of his participation in one of the famous post-War Salzburg Seminars at Max Reinhardt's Schloss Leopoldskron, from which he came believing that an Irish writer had 'no active sense of European culture, but a kind of self-conscious, isolated bravado with the artist in the invidious position of spiritual director to the intelligentia'.

A Fulbright Fellowship at Yale removed him from the Dublin scene in 1953 before he could become either a spiritual director or the scourge of local theatre. From Yale he moved to the University of Iowa where he became part of Paul Engle's famous writing programme, submitting his first, unpublished collection, *The Mad Priest and Other Poems*, as his required MFA thesis. It was while at Iowa that he met 'a titled young Frenchwoman with an eager grin and golden-brown eyes, called Madeleine de Brauer', who became his first wife. America, his birthplace but not his mother country, rushed into his consciousness with its campus rhythms and social habits, rhythms that would be enhanced by a sojourn in California in the mid 1960s:

> *Lines of protest*
>   *lines of change*
> *a drum beating*
>   *across Berkeley*
> *all that spring*
>   *invoking the new*
> *Christ avatar*
>   *of the Americas*
>   ('A New Siege')

That American strain, a playfulness and delicacy of line that comes from Snyder and Duncan, permeates even his most traditional poems. The tension between deeply embedded Irish myths and archetypes, combined with a Dave Brubeck-like twist and turn in the line, is at the heart of his personal music. The 1961 collection, *Poisoned Lands*, carries the weight of the British Movement in its verse structure but his ideas and experiences are too well travelled and complex to be deceived by a small ambition.

Montague's wanderings in America were followed by his sojourn in that basement flat at 6 Herbert Street where the younger Doris Lessing played with her coloured notebooks. In the late 50s he'd assembled his tyro-collection, *Forms of Exile*, for the Dolmen Press. These were the intense years of Thomas Kinsella, Seán Ó Riada, Liam Miller, Garech de Brún and Brendan Behan's late night visits in search of company. Miller, printer and architectural draftsman, and Garech de Brún, aristocrat and patriot like Dr Douglas Hyde, were the two pivotal figures of Montague's early adult years. Montague and Kinsella would spend many hours going through Dolmen

Poet of Exile and Return

submissions and proofs while Montague and de Brún would spend days and nights driving through the Irish countryside in search of music and voices for Claddagh Records. Those Dolmen days of the 1950s and the 1960s combine in his two books of memoir to create a golden commonwealth of Irish poetry and music. Yet, between two distinct Dolmen phases, Montague spent a crucial spell in Paris, at 11 rue Daguerre, where the poet Claude Esteban and the painter-engraver Bill Hayter filled a chasm created by the absence of Miller and Kinsella. Paris and its political ferment energized Montague's poetry and flooded his love lyrics with a particular light:

> *Such intimacy of hand*
> *and mind is achieved*
> *under its healing light*
> *that the shifting*
> *of hands is a rite*
>
> *like court music.*
>   ('The Same Gesture')

That poem is from *Tides* (1970), an exquisitely printed book from the Dolmen Press. *Tides* in its structure and language was a refinement of the style in *A Chosen Light*, published in 1967. Both collections are a successful blend of art and literature, a seamless dance of Louis le Brocquy in 1967 and William Hayter in 1970. Both books still stand as portals to a new kind of Irish poetry, to a new possibility. Their importance has never been diminished. Younger Dublin-based poets such as Richard Ryan, Hugh Maxton and Thomas Dillon Redshaw skipped through the Montague portal for several years. In those days Montague was also the Paris Correspondent for *The Irish Times*, filing his reports from a city that rocked with student protests and post-colonial angst. It was in the ferment of Paris, then a vast political street theatre, that the poet met the second great love of his life: 'And now I was confronted by a representative of this new class war; she was also beautiful, and beauty, along with fiery youth, can be a powerful potion,' he wrote in *The Pear is Ripe*.

It was with this fiery beauty, Evelyn Robson, his new wife, that Montague settled in Cork as a lecturer in UCC's English Department. An equally youthful Montague was also at the height of his powers having finally assembled *The Rough Field* and begun work on *The Faber Book of Irish Verse*, a task he had inherited from Valentine Iremonger. It was Seán Lucy, the affable and charismatic Cork poet, who arranged Montague's appointment at UCC. The two poets had been united by Seán Ó Riada's death and funeral. Ó Riada became a shadowy but permanent presence in Montague's poetry over the next ten years, as indeed he shadowed Seán Lucy to the end of his days. The early loss of the composer became a motif and symbol, a prophecy, of worse things to come in 1970s Ulster: 'Beyond the flourish / of personality, peacock / pride of music or language: / a constant, piercing torment!' ('Ó Riada's Farewell'). I can still remember the evening in the mid-70s when Montague read that newly composed poem to Evelyn, Theo Dorgan and me by his fireside at Grattan Hill. The Montagues had a bevy of devoted literary students who haunted their house in Cork, students who included Gregory O'Donoghue, Dorgan, Maurice Riordan and Patrick Crotty. In his UCC lectures Montague also had two brilliant women who would go on to do extraordinary things: Nuala Ní Dhomhnaill and 'Fifi' Wilson (now better known as the actor 'Fiona Shaw').

It was easy to be devoted to the Montagues, the poet with his tall, graceful stride, and Evelyn with her beauty and Gallic flair. Montague communicated an uncompromising view of the poet's life to all his students, including the would-be poets: to be a poet was not something to be taken lightly; it was not a hobby, it was a serious way of being in the world. But, exiled so far south, he also embodied the growing glamour of Ulster poetry, its world-beating and globetrotting nature. Through him we learned that Ulster poets stood no nonsense and that they were the true inheritors of the spirit of Yeats. He was extraordinarily generous with his time while he taught at UCC, and generous in practical ways too, dispatching his best student-poets on Canadian PhD trails and introducing our manuscripts to the harassed and weary Liam Miller. It was no accident that Seán Dunne, Greg Delanty and I were first published by the Dolmen Press.

In the late 1980s Montague, grown weary of Ireland and UCC, I think, moved to SUNY Albany where he became writer-in-residence at its famous Writers' Institute. In 1998 he became the first Ireland Professor of Poetry. In these recent and very social years he published a series of powerful collections including *Mount Eagle* (1989) and *Smashing the Piano* (1999). His energy, power and belief in the poet's vocation grows in intensity with every passing year. Along with that energy is a familial delicacy, an ability to capture microcosms of love:

> *In my sick daughter's room*
> *the household animals gather.*
> *Our black Tom poses lordly on*
> *the sun-warmed windowsill.*
> *A spaniel sleeps by her slippers,*
> *keeping one weather-eye open.*
>
> ('Guardians')

Now he contemplates the ebb and flow of Irish reputations from the warm perch of a Nice apartment with his belovèd Elizabeth Wassell, the American novelist. He still writes shrewd reviews for *The Irish Times* and assembles new collections. On the evidence of his recent memoirs his belief in the poet's life is undiminished and unbowed: 'For now it seemed I had found a haven.'

The Irish Times,
2009

John Montague

John Montague, the great Ulster poet, first Ireland Professor of Poetry and a former *Irish Times* correspondent in Paris, who has just died in his belovèd France, will be mourned by everyone who understands Irish poetry. We have now forgotten how it was that the charisma of France pulled the Irish establishment into the European Union and Montague belonged to an educated Irish generation of poets and diplomats who embodied this Francophile ideal. France was what Irishmen and women might aspire to, and Montague's treatment of love, history and politics in his poetry always had a Parisian edge and flavour. He was married to two high-born Frenchwomen, and his late third marriage to the American novelist Elizabeth Wassell was spent almost entirely in Southern France. Like Samuel Beckett Montague died in the place that defined his art, his loves and his life:

> *Rue Dageurre, how we searched*
> *till we found it! Beyond*
> *the blunt-pawed lion of Denfert...*

John Montague was born to Ulster Catholic parents in New York in 1929. He was sent back home to the family farm in County Tyrone at a very young age. This sense of dislocation remained with him for the rest of his life, and the urgent effort to integrate dislocated elements in his own nature would become a key signature in his work. He was educated at St Patrick's boarding school in Armagh, at UCD and at the influential MFA writing programme of the University of Iowa. He was an industrious and ambitious young poet taking part in the famous Salzburg Seminars and writing criticism and commentary as part of a brilliant UCD generation that included Denis Donoghue, Anthony Cronin and Thomas Kinsella.

He was also at Berkeley in the early 1950s, working as a University Teaching Assistant and absorbing the values and methods of Bay Area poets like Robert Creeley and Robert Duncan. Montague's first collection of poems, *Forms of Exile*, was published by the Dolmen Press in 1958. This book was followed by the masterful *Poisoned Lands* in 1961 and then by one of his greatest books, *A Chosen Light*, in 1967. This book contains two of his most popular poems, 'The Trout' and 'All Legendary Obstacles'. By the time Montague published *Tides* in 1971 the high aestheticism of France, its humanism and cosmopolitanism, was fully developed in his work. By then in his early forties he had achieved the line, the pacing, the grace notes and tonal qualities, that would animate his best poetry for the rest of his career.

John Montague had also reached a point of crisis and re-definition in his personal life. He met and fell in love with a young French scholar, Evelyn Robson. The youthful and attractive couple moved to Cork where he took up a post as Lecturer in the English Department at UCC at the invitation of the poet Seán Lucy.

His crucial work, *The Rough Field*, a poetic analysis of Ulster tensions, was published to great acclaim and argument in 1972. The image of an Ulster Catholic population left rudderless and unrepresented after Partition haunted him and he mourned for this community in the way George Seferis mourned for the lost Greeks of Smyrna. Most UCC English students will remember the poet from this era: tall, charismatic, full of fire and brilliant impatience. His aristocratic manner, strenuously keeping a childhood stammer under control, like Elizabeth Bowen. His two daughters, Oonagh and Sibyl, were born at this time and their presences would weave in and out of all future collections: 'Daughter, dig in,

Thomas McCarthy

with fists like ferns / unfurling, to basic happiness!'

In the late 1980s Montague was invited by novelist Willliam Kennedy to work at the New York Writers' Institute. He spent many years in Albany, teaching and writing, and publishing such influential books as *Mount Eagle* (1989) and *Time in Armagh* (1993). By this time also he had found a new publisher, Peter Fallon of The Gallery Press, who would completely revitalize his career and create a much wider audience for his work.

John Montague wrote fiction and memoir as well as poetry. Books like *Death of a Chieftain* (1964) and *The Pear is Ripe* (2007) brim with energy and precision and are still widely read. Living with his wife Elizabeth Wassell in Nice he had a dramatic, engaged, fruitful literary life right to the end of his days. John Montague won many awards, from the Martin Toonder Award in 1976 to the Bord Gáis Energy Bob Hughes Lifetime Achievement Award, presented just three weeks ago. He was a founding director of Claddagh Records, founding member of Aosdána, founding President and lifelong supporter of the Triskel Arts Centre, Cork, President of Poetry Ireland and a Chevalier de la Légion d'honneur. A long and wonderful life in literature, a noble procession of poems and stories, has just passed out of Irish life.

The Irish Times,
December 2016

The Prince of the Quotidian by Paul Muldoon

In the New Year of 1992 Paul Muldoon decided to write a poem every day. He was newly arrived at Princeton where he had become Director of the Creative Writing Program. The result is this forty-two-page poetry journal. If the project sounds Louis MacNeice-like, that is no coincidence. Muldoon, more than any other Ulster writer, has inherited many of the qualities and stylistic mannerisms of MacNeice.

And what are those qualities? Well, an acquisitive intelligence, a comfort with the detritus of modern life, an ability to absorb non-Irish experiences without the tendency to flee back into a set of Irish references. He also shares with MacNeice a healthy dose of self-irony and a belief in friendship: 'I insert myself like an ampersand / between Joyce Carol Oates & Ingemar Johansson', 'To Deane I say, "I'm not in exile", / though I can't deny / that I've been twice in Fintona.' Johansson was the Swedish boxer who knocked out Floyd Patterson. In company with Joyce Carol Oates he would certainly be as threatening as the day spent in Fintona. Muldoon's rejection of the heroism of exile plays an important part in setting the record straight. Like MacNeice's move from Ireland to London to Cornell, Muldoon's move is also a kind of intellectual's commuting. To be genuinely 'exiles' is to be permanently removed from one's context. A poet like Muldoon has established any number of contexts for his work and his life. Long before he removed himself physically from Belfast Muldoon had been surfing the poetry internet. His world is not lyrical, like Austin Clarke's or Kavanagh's, but it is intertextual, dependent upon educated guesses, like the work of Beckett or Flann O'Brien. He creates powerful

Thomas McCarthy

localities, but he's not provincial:

> Much as I'm taken by Barry Douglas playing
>   Rachmaninov
> with the Ulster Orchestra
> I remember why I've had enough
> of the casuistry
>
> by which pianists and painters and poets are proof
> that all's not rotten in the state . . .

Muldoon's work reminds us — the word 'remind' is too imprecise here — that poetry is a relative thing. His resolve to write a poem a day was in itself a challenge to the notion of inspired genius. His poems are 'given' but not in the traditional sense; rather, they are an accretion formed around his literary life. Like contemporary works of art they are both poems and possible technical ideas about the nature of poems. They resonate, and then only when they are studied. He writes:

> We followed Lafitte and the great McIlhenny
> and all that pirate krewe
> on a flat-boat through Honey
> Island swamp in search of the loup garou.

These lines are reprised: 'The moon hangs over the Poconos / like a madeleine. / Warren Zevon. "Van the Man". Bob Dylan.' Warren Zevon's big hit was (you guessed it) 'Werewolves of London'.

Food, travel, books, music — these are constant references in *The Prince of the Quotidian*. The 'okra/monious gumbo' is more than a slimy Southern vegetable and Paul Prudhomme is surely more than a famous Cajun chef. Yet 'the bittern and curlew' of home reminds us of the two Irish soldiers in exile, General Alejandro O'Reilly and Francis Ledwidge.

The Prince of the Quotidian by Paul Muldoon

Muldoon warns us not to seek patterns in his 'crazy quilt'. But this is a daft warning, possibly tongue-in-cheek. This book is its own kind of health warning; it is a picture of the poet's intellectual context, our context as well as, quite simply, a journal of poetry.

Éire-Ireland,
Winter 1995

Seamus Heaney's First Anniversary

It was a catastrophe that fell upon us all, the day Seamus Heaney died. I attended his removal at Donnybrook church that Sunday night and the funeral mass the next day. I didn't travel north to County Derry but a huge contingent of Southern poets did make the journey across the border behind the Presidential cavalcade. A long line of poets, journalists, politicians and rock stars crowded around his coffin and hospitality was shown to all strangers by his belovèd Bellaghy GAA club. The quality of the huge crowd at his funeral mass in Donnybrook — the grandeur of the audience, as Micheál Mac Liammóir used to say — was proof that something prodigious in Irish life had passed away. The day had the atmosphere of a state funeral, but with Seamus as a kind of matinée idol, the Valentino, the John McCormack or Jack Doyle, as well as a man of the people: but always a Bellaghy GAA man.

What a beautiful life he had, and what a beautiful adventure in poetry he and his belovèd Marie had together; an adventure from which we all received postcards and were made to feel included. It is too early, yet, to think about the literary meaning of his sudden passing nearly a year ago. It may take decades for the full force of his work to be absorbed. Slowly it dawns upon us what a giant passed by. A Yeats has died, certainly. Each generation seems to need a true adventurer, a knight who will ride out and slay all the dragons of the literary world, while we stay at home in Éire and do little chores about the house. Heaney was the dragon slayer, bringing entire poetry scenes from Oxford to Harvard within his dominion.

Seamus Heaney's First Anniversary

Nearly ten years ago he came up to me after a reading, full of praise for my book *Merchant Prince*: 'The whole enterprise, the whole imagined achievement, deserves great attention,' he said; and then we went off together to the bar and chatted about poetry and politics. His plate was full from the beginning so that he grew up with the habit of encouragement. Later that year Nuala Ní Dhomhnaill and Seamus and I were drinking in the Stag's Head in central Dublin after an Ireland Funds meeting, staying about one and a half hours, chatting about his new manuscript, *District and Circle*. In a TV interview upon the book's publication he credited both Nuala and me with giving him the title. I don't think we did, but he would say it just to namecheck younger poets, to give them a boost.

'Yeats has died, already having the rating of a major poet,' wrote John Crowe Ransom in *The Southern Review* of Winter, 1942. It had taken over two years from the death of Yeats to consider the meaning of that death — to place it, somehow, in the context of world literature. Ransom in his great essay also tried to define 'greatness' in a poet. He praised Yeats for his personality, his useful as well as unprofitable journeys, his themes and metrics, and his magnificence. Heaney is remembered for all those qualities as well, especially 'magnificence'. And 'magnificence', it is accepted, can only be achieved in an artistic life that contains a religious quest. Each of his collections was another layer in an archaeology of belief; each poem sets the darkness echoing.

With his death the Irish cultural economy has certainly deflated and Irish Studies internationally has suffered a terrible blow. There are grand talents still among us. One thinks of the great poet Montague, or Mahon, Muldoon and Boland. But these are poets' poets, rare earth creatures, with no interest in swimming into that rich bazaar of public relations and august American foundations. Heaney was a political person, a public teacher in the manner of John Hume or Bill Clinton. Abroad, and especially in America where our current government

Thomas McCarthy

urgently needs to butter some Washington bridges, Heaney will be sorely missed. So who can replace him? The answer: nobody. When a great poet dies the tide goes out a very long way. Even a year after his death the light from Heaney's prodigious star still illuminates our Irish tides.

Irish Examiner,
2014

The Translations of Seamus Heaney
Marco Sonzogni (ed)

The late and much loved Seamus Heaney had a phenomenal life and a phenomenal career as poet. I use the word 'phenomenal' advisedly. The sheer scale of his achievement as poet in the English language already looks to us like a sequence of phenomena, a succession of Northern Lights in a dark sky, something magical and unexpected that changed the temperature and reading habits of my generation of Irish poets. His books were a succession of starry appearances and there are many traces still of the light these stars left behind. In his aftermath many of us now read history differently and have rearranged our view of Ulster in a vigorous, intensely familiar light. Marco Sonzogni, in his brilliantly researched and lucid Introduction to this latest book, charts the geography of Heaney's translating life and explains the great poet's method and purpose as translator: 'When a text was published, it was invariably in a state of advanced completion. Still, the "double-take of feeling" influencing the poet-translator — being simultaneously accountable to "the inner literalist" and to "the writer of verse" — is a force that is always operating upon the author to an extent that can be considered "self-revealing". The line between completion and abandonment is not always a clear one.'

This revelatory statement is more than reaffirmed by the scale of Sonzogni's completed anthology. Here was a giant effort of translation by Heaney, a parallel lifetime spent by a great poet among the lives of others. Heaney was saturated by others, translating from the word go, as if translating was part of the writing of poetry — not a duty, but an aesthetic

Thomas McCarthy

anxiety quenched only by the act of possession and repossession that occurs when one poet carries another across the treacherous waters of language. A fine scholar, Heaney was insatiably curious about clusters of information contained within other languages, information that might stretch and illuminate his own prodigious talent. He almost overdosed on these vitamins of information, almost but not quite because his inner editor, his flawless gyroscope, always spun him back into that airy, confident sureness of his own voice. And it was when that sureness of touch also touched upon Ana Blandiana or 'Anonymous' (that great Gaelic poet), Pascoli or Dante, that the sheer malleable giftedness of Heaney revealed itself. In Dante's tragic storytelling, in that story of Ugolino who was condemned to starve to death in the tower with his children, Heaney conjures an ether of hunger and protest:

> *Others will pine as I pined in that jail*
> *Which is called Hunger after me, and watch*
> *As I watched through a narrow hole*
> *Moon after moon, bright and somnambulant,*
> *Pass overhead, until that night I dreamt*
> *The bad dream and my future's veil was rent.*
> *I saw a wolf hunt . . .*

In Dante Heaney could see the living metaphors of his own life at that moment. He had moved south into County Wicklow, an inner exile on the island of Ireland. He had moved, not to save his own life but to save his poetry. Flight, hunger, blame, warring cities, princely factions, were all in his mind and what was in his mind at that moment could settle inside Dante's work and Dante's biography. Most of Heaney's poetic decisions were emotional and aesthetic rather than political; he was always true to some deep part of himself, that inner voice of sureness never overheard by others, especially poetic rivals, but revealed elliptically through his choices of translation. Then, of course, there was his curiosity, a sort of youthful questing among books that was part of his lifelong character. More than many others he would succumb to a challenge. Therefore *Sweeney Astray*, his first major work of translation, would be tinkered with and fascinated over until he arrived at a text that somehow fulfilled 'the aspiration of all translation to live a free and independent life':

> *The bushy leafy oak tree*
> *is highest in the wood,*
> *the forking shoots of hazel*
> *hide sweet hazel-nuts.*
>
> *The alder is my darling,*
> *all thornless in the gap,*
> *some milk of human kindness*
> *coursing in its sap.*

The character of Sweeney astray in the woods is the first truly redolent invented character of the Heaney oeuvre. There would be many other such invented and inhabited characters, saints, skeletons, chroniclers, heroes and sacrificial victims in Heaney's translations, none more powerful or real than Beowulf:

> *Beowulf, son of Ecgtheow, spoke:*
> *'Wise sir, do not grieve. It is always better*
> *to avenge dear ones than to indulge in mourning.*
> *For every one of us, living in this world*
> *means waiting for our end. Let whoever can*
> *win glory before death. When a warrior is gone*
> *that will be his best and only bulwark.'*

Heaney was born to make this version of *Beowulf*. His love of Old English and his understanding of the *Beowulf* epic and its lesser but luminous satellites were truly compelling and infectious. He spoke of Beowulf's world as easily as Ausonius played with Greek texts; he knew the material with astonishing comfort, having had the most brilliant teachers at Queen's University. The ease with which he could quote and refer was priest-like. There was something moral in his relationship with this deep material; in it he relived an heroic code and he wanted to bolster our courage as readers the way Beowulf bolstered Hrothgar. In *Beowulf,* as in Columcille's Derry, Heaney found 'transparent angels in every / breath of air'. For Heaney this act of translating was both a shield and a charm.

Heaney's stage instructions for the Chorus in his Field Day *The Cure at Troy* are precise and very Heaneyesque: 'CHORUS discovered, boulder-still, wrapped in shawls. All three in series stir and move, as it were seabirds stretching and unstiffening.' He was not a theatre person as Yeats was, Yeats who knew every nuance and trick of stagecraft. But Heaney knew what theatre design-effects best suited the tone of his own translation: he would insist upon 'a gradual, brightened stillness'. Heaney's version of Sophocles' *Philoctetes* was many years in the writing and reviving. It will probably endure in a kind of shallow public posterity because of the tiresome repetition by politicians on both sides of the Atlantic of those words upon which hope and history rhymes. Soon that phrase might be mercifully placed back upon its shelf to regain its full Sophoclean dignity, for it belongs very specifically and dramatically to its theatrical context. Sonzogni does a superb job here in his historic analysis of the Heaney texts, the multiple versions, excerpts and editions between 1990 and 1997. As Sonzogni notes Heaney's 1990s were 'punctuated by poem-length and award-winning book-length translations from a staggering number of languages: Classical Greek, Czech, Dutch, Old English, Irish, Latin, Polish, Romanian and Russian'. It was a remarkable range and rate of work, punctuated not insignificantly by all the responsibilities created by a Nobel Prize in Literature. In the middle of this noisy decade Heaney published the much quieter 'Lament for Timoleague', his sublime translation of Seán Ó Coileáin's 'Machnamh an Duine Dhoilíosaigh: Caoineadh Thigh Molaige':

> *No meals in refectory,*
>   *No beds in the sleeping quarters,*
> *No order in possession,*
>   *No mass being said at altars.*
>
> *No abbot, rule or office,*
>   *No round of disciplines.*
> *All that remains is a pile*
>   *Of sticky, clay-streaked bones.*
>
> *And then I saw myself*
>   *Like the monastery I mourned for,*
> *Buffeted, exposed,*
>   *And fated to endure.*

This Heaney version is a thing of beauty and a treasure. The great West Cork friary of Timoleague had been founded by the Franciscans in the early fourteenth century and it is celebrated still for the great illuminated Codex prepared by the friars for Finghín Mac Cárthaigh Riabhach. It was taken from the defeated McCarthy prince as a booty of war by Lord Inchiquin's English forces and stored for centuries in Lismore Castle. The Duke of Devonshire, owner of the Lismore Estate, presented the book to the Boole Library at UCC in recent years so that it has, astonishingly, been restored to a house of the Gael. Heaney's translation captures the intense music and the animated religious spirit of the original. The translation is poignantly dedicated to that great old Northerner and early Heaney supporter, Benedict Kiely, and it is lovely to find it here, to see Kiely remembered and a friendship celebrated through one act of deep translation.

There are many such jewels in this book, an important

Thomas McCarthy

book of summation and restoration, this Codex, if you like, of a poetic art illuminated by the golden threads of Heaney's fame. A great deal of the pleasure of this book derives from Marco Sonzogni's Norman Jeffares-like thoroughness of research and note making. How fascinating to discover that the origins of Heaney's lovely poem, 'A Kite for Aibhín' — his last poem in his last collection — lie in the Giovanni Pascoli poem 'L'aquilone' of 1904? Sonzogni tells the full story of this translation superbly, how its origins lie in Heaney's full translation of the Pascoli poem, work done as a gift to Mary Kelleher 'because of her love of Italy, Italian people and Italian culture'. While being honoured at the University of Urbino Heaney was given the text of the Pascoli poem by Professor Gabriella Morisco. The Yeatsian 'Urbino's windy hill' and Heaney's kite are lurking in the Pascoli text. When Heaney read the translation at the 92NY in New York on September 26th, 2011, he told the audience that his poem was 'a translation that has been appropriated' and 'Hibernicized':

> *So now we take our stand, halt opposite*
> *Urbino's windy hill: each scans the blue*
> *And picks the spot to launch his long-tailed comet.*
>
> *And there it hovers, flips, veers, dives askew,*
> *Lifts again, goes with the wind . . .*

The thrill of Heaney's work is that it contains so many such appropriations, fantasias, borrowings and reincarnations. The feel of a poem, the music inside it that should set the water diviner's fork quivering, the soul music that can be carried over from one language to another — all of these things are in Heaney's complete aesthetic, whether in original texts or translations of other texts. It is not so much that poems have been rendered into English but the best, the very best, have been rendered into Heaney-language. His language, so compressed and intense, was the *lingua franca* of a republic with

The Translations of Seamus Heaney

one citizen.

Yes, such a treasure, this book. Here, all of Virgil's *Aeneid Book VI*, published posthumously in 2016, and here, also, a marvellous version of Mario Luzi's 'Il pescatore/The Fisherman' accompanied by Sonzogni's wonderful notes. The complete text here is taken from Luzi's *Persone nel viaggio/ People on a journey*, edited by the indefatigable Alessandro Gentili and published by Valigie Rosse in 2021:

> *I crane my neck*
> *to follow with anxious eyes the fisherman*
> *who comes over to the breakwater and hauls*
> *from the sea what the sea allows,*
> *a few gifts from its never-ending turmoil.*

'What the sea allows' is pure Heaney, with its heroic Norse echoes. But there are many other scattered poetic voices, each voice given a second voice in the mead hall of making as Heaney makes his noble call after noble call, each chosen poet standing a moment in the limelight of his life. No voice is more poignant or beautiful than that of Blandiana, the great Romanian poet. Heaney's marvellous and important versions of Ana Blandiana are a joy to come upon again:

> *Let's talk about*
> *The country we come from.*
> *I am from summer,*
> *A homeland so frail*
> *The fall of a leaf*
> *Could crush it to nothing.*

In translating Blandiana Heaney was responding to literary Romania's urgent need to be heard in its moment of fragmentation and delivery out of communism. That he was there at that historic moment for a Romanian poet, waiting to carry her over into an English audience, speaks volumes for his

Thomas McCarthy

integrity and sense of solidarity.

His sense of duty to others never diminished through his entire life and this is why he responded to John Farleigh's ambitious and unexpected Bloodaxe project in Romanian poetry. Such Heaney commitment is part of the animating power of this book. This is an anthology not just of texts but of encounters and proclamations, all of them detailed here in over 680 pages of translation, notes, bios and bibliographies. Sonzogni's scholarly thoroughness is equal to Heaney's demanding, clairvoyant music. In working so thoroughly upon the Heaney materials Marco Sonzogni has created a powerful assertion of the truth of poetry, and above all things poetry's enduring truth in our age of scoundrels. This book is an important document, therefore, and its ownership should be one of the essential possessions of your literary life.

Poetry Ireland Review,
Summer 2023

Collected Poems: Volumes One and Two by Ciaran Carson

To glance at these two powerful and hefty volumes from a great Ulster poet is to be consumed by an intense sadness. Like Seamus Heaney Ciaran Carson died too young and too soon. He was at the height of his powers as poet and thinker; though it must be said that he was at the height of his powers for many years, almost from the beginning of his life as a published poet. And there wasn't only this fine poetry, but fine music, very fine theoretical writing and very fine descriptive writing on his terrifying, belovèd Belfast. His life and work spans the entirety of the Troubles, the worst and darkest days, the unremitting cruelties and hatreds based upon a slight difference in the interpretations of our one Christ. What he witnessed in his native city was a scandal before God and he wrote to create and perpetuate an alternative poetic music, to capture and assert feelings and belief systems that were more embracing and humane. He was the George Seferis of the Falls Road, a luminescent Mathios Paskalis wandering among the McGredy thorns and roses of this Ulster reality. In truth the 'confetti' he wrote about was not as light as petals:

> *'The subversive half-brick, conveniently hand-sized, is an essential ingredient of the ammunition known as "Belfast confetti", and has been tried and trusted by generations of rioters; it is also known here as* hicker *or a* heeker, *a word which seems to deal in the same currency as* hick, hack *and* howk, *pronounced* hoke *in these parts, meaning to dig or burrow; perhaps*

Thomas McCarthy

> *the defiant badger is in there somewhere after all, related to the superlative* wheeker, *which is another way of saying a* cracker, *something which is outstanding or* sticking out.'

The above quote, which is a single sentence of two semi-colons and ten commas, resonates with Carson's expansive character. The words have a musical quality; there is also an expectation of attention, as one might attend to a complex piece of traditional music. There is always a musician's confidence in this poet: confidence that you will pay attention until the full meaning is revealed. There was almost nothing elliptical in Carson; there was no avoidance. He really meant to be here, with a firm grip upon the instrument played. This is part of the demanding reality of both his poetry and his prose. Even before the long line, before he got into his full stride, Carson knew what he was doing. He was sure of his effect, as in this poem, 'Stitch', from *The New Estate and Other Poems* (1988):

> *A hailstorm drum-roll*
> *Heralded a glimpse*
>
> *Of what I had been*
> *Looking for: not the twin*
> *Of this lost button,*
>
> *But something very like,*
> *Near enough to do,*
> *To speak*
>
> *That moment when the thread*
> *Was loosed, that look.*
> *Lethargic Adam*

Collected Poems: Volumes One and Two by Ciaran Carson

In the Sistine Chapel,
I extend my dangling
Cuff to her:

She sews the button
Back, then snips
The thread.

This Heaneyesque moment predates Heaney's poem of peeling potatoes by about a decade. But it is the same idea, a poet's moment with a mother, a button replaced from the many buttons and threads in her *Quality Street* sweet tin. The delicacy of it and its intimacy is part of Carson's magic. It is very interesting that in later years the poet would return to this shorter line, sometimes a line of one word, more in the manner of William Carlos Williams than C K Williams. Both *On the Night Watch* (2009) and *Until Before After* (2010), as in 'The hinge as hinges':

go
becomes until

between
the one next

and the next
each step

diminishing
the further

on
you go

Such minimalism would have pleased Beckett. In those later years Carson was struggling to reach essences, to write down what was only absolutely essential in both language and recorded feeling. But at this stage it is as well for us to go back, to recap, to map the life of the man who created this prodigious work.

Ciaran Carson was a poet of the Falls Road, born a postman's son, working class and Irish-speaking, fluent and serious about the language. Music was also in the family bloodline, skills with instruments and an easy, very elaborate confidence in the Gaelic song tradition. So this isn't your normal Catholic working class; these were superior people in the social tumult of Ulster life. Carson carried that sureness of touch through his entire life; elegantly attired like a superior jazz musician he proclaimed the grandeur of the Irish race. This cultural centredness, yet outward looking and inclusive, was a towering achievement in his life as Northern Ireland Arts Council's Traditional Arts Officer and Literature Officer, poet and Professor. As a poet he struck early, publishing *The New Estate* with Blackstaff Press in 1976. The Gallery Press published his *The Irish for No* after an interval of a decade and *The New Estate and Other Poems* in 1988. This was the book that consolidated his presence on the Irish literary scene; it was the collection my generation read very carefully. A year later Gallery published *Belfast Confetti* and this book really did extend his influence and his audience. It was a thrilling and original work, a map, a history and a biopsy of the Laganside city in lines that had been stretched and wracked by a frenzied mob of alexandrines:

> *For the present is a tit-for-tat campaign, exchanging now for then,*
> *The Christmas post of Christmas Past, the black armband of the temporary man;*
> *The insignia have mourned already for this casual preserve. Threading*
> *Through the early morning suburbs and the monkey-puzzle trees, a smell of coffee lingers,*

Collected Poems: Volumes One and Two by Ciaran Carson

Imprisoned in the air like wisps of orange peel in
  marmalade; and sleigh-bell music
Tinkles on the radio, like ice cubes in a summer drink.
  I think I'm starting, now,
To know the street map with my feet, just like my father.
('Ambition')

It is difficult to describe the effect of this kind of poetry. It is not Muldoon as some reviewers seemed to imply, most definitely not. It is another voice, different, attempting to stretch language with added information, which is what the best poets do, adding to our handbook of descriptions so that language seems new woven. A good poet renews the language of poetry and by the late 1980s Ciaran Carson was that good. As poet he had sidled up to the First Class cabin to share MacNeice's august company. At this stage he must have understood how good he was. Certainly there were poets in my orbit who knew how good he was, poet Theo Dorgan, for example, who has remained a fervent advocate of Carson's poetry and prose. Carson's memory of music may have been a memory of last night's fun, but it was also the memory of a way of life, as he would write in *Last Night's Fun*:

> '*So, I remember fiddle-players with cigarettes poised between two fingers of their bow-hand, and the ash would wave and sprinkle in a silent musicology across their trouser-knees; or the cigarette that drooped between a player's lips would let drop a little grub of ash into an f-hole of the fiddle, where it disintegrated as it crashed into the ersatz 'Stradivari' label. Then knees were dusted off, someone rosined up, and a fitful shaft of sunlight would illuminate the dust-motes like a dissolute snowstorm souvenir.*'

His collections, this two-volume *Collected* here, buzz, swing and syncopate with musical intensities, but it is the deep music of the human voice that was his first and last instrument. Many poems begin when a conversation begins, in real time or in reported speech. Life happens in the intervals between music:

> *You're not from around here, I said. No, from elsewhere,*
>   *you said.*
> *As from another language, I might have said, but*
>   *did not.*
>   *('Pas de Deux')*

or

> *And I've this problem, talking to a man whose mouth is*
>   *a reflection.*
> *I tend to think words will come out backwards, so I'm*
>   *saying nothing.*
>   *('Queen's Gambit')*

Of smoking, of the willingness to speak, of offering the companionship of conversation, these are the perpetual Carson loops:

> Cast a spell
>
> *on me*
> *wrap me in*
>
> *whatever*
> *warp of words*
>
> *come to*
> *your mouth*
>
> *until I gulp*
> *them whole . . .*

Collected Poems: Volumes One and Two by Ciaran Carson

Those changes of line length, switching of poetic key, accumulate over time into a thrilling range, a sure sign not just of extensive and thoughtful reading, but of an ear constantly alert to cadences, to ebbs and flows in a poem's possibility. All the while he 'was trying to complete a sentence in my head, but it kept stuttering, / All the alleyways and side streets blocked with stops and colons.' His work is a truly fine elocution, but with effort: language in his work is always elegantly attired and fiercely prepared for its public moment.

It's not surprising that Carson became a highly respected Professor at Queen's University, but that was after his long cigarette-saturated career as Traditional Music Officer with the NI Arts Council. He was an able poet, never a shrinking violet, and he did astonishing work to stretch and expand the Ulster scene. There was always a public service element in his view of necessary action and he was a true master of public instruction. There were urgent, hidden things that he wished to be known, not just about poetry but about the universal nature of all music. He was an advocate as well as a poet; in this public advocacy as in his poetry he was sure and fearless.

The two Gallery Press volumes here are also sure and fearless. They claim their space on our bookshelves as of right. They are also a magnificent event in Irish publishing, over a thousand pages of poetry and translation from one of the finest poets of Northern Europe in the late twentieth and early twenty-first centuries. They fit perfectly into that great Gallery Ulster canon of the Montague *Collected* and the Mahon *Collected*. In Volume Two we get not just the last moving collection, *Still Life*, from 2019, but the poems of *From Elsewhere* (2014), his incomparably beautiful versions of the dense and elusive French poet, Jean Follain, a collection poignantly dedicated to his students at Queen's. He had come to Follain by accident, through a conversation on the poetry of Ponge with Frank Ormsby at Dennis O'Driscoll's funeral. Alerted to Follain's existence through a subsequent study of Ponge materials he found his first Follain poem on the internet — the poem 'Soulier renouée/Shoelace Tied' which is the first poem in his collection from Follain:

> ... and a boy in an iron-grey smock
> bows to a rut
> to tie his shoelace
> no slack in his life
> no trace of absence.

In a 2016 *Ploughshares* (Emerson College) interview Carson emphasized the visual quality of Follain's work, of Follain's ability to create vignettes in a landscape haunted by ghosts. He was also attracted by Follain's 'avoidance of any straightforward resolution to the ominous and resonant situations set forth in his poems'. That Follain could speak through 'things', whether a shoelace or a poster or a globe, was also immensely attractive to Carson whose poetry is saturated with not so much 'things' as *possessions* like a biscuit tin, an Omega watch, a violin or a 1931 Waterman fountain pen. For Follain, stubborn and legalistic, language could only mean the one thing, words were the French thingness of things such as bread 'Le pain' or wine 'Le vin', and there was no English equivalence: the object in the word belonged to its own 'terroir' only. This refusal to accept the reality of any translated world must have been both provocative and thrilling to a poet like Carson: a poet who lived easily in two languages. But *From Elsewhere* is not just a series of translations of the Normandy master poet, it is a dialogue between these two poets of two worlds, carefully, even obsessively, arranged. His act of translating is an act of 'fetching', as he goes on to explain the act in nautical terms: 'I fetched myself in the wake of Follain, and hence fetched my course, like a sailor who after a long fetch at sea comes home with a farfetched tale ... So I find myself in the other of Follain, questing and fetching the poems from another language, from the elsewhere of his poetry.' That Jean Follain, aged 68, was knocked down and killed by a car on Place de la Concorde while returning home from a dinner dedicated to collectors of printed ephemera only added to the sacerdotal importance of a poet's possessions:

> A rooftop then the star
> paling over
> caught the eye of a man
> who felt himself taken back
> to the endgame of a legal process
> the signs below
> unveiled their words of gold,
> wood, iron, stone
> imposed their presence
> ('L'aube: The Dawn')

The whole farfetched project had created a terrifically ambitious book and re-reading the poems now in the *Collected* is to be reminded how successful that encounter between Carson and Jean Follain really was. It was a recognition of similar instincts, a poetic marriage made through things. The rightness of the encounter has only deepened over time, the wine of the French poetry grown richer in its Belfast cellar, waiting in hope for *Le belle journée* of an Ulster readership. And it only added to that impressive fetching from the French as, in 1998, Gallery had published his *The Alexandrine Plan*, those very individualistic and vexatious renderings of Mallarmé, Bauledaire and Rimbaud. In 2002 he translated *The Inferno* of Dante, a book that won the Oxford-Weidenfeld Translation Prize. In 2005 he published a version of Merriman's Rabelaisian *Cúirt an Mheán Oíche*, and two years later his version of *The Táin* became a Penguin Classic. So those years of late middle age were intensely creative years for Carson, a kind of harvesting of everything that was latent within. Those years from 1998 to 2008 were sensationally productive; in that decade he blazed a vapour trail of superb books, including *The Alexandrine Plan, The Twelfth of Never, Breaking News* and

Thomas McCarthy

For All We Know.
   By the time he reached his sixties his poetic line had shortened again as if he'd been restored to a much earlier poetic. *On the Night Watch* (2009) and *Until Before After* (2010) both make use of a much more modernist East Coast American line; both books are characterized by a poetry of essences and essentials. Long-lined garrulous conversation has ended for the poet and a bone-dry, rinsed poetic is at play:

I Ask Myself

what are you
eyebright

flower
of the field

that speaks
her name

without a word
to me . . .

This is an essential poetic, the placing, pacing and pausing absolutely crucial in the vast unforgiving acreage of white space on each page. There is no room for error in this kind of poetry; sloppiness of both thought and pacing is quickly exposed. A musical training, the sure placing of pause and interval, works wonders for Ciaran Carson in these books. The sure placement of 'eyebright' and 'flower' and 'that speaks' is a signal that we are in the hands of a master; no line is arbitrary because every phrase has to be essential. In either of these collections a reader could choose any three poems at random, re-read them, and then realize that the effect is the same. The poet has not so much abandoned the long line as changed a key in music. But the key is consistent, the pacing no longer one of easy fluency but one of adamant high pitch. Look, here:

> It's one of those
>
> *tunes with*
> *a backstitch in it*
>
> *into its*
> *beginning re-*
>
> *negotiating what*
> *you thought*
>
> *it was eluding*
> *you the first time*
>
> *round the scale . . .*

There are poems that mirror and echo this effect everywhere in both collections. The voice is pure and the method is sure. Imaginatively those must have been great years for Carson. Which brings us to the last collection of this monumental *Collected*: 'Strange how a smear of colour, like a perfume, resurrects the memory / Of another, that which I meant to begin with.'

What he meant to begin with, in *Still Life* (2019), was a recollection of William Carlos Williams' poem upon the Asphodel, 'that greeny flower'. With an old pencil in hand he writes 'Claude Monet, Artist's Garden at Vétheuil, 1880':

> *The days are getting longer now, however many of them*
>   *I have left.*
> *And the pencil I am writing this with, old as it is, will*
>   *easily outlast their end.*

Thomas McCarthy

That the pencil would keep going on was important, though the smear of colour, the green and yellow of a pot of daffodils upended in the front garden at Glandore Avenue is what inspires the poem; the poem is not just a meditation upon Monet's garden but a meditation upon things that survive beyond time and accident. Like Seán Ó Ríordáin detained in his sick bed at Inniscarra this Belfast poet of the Gael also considers the delicate universe: 'Because when looking at a thing we often drift into a memory of something else, / However tenuous the link.' The poet is detained by illness and physical decline but his bed is placed in a cathedral of art: 'And so we come to talk of how we take our bearings from the moment / Of a painting, where everything is at a standstill,' he writes, now drifting, afloat on painted canvas, fetching epiphanies from Monet, Poussin, Canaletto, Angela Hackett and a host of others. The poems are marvellous, unfailing, crowded with good company. Art speaks through him and he speaks through art, creating a world as companionable as a book of Sholem Aleichem stories.

These two volumes of Carson's *Collected* are important books, not just as teaching instruments upon the writing of very fine poems, but as the true, authentic memoir of a Belfast genius. They soar and take flight before your eyes so that a reader would need to be both tone-deaf and culturally ignorant not to respond with a sense of immediate belonging, of instant recognition. Here is all of the art of poetry you will ever need, powerfully assembled by The Gallery Press. With Ciaran Carson the bow was well rosined, 'The sax's bell was beaten gold.'

Poetry Ireland Review,
Summer 2024

PART FIVE
THE QUESTION OF CORK

James Barry, 'Self-Portrait as Timanthes'

All through the 1990s each train journey I made became a pilgrimage to this one painting. I visited Dublin regularly to attend Board meetings of Poetry Ireland, a national organization that was then expanding its influence under its Director, the poet Theo Dorgan. I always tried to arrive at Heuston Station well ahead of our meetings because I needed to commune with that other innovative native of Water Lane, Cork, the artist James Barry. Theo Dorgan had been born at the top of Water Lane, now Redemption Road, close to the Palace of the Bishop of Cork and Ross, while the fiery and troublesome James Barry had been reared near the base of the same road. Each time on my Dublin pilgrimage I ran straight through the door of the National Gallery, then left . . . left again . . . and there it was, in all its orchestral, romantic glory, one of the most naked self-portraits ever imagined by an Irish genius. Here is art as European as anything by David and as vulnerable as anything by James Joyce. The shocked and haunted eyes of the mythical and elusive painter Timanthes interrogated me and found me wanting. None of us could ever measure up to the ambitions of Barry; none of us could ever answer such yearning from this furtive agent of the Enlightenment. Here the artist stands back, rudely interrupted by our ignorant presence, holding the oils of the gods at the feet of Hercules who tramples the serpent of Envy. This is not the smooth Barry with Paine and Lefevre, painted in 1767, or the Barry seated beneath the heroes of his great Royal Society of Arts wall painting 'Crowning the Victors at Olympia' from 1777-84. This is a mythic and dramatically self-aware Barry; this is the self-aggrandizing artist, the allegorical creator who has suffered for us — in the manner, as William Presley points out, of Angelica Kauffmann's 'Self-Portrait of the Artist Hesitating between the Arts of Music and Painting'.

We must all stand back from this work and feel ashamed that we have not done more for art and truth. Scholars have construed the loosened black ribbon at Barry's neck as the shadow of the guillotine, the fate that awaits all counter-revolutionaries. I beg to disagree: I've never bought that. Surely it is art unbuttoned, bindings loosened, the breath of life upon an exposed neck. The head of Envy's serpent barks like a dog against Barry's/Timanthes' right ear, but the artist's eyes appeal to us not to heed this voice of Envy, but to accept Pan's pipes and the timeless offering of the Greek landscape. Barry took his Hercules and his Envy from a reading of Horace, but the extraordinary juxtaposition of antiquity and informality, of Art within art and of the troubled Corkman himself as a mythical character, are pure Barry — the product of a desperate provincial auto-didact. Hercules would triumph over Envy by dying as Barry triumphed over orthodoxy by suffering various kinds of expulsion. Explaining himself, Barry wrote, 'envy should continually haunt and persecute the greatest characters; though for the time, it may give them uneasiness, yet it tends on the one hand to make them more perfect, by obliging them to weed out whatever may be faulty . . .'

Nothing painted by James Barry was ever flawless — his drawing of hands is always poor — yet every oil of his contained more ambiguous brilliance and politics than anything by Reynolds or Fuseli. (See! Just a few minutes with Barry and I am making aggressive and unsupported observations!) He conversed only in extremities and his ambitions for British art were unhinged by the breadth of his vision. He was an Irishman, yet he wanted the best for the English mind. His London efforts to extract the best from British possibilities would destroy him mentally and vocationally. This is the portrait of an artist who has suffered from an extreme

James Barry, 'Self-Portrait as Timanthes'

ambition. The eyes tell us that he has been painted into a corner. Here the artist as a cornered Timanthes marks a point of irreversible decline in the fortunes of the painter. Despite the exceptional kindness of friends in the RSA, whose Great Room he had immortalized in the 1770s, Barry would isolate himself and retreat down the Thames to Greenwich, into a house with broken windows and darkened printing presses.

Nearly a decade has passed since we all stood around the plaque in the crypt of St Paul's Cathedral in London to commemorate the bicentenary of Barry's death. Now the scholar William Presley's words are ringing in my ears: his belief that Barry's huge wall paintings in the Royal Society's Great Room are actually a piece of sustained Roman Catholic propaganda. Great art forces us to grapple with its content, rather than merely look and say 'oh' and move on. But I'm not sure if it matters, or let me put it another way: it doesn't matter to me. I'm never too worried about what art means; I've always been more conscious of what it does to me, what it says in a human way. I'm constantly saying 'oh' and refusing to move on. A poet could be saturated with Barry; I mean any poet could come away dripping with history and historic associations. But that would be to miss the point, and the power, of this great painting of Timanthes. This is a deeply personal work of art; it is full of yearning and human wariness. It is very much the metaphor for an artistic life of any kind. And it doesn't have a citizenship or a religion: we are all hunted, as Timanthes was, and we are all nervously awaiting our destiny, as Barry constantly was. I feel for him and I feel for this painting because I know his luck ran out several times. I still love to come upon it. It speaks to me of many lost connections and that foolish yearning to hurry up and finish some all-consuming work of art.

This painting is one of the gems in our National Gallery. It is worth taking any long journey to come upon this triumph of antiquity and revolution, of political camouflage and artistic nakedness. When I stand by this painting my political faith

Thomas McCarthy

in the artistic life is restored completely.

*Lines of Vision: Irish Writers on Art,
Janet McLean (ed),
2014*

'Like Maginn, a Corcagian': Bad Company for Daniel Maclise

'A word as to the etchings of D Maclise, R A. This great artist in his boyhood knew Prout and has fixed his true features in enduring copper. The only reliable outline of Sir Walter Scott, as he appeared in plain clothes, and without ideal halo, may be seen on page 54, where he "kisses the Blarney Stone" on his visit to Prout in the summer of 1825.'

Thus wrote Francis Sylvester Mahony in his Preface to the 1860 edition of his *Reliques of Father Prout*, published in a single volume as part of Bohn's *Illustrated Library*. The work had been originally published in two volumes in 1836 by James Fraser of Regent Street, London, and neither author nor illustrator had placed their names to that edition. Maclise then signed off as 'Alfred Croquis, Esq' and Mahony as 'Father Prout', the fictional parish priest of Watergrasshill, County Cork, whose writings had been 'edited' by the equally fictitious Oliver Yorke of the minor nobility. There was once a real parish priest called Prout but his death before 1830 provided the mischievous Frank Mahony with a pretext for a complex fiction worthy of Flann O'Brien. In his essay 'Dean Swift's Madness' Mahony's fictional Father Prout recounts how he was a love child of Dean Swift and 'Stella' who was kidnapped from his doting mother by Woods of the infamous 'Woods' halfpence' and deposited in a ditch near Watergrasshill: 'I had an appendage round my neck — a trinket, which I still cherish, and by which I eventually found a clue to my real patronage. It was a small locket of my mother Stella's hair, of raven black (a distinctive feature of her beauty, which had especially captivated the Dean): around this locket was a Latin motto of my gifted father's composition, three simple words, but beautiful in their simplicity — "Prout Stella Refulges". So that, when I was taken into the Cork Foundling Hospital I was at once christened "Prout" from the adverb that begins the sentence . . . ' Eventually, in a Dickensian twist, the child Prout steals away from the Foundling Hospital in a milk churn, after which he is taken in and reared by the good people of Watergrasshill, that parish where he will eventually become parish priest.

This was the era of high mischief in London journalism and fiction writing, an era of journals, clubs, circles, Whig and Tory factions, invective and baroque excess of language, humour, quotation and random translation. The first edition of *Reliques* does not contain Prout's remembrance of James Barry in Rome, perhaps in deference to the presence of a real Cork artist, Maclise, among the staff, nor did the original two-volume edition of Mahony's work contain the great cartoon of the contributors to *Fraser's Magazine*. The Fraserian circle, at that moment, was still lost in the excessive energy of itself. Maclise's famous etching, published in *Fraser's* in 1835, was only added to Mahony's *Reliques of Father Prout* in 1860, thus intensifying and extending the myth-making and retrospective glory of the serious writers, as well as the hacks, who contributed to that famous magazine in its glory years of 1830 to 1838.

> 'The banquet he has depicted was no fiction, but a frequent fact in Regent Street, 212. Dr Maginn in the chair, addressing the staff contributors, has on his right, Barry Cornwall (Procter), Robert Southey, Percival Banks, Thackeray, Churchill, Sergeant Murphy, Macnish, Ainsworth, Coleridge, Hogg, Galt, Dunlop and Jerdan. Fraser is croupier, having on his right Crofton Croker, Lockhart, Theodore Hood, Sir David Brewster, Dr Moir (Delta), Tom Carlyle, Count D'Orsay (talking to Allan Cunningham), Sir

'Like Maginn, a Corcagian': Bad Company for Daniel Maclise

Egerton Brydges; Rev G R Gleig, chaplain of the Chelsea hospital; Rev F Mahony, Rev Edward Irving (of the unknown tongues), a frequent writer in Fraser, and frequenter of his sanctum, where 'oft of a stilly night' he quaffed glenlivat with the learned Editor.'

When Mahony wrote that second Preface in Paris on 20 November 1859 only nine of the 27 Fraserians captured by Maclise were still living, including Thackeray, Sir David Brewster, Rev G R Gleig, by then Chaplain General of H M Forces, and Mahony's old Clongowes' friend, Sergeant (Stack) Murphy, by then an insolvency commissioner. (Mahony had only counted eight as surviving in 1860, but he forgot that William Jerdan, who lived to the ripe old age of 88, was very much alive.) Jerdan would recall Maginn vividly in volume three of his four-volume autobiography, published in 1852. These writers had been distinguished company for the young Daniel Maclise from Sheares Street, Cork, to fall upon in the early 1830s, but by 1860 Maclise's name could hold its own with any distinguished artist or writer in England.

The Fraserian circle was a motley but spiritually rich crew. Jerdan had established *The Literary Gazette* in 1817 and was a famous party giver. There is a letter from Maclise to Crofton Croker who was, at that time, visiting Cork, describing a Jerdan party: 'I was at another party at Jerdan's which, for length of duration, fairly rivalled the preceding one; dancing until the cool blue gleam of morning intruded through the crevices of the shutters into the hot yellow room.' Another Fraserian, the dandy Count D'Orsay, had famously married the daughter of Lord Blessington and run up debts of £120,000, while another, Lanarkshire-born John Lockhart, had married the eldest daughter of Sir Walter Scott and was long-time Editor of the *Quarterly Review*. John Galt was the author of *A Life of Byron*; Percival Banks, the lawyer, married Maclise's younger sister, Anna; Thomas Carlyle, born in Dumfriesshire, became an overwhelmingly powerful, provocative and brilliant essayist; Thackeray had begun contributing to *Fraser's Magazine* when he was only 23; there he wrote under five pseudonyms, including Ikey Solomons and Michael Angelo Titmarsh. While living in Paris in the 1830s Thackeray had married a Doneraile woman, Isabella Creagh Shawe, and it was Rev Francis Mahony who 'got the little house together for the young couple'.

But there were many other contributors with a very strong bias towards Scotland and Scottish education. Presiding over that ménage of brilliant, over-educated talkers in Regent Street was the caustic and clubbish Corkman, William Maginn, son of the famous Dr Maginn of Cobh. Maginn had taken a doctorate at Trinity College, Dublin, in 1811. After working for several years in his father's famous school in Cork (where a young Maclise could have been his student) he moved to London where he worked on Blackwood's *Magazine* and began his execrable *Homeric Ballads* which were eventually published in *Fraser's*. These were Homeric poems translated into popular ballad metre instead of the more usual iambic pentameter. They were praised by Gladstone and Matthew Arnold but, as W B Stanford observed in *Ireland and the Classical Tradition*, 'When one reads them now it is hard to see how they escaped instant condemnation.' But Maginn was an indefatigable worker who could write, on average, 2,500 words in a single sitting. It was partly due to his prodigious work rate that *Fraser's* was a huge success, selling 8,700 copies per issue by the end of its first year. In *Rebellious Fraser's*, Miriam M H Thrall has written:

> 'Among Maginn's most engaging triumphs was that of employing the magazine's young artist, Daniel Maclise, to sketch the more prominent of the Fraserians seated about the round table at a staff dinner in the publisher's back parlour... From the first, Maginn had liked the Round Table. It had, he explained, literary association of high and ancient story, making

'Like Maginn, a Corcagian': Bad Company for Daniel Maclise

for equality and fraternity, like its prototype in King Arthur's hall at Camelot. Above all, it was a big and hospitable board, around which any of the Fraserians who happened to be in London could sit at convivial ease till dawn streaked the east and even James Fraser's goodly supply of drink and meat ran low. For they were great trenchermen, this gay, brilliant staff of "Regina". And the best man among them was perhaps that famous concocter of whiskey punch, the blithering Irish editor, alias Sir Morgan O'Doherty, Adjutant — Billy Maginn, the "Doctor" himself.'

After his arrival in London Maclise fell firstly into the benign circle of Thomas Crofton Croker, 'to give him his whole name', as William Bates wrote. He was, like Maginn, a Corcagian, and was born in the 'beautiful city' on the 15th January 1798. His first visit in England was paid to Thomas Moore in Wiltshire and, soon after his arrival in London, he received from John Wilson Croker, a namesake (but no relation), the appointment at the Admiralty, which he held for nearly thirty-five years, retiring in 1850 as senior clerk of the first class. At first Croker had hero-worshipped Tom Moore, even inscribing a chair he owned that Moore had sat upon, an act that led Rev Francis Mahony (who hated Moore) to write:

This is to tell o' days when on this cathedra,
He of the 'Melodies' solemnly sat, agrah!

Croker's circle included Mr and Mrs S C Hall (poor Mr Hall had been hounded into exile by William Maginn's insults over his heavy Cork accent, only to discover that Maginn had also moved to London to continue the torture), Miss Edgeworth, Samuel Lover, the poet Miss Landon ('L E L was one of Maclise's most enthusiastic worshippers. The friendship between them was honourable to both. The Painter has drawn for posterity the only portrait of the Poetess that exists — a perfect gem of art; and the Poetess has repaid him by this, one of the sweetest of her poems) and last, but not least, Father Prout (Mahony).

But Maclise also made the acquaintance of 'The Doctor', Maginn, who had moved from Blackwood's *Magazine* to found *Fraser's*. In his entry on Maclise in the *Dictionary of National Biography* John Turpin wrote 'Maclise was thoroughly at home in the world of writers and literary culture . . . ' The first of Maclise's contributions to Maginn's new magazine appeared in the fifth volume in June 1830. It was an outline portrait of William Jerdan, the first of that famous 'Gallery of Illustrious Literary Characters'. (As Maginn noted, 'William Jerdan was born in Scotland about the year 1730. The first seventy or eighty years of his life he spent in the usual dissipations of youth . . . ' The misinformation was typical of *Fraser's*: Jerdan was born at Kelso in 1782.) Maclise's portraits, a perfect foil to Maginn's commentary, became a unique selling point for the journal creating, as it did, a distinctive flavour of a milieu, a true companionship in letters. By the time the magazine had reached its fifteenth volume eighty-one portraits had appeared. But Maginn began to fret that some of the subjects were not that *illustrious*, so he let the Gallery lie fallow. No portraits appeared in volumes fifteen and sixteen, and only two in volume seventeen. Both the portraits and the captions were without signatures until February 1832 when 'Alfred Croquis' appeared beneath the portrait of Ettrick Shepherd. When Maclise finally withdrew from the task of literary portraiture Maginn paid tribute to him in volume twenty-one of *Fraser's Magazine*:

> 'But can we part from our Gallery without saying a word or two about him to whose pencil we are indebted for it — our old and much-honoured friend, Croquis? . . . He is rising every year to higher honours and renown, and displaying fresh proofs of unwearied genius; and though the pictures which he exhibits are

> *of greater splendour and loftier aspiration, yet, in their own way, we maintain that the sketches of Croquis display as much talent as any production of the best RA or ARA of the lot, '-ay, even if you named Maclise himself.'*

The 'Portrait Gallery' of Maclise was an innovation in British publishing as Miriam Thrall has pointed out. It was the first attempt by a London magazine to give intimate, informative and provocative portraits of prominent living writers. Maginn's notes to each Maclise sketch were sharp, barbed, humorous and pitiless in their exposures of writers' faults and foibles. And 'Maclise's pen-and-ink drawings of the victims are scarcely less punitive,' wrote Thrall. 'Although at the time a boy, and entirely unknown, the nimble satirist was already at the height of his power. Nowhere in his later work was he to show more delicacy and firmness than in these early drawings for *Fraser's*.'

Years later Paris-based Mahony's Preface to his 1860 edition of *The Reliques of Father Prout*, along with the insertion of Maclise's group portrait of the Fraserians as a folding-paper frontispiece, reawakened interest in the pencil portraits of Daniel Maclise. William Bates, then Professor of Classics at Birmingham, replied to a query in 'Notes and Queries' on 11 March 1871, and D G Rossetti presented a paper in the Academy of 15 April 1871 in which he wrote:

> *'... no such series of the portraits of the celebrated of any epoch, produced by an eye and hand of so much insight and power, and realised with such a view to the actual impression of the sitter, exists anywhere... Both in rendering of character, whether in its first aspect or subtler shades, and in the unfailing knowledge of form, which seizes at once on the movement of the body beneath the clothes, and on the lines of the clothes themselves, these drawings are on an in-*

calculably higher level than the works of even the best professional sketchers. Indeed, no happier instance could well be found of the unity for literary purposes of what may be justly termed 'style' with an incisive and relishing realism.'

Indeed it was Maclise's sketch work that had first brought him to the light of day as a youth in Cork. Richard Sainthill, merchant and antiquarian, or it could have been the humble Mrs Spratt, had spotted a sketch by Maclise in his father's cobbler's shop in Nile Street (Sheares Street) in 1821. A Sainthill led to a Penrose of Woodhill House, owner of Barry's 'Venus Rising from the Sea' and Angelica Kauffman's 'The Return of Telemachus'. All of which led by various routes of Newenham, Dr Woodroffe and Bolster's Bookshop, to a famously elaborate pencil drawing of Sir Walter Scott in August 1825. In his essay 'Daniel Maclise and Cork Society' John Turpin has written:

'On Bolster's advice, Maclise decided to have the portrait lithographed as it had attracted some attention, but since there was no press in Cork, he prepared tracings, which were used in the making of a lithograph in Dublin. Apparently, five hundred copies were printed and sold rapidly . . . The exhibited drawing of Scott and the subsequent edition of lithographs established Maclise's local reputation in Cork as a portrait draughtsman.'

In 1873 the *Maclise Portrait-Gallery of Illustrious Literary Characters*, with the old Fraser notes chiefly by William Maginn, was collated and edited by William Bates and published by Chatto & Windus, London. It was reprinted twice. But it was through the connection with Rev Francis Sylvester Mahony's *Reliques of Father Prout*, published in several editions in London and New York in 1836, 1860, 1873, 1886, 1901

'Like Maginn, a Corcagian': Bad Company for Daniel Maclise

and 1904, that the Fraserian circle, including those 'youthful Corkers', had their posterity extended at a time when a more urgent, Nationalist posterity was being created within Ireland and Irish America. By the time Douglas Hyde's Gaelic League (where the round table was now occupied by a sworn knighthood of IRB men) had completed its national task, and the almost simultaneous fictional-rhetorical reaction of O'Connor and Ó Faoláin had burgeoned forth, the political ambiguity, loquaciousness and Englishness of Maclise, Maginn and Mahony had caused an entire generation of real literary life to slip beneath our aesthetic Catholic Irish (patriotic or revisionist) radar. Neither Corkery nor O'Connor, Peadar Ó Laoghaire nor Seán Ó Ríordáin seemed aware of what had gone on in Cork, mainly Protestant Cork, in the century before them.

It was the outsiders, the technical desperados of Irish literature, Joyce and Beckett, who would interiorize the linguistic, classical pyrotechnics of Mahony and Maginn. Clongowes-educated Joyce would have Stephen Dedalus deconstruct 'The Bells of Shandon' in *Portrait of the Artist*, even as his father had tears in his drunken eyes, and parody Mahony's anthology of styles in *Ulysses*, while Beckett would make a pilgrimage to Prout's tomb before leaving Ireland and set a chapter of *Murphy* in Shandon churchyard. Those linguistic men, the language writers, knew of a more luminous, Irish, narrative possibility than our politically-driven fiction writers. Insight, as classically trained Mahony and Maginn well knew, could be contained within the style of Beckett's 'Precordial,' said Murphy, 'rather than cordial. Tired. Cork County. Depraved.'

Today, we are neither politically not aesthetically equipped to appreciate the extraordinary first impact of *Fraser's Magazine*, both its literary and its graphical impulses and power. Our Cork-born children will be even less inclined to understand them. But the achievement of that circle of ambitious Corkmen stands firmly still as a monument to the crowded early nineteenth century — that ambiguous cultural space between the Act of Union in 1800 and *The Nation* of Thomas Davis in 1848. There was a particular historic moment, among a few others, perhaps, when a bridge into the Catholic life of Ireland (the people of O'Connell and Davis) presented itself for Maclise and his intellectual London companions. That was the excursion to, the retreat from, and the memory of Maclise's work, 'Snap Apple Night, or All-Hallow' Eve', engraved by James Scott and published in 1837. This was a picture of Father Matthew Horgan PP's wonderfully open-spirited gathering in Blarney on All Hallows' Eve, a festive night where gentry and ordinary Irish country people gathered unselfconsciously. Exhibited in 1833 the picture is a crowded tableau of Irish celebration — buxom girl and stalwart Blarney boy, fiddler and piper, and happy chaos. In many ways it created in the work of Maclise a permanent acceptance of Ireland as a backdrop, a theatre curtain, because the real actors, the faces that speak personally to the onlooker, the figures foregrounded, are Sir Walter Scott, Percival Banks (Maclise's brother-in-law) and Crofton Croker. Years later, in a typical Irish political act of readjusting the biography of the image, the folklorist-scholar Séamus Ó Casaide 'tackled' Maclise's painting in *Béaloideas*:

> 'Father Matt was a lover of Irish poetry and music and of Irish games, outdoor and indoor. He was the soul of hospitality, and maintained a permanent sean-chaidhe *(storyteller) in his house, a man named Ó Súilleabháin. On the occasion of Sir Walter Scott's brief visit to Cork in 1825, it is more than likely that Father Matt intended to entertain him at a typically Irish gathering in Blarney, such as that so well depicted by Maclise. But Scott had only time for a hurried visit to the famous Blarney Stone.'*

Through personal memory, naming, contextualizing the

'Like Maginn, a Corcagian': Bad Company for Daniel Maclise

estranged text of an Academy painting (a depiction of his people), Ó Casaide aimed to restore the complete, as opposed to caricatured, likeness of an Irish snap-apple night. Up the road in Bowen's Court and at her London flat Elizabeth Bowen was reaffirming at that very moment during the War the centrality of her own class experiences in Irish history by writing the definitive social history of her Cork Ascendancy family in Bowen's Court. Big House, Fraser iconoclasts and Blarney barn, all contained versions of Irish life. Each life, in turn, would be subject to versions of caricature, to a vectored, politicized description. But Maclise's Fraserian sketch work survives for all of us, beneath the mythologized canvas and oil, as a simple neoclassical footbridge between the literary and geographical heritage of Ireland during that special half-century, 1800 to 1847. Maclise took directions like a stonemason: while no writer could cut the stone like him, he depended upon others for the arrangement of the plaques.

Maclise's sketching, pen portraiture and illustration is as much a matter of temperament as of business. As a Corkman, son of a Presbyterian shoemaker, he had more than one Irish story to tell. He needed instruction to complete mythologies, to organize his artistic impulse. His work reminds us of how Irish writers so completely dominated the thinking of Irish artists. Irish pen and pigment, at moments of severe national stress, seem incapable of creating their own narratives. Irish artists do seem to gravitate towards writers in a kind of Pavlovian, legitimizing response. Should Irish artists have a subject matter without poets, a non-mythologized aesthetic that arises only from a hermetic relationship with pen, clay, canvas and pigment? These questions are as urgent in Maclise and Mahony/Maginn as in Joyce/Yeats and Louis le Brocquy. While the duty of literary historians may be to collate and remember it may be the more radical duty of Irish art to learn forgetfulness, to disengage from national narratives of any kind. Perhaps because we live in such a small country where there is a narrative cross-infection and a cramped personal politics, literature and talk will always dominate and colour the other artforms and disciplines. Even at the present time the continuous dialogue in the nomination for membership and speeches from the floor of Aosdána does indicate an affecting warmth between literary and visual disciplines in Irish life.

Certainly, at various stages of his career, Maclise came to fame through literature — by sketching Scott, by learning how to create effective caricatures in ink through reading caricatures in paragraphs by Maginn and Mahony. His work can never be disentangled from those luminous narratives. It is crowded with history: Catholic and Presbyterian histories swill around inside his work like pieces of lemon and cloves in an Irish hot whiskey. Like whiskey the art has both warmth and intoxication. The imprint of literary activity does saturate his life, as it saturated his youth. As Nancy Weston has observed, 'Mahony's witty and playful personality pointed him in a clearly satiric direction and Maclise's drawings followed suit' and, 'Although his admiration for living authors kept Maclise from entering into Maginn's jibes and sarcasms in *Fraser's*, he joined wholeheartedly with Mahony in *The Reliques of Father Prout*.'

Weston points out that while at work on illustrating Mahony's essays Maclise was also working on illustrations for John Barrow's *Tour Round Ireland, through the Sea-coast Counties in the Autumn of 1835*. (Barrow, like Crofton Croker, also worked at the Admiralty.) But, without Rev Francis Mahony's witty and domineering personality to guide him, Maclise failed, according to Weston, to create a consistent visual narrative. As an illustrator Maclise needed instructions rather than a free hand. Unlike James Barry Maclise disliked journeys into the unknown; dialogue around subject matter was crucial to his art. The decline of his later life, the exhaustion and depression, is certainly characterized by the loss of important youthful dialogues. Of Maclise's relationship with *Fraser's Magazine* Weston has written:

'Like Maginn, a Corcagian': Bad Company for Daniel Maclise

> '*Maclise's subordination to the commanding personality of the older Maginn was noticed by contemporaries. Rossetti wrote of Maclise that " . . . he was doubtless as a young man then, a good deal under the influence of association with the reckless magazine-staff, among whom he worked in this instance."*'

John Turpin has, on a number of occasions, emphasized Maclise's particular gift as an illustrator, but not merely of books by Irish authors like Mahony, Thomas Moore and Crofton Croker: 'Maclise distinguished himself as a book illustrator of texts by British writers, illustrating Edward Bulwer Lytton's *The Pilgrims of the Rhine* (1834) and his *Leila, or The Siege of Granada* (1838) — an orientalist romance — and Milton's *L'Allegro* and *Il Penseroso* in S C Hall's *Book of Gems* (1836).' In his essay, 'Maclise as a Book Illustrator', Turpin has noted that:

> '*There is a strongly satirical and anti-clerical slant to Mahony's writing which is reflected in Maclise's varied illustrations which have a sharp bite without any romanticism. Most of these illustrations are very tightly composed without borders. They were wood engravings, placed in the body of the text (not steel engravings printed on separate sheets).*'

Physically, therefore, the work of the Cork essayist and the work of the Cork artist were bound together in a specific, organic unity. The illustrator existed without the protection of borders; the relationship on the page was intertwined.

It is ironic, then, that time played havoc with the play of influences. While *Fraser's Magazine* would survive for fifty years, anticipating *Punch* in its satire and graphical impact, the great Cork Fraserian circle that included Crofton Croker, Stack Murphy, Maginn and Mahony waned and aged just as Maclise's fame grew — so much so that by May of 1847 the

Thomas McCarthy

Dublin University Magazine was writing effusively and romantically of Daniel Maclise in its own Portrait Gallery, and by 1870 the *Illustrated London News* was featuring his house in Cheyne Walk, Chelsea, and lamenting his lack of honour by an ungrateful nation. The 'nation' in this case was, of course, Queen Victoria's, not the nation of O'Connell or Thomas Davis. By February 1882 *Hibernia*, while printing 'an unpublished relique' of Father Prout and Thackeray, noted the passing of the last Fraserian:

> 'Lately, the most daring of these Knights of the Round Table — Carlyle — died in harness; and now the last of the Fraserians has answered the muster-roll, Harrison Ainsworth, whose defection from the 'legitimate' in fiction the good Father had lamented with such tender melody in the 'Redbreast of Aquitania'. All, all are gone, the old familiar faces! — The Priest now rests in his own land, among his people, for whom he zealously faced death in the terrible days of cholera.'

Ainsworth had been a typical Fraserian, a man of the world, a discharged debtor, a failed lawyer, a wanderer in Europe and Canada, a proprietor of magazines (he purchased Dickens's *Bentley's Miscellany* for £1,700, but also owned the *New Monthly* and *Ainsworth's Magazine*), author of a spectacularly successful crime novel, *Jack Sheppard* (1839), and, as well as the Byron biography and others, author of a two-volume autobiography and three-volume *The Literary Life*. The Fraserians had much to say, and usually said it all.

But Maclise's anthology of images was increasing in influence, thanks to Mahony's famous book that circulated for nearly a century through a huge Irish Catholic network in the British Empire and the Americas. What the bookish Irish parish priest in his presbytery in Boston, San Francisco, Melbourne, Cape Town, Glasgow or Shrewsbury would read as he opened any late edition of the *Reliques of Father Prout*

'Like Maginn, a Corcagian': Bad Company for Daniel Maclise

would be these fateful words: 'This great artist in his boyhood knew Prout and has fixed his true features in enduring copper.' Biographically at least, what was visual, Maclise's minimal sketching, had extended the reach of a once powerful, mainly Protestant, Scottish and London-Irish Cork milieu.

Daniel Maclise, 1806-1870: Romancing the Past,
2008

A Quiet Voice that Lingers On

The poet and essayist Seán Dunne died in Cork City on the 3rd of August this year. His sudden death at the age of thirty-nine seems unreal, unjust and cruel. Even as I write these words I expect a phone call explaining that it was a mistake and that he'd merely gone away for a rest. Only yesterday as I stood in Waterstones in Patrick Street I thought I heard his voice. But these are only the hallucinations of the recently bereaved. Seán Dunne is dead, and with him has gone a good deal of the energy and focus of literary Cork. The poets of the South needed his provocative presence as well as his critical and anthologizing energy.

His death is first and foremost a personal tragedy. He is survived by three children, Gavin, Eoghan and Niamh, as well as by his belovèd Trish Edelstein and her son Merlin. Trish was with him when he died of a heart attack in his home at Kilcrea Park, near University College Cork. It is Trish and the children as well as Seán's father, Ritchie, who must carry the real pain of loss. As Seán himself might observe, the poets can work out their loss in their own highly subsidized, highly pampered good time.

Dunne was born in Waterford City in 1956. He grew up in St John's Park, a bustling, working-class neighbourhood. During his childhood Waterford was a busy and prosperous port, a town of thriving warehouses and glass factories. It was the home of Munster champion hurlers and the mighty 'Blues' soccer team. It was also the spawning ground and nurturing home of the Royal Showband, Brendan Bowyer and Val Doonican. In his memoir *In My Father's House* (1991) he captures the flavour of that blue-collar world as well as the

A Quiet Voice that Lingers On

personal tragedy of his young mother's death.

Seán graduated from University College Cork in 1976. His degree didn't mean much, other than that he had spent the previous few bohemian years in the vicinity of a university. He was immensely popular at College. Professors and undergraduates loved him, despite the fact that most of his seminars were held in The Long Valley bar.

After graduating from UCC Seán drifted between Waterford and Cork. He published a pamphlet, *Lady in Stone*, and was thrilled when he sold two copies to Leland Bardwell and Macdara Woods in a Dublin pub. After that he got a temporary job in Cork City Library where he survived for more than a year. All the while he was writing poems, sending work out, getting published. In 1983 a selection of his poems was published in Raven *Introductions I*. In the same year he began to compile his ambitious *Poets of Munster*, the first of his major local anthologies. In his Introduction he published an early Southern grumble against the hegemony of the Northern poets: 'They (Munster poets) come, in fact, from the wrong side of the tracks, though perhaps it would be more precise to say they came from the wrong side of the border. *Aquarius* is the only London journal to give them adequate space.' In later years he would modify that simple reading of the situation: indeed his last essay, published in *Graph*, castigates the inflated reputations and notions of Southern Irish poets.

His own early poems are precise and modest:

> *Stacked in jars on shelves, the beans*
> *diminish in time to favourite recipes.*

These poems were collected in his first collection, *Against the Storm* (Dolmen Press, 1985). Ironically, it was his admiration for two Ulster poets, Derek Mahon and Gerald Dawe, that led him into a new strategy for writing. The technical precision of Mahon's *Courtyards in Delft* shocked him out of his first easy ballad rhythms and rhyme into a colder and finer syllabic metre. Dawe's work on *Krino* and in particular his critical writing taught Seán how to clarify poetic subject matter before proceeding with the making of a poem. By the time Seán published *The Sheltered Nest* (The Gallery Press, 1992) he had grown intellectually and emotionally. But he had also discovered a myth, an enabling myth for his poetry: the myth of silence. 'I found that to live without such an inner silence seemed like an amputation of some vital part of myself.' Last year he published an account of that spiritual journey in the brilliant *The Road to Silence* (New Island, 1994).

Seán Dunne's poetic journey was more brief than it should have been. Its brevity is a bitter injustice. But I have no doubt that he had already discovered an equilibrium, following the journey of the poet Seán Ó Ríordáin who also voyaged away from the crowd and found a poetic silence among the Cistercians of Mount Melleray Abbey. As John Montague observed at his funeral: 'I was sustained by him and other brilliant students. We have lost the poet but we have the poems.'

Fortnight,
October 1995

Seán Dunne, A Memory

I kept thinking of the poet Seán Dunne as I wandered through the vibrant Book Centre in Waterford City recently. This place was one of his haunts and he was proud of it as a beacon of culture in the sunny South East. Dunne's Waterford was a dazzling, sunlit city of busy glass-factory workers and of secure, sunbathing St John's Park mothers. It was also a place of serious writers, his close friends and first supporters whose work he admired enormously, Jim Nolan, John Ennis and Liam Murphy. Everywhere I walked with him in Waterford there seemed to be sunlight and music. Gifted with a resonant voice he had an instinctive feel for music, both classical and popular — he loved the Vanbrugh Quartet as much as he admitted the efforts of Brendan Bowyer and Val Doonican. The sunlight and sounds of 1960s and 1970s Waterford is everywhere in his poems and memoirs. He relished the sounds made by crowds at a match in Walsh Park or the sound of children playing on bone-dry urban footpaths, the sound of the waves at Dunmore East or of the Iron Man in Tramore. All of these sounds caressed his ears and impinged upon the rhythm and style of his verse-craft.

His warmth and joyousness, his flawless memory of song lyrics, his mimicry and laughter when very young, all of these things in his nature seduced and delighted people. He was one of the most loved people I ever knew. And there was a lot to love, that gregarious instinct and, of course, a poet's depth and darkness that revealed itself inexorably in the published poems. There was his ability to sing Kavanagh's 'Raglan Road' with much of the skill of Luke Kelly, and with the same ballad singer's tilt of the head; there was his standing on a table in a

Thomas McCarthy

lecture room of UCC's old West Wing to recite more clearly, to declaim passionately, the poems of Rimbaud. There were his constant rages against injustice in Central America and his passionate support of trade unions, their purpose and history. Like the same Luke Kelly or poet Patrick Galvin he had an instinct for the underdog and the barricades. Then, much later in what was too brief a life, there was his discovery of Mount Melleray Abbey, Thomas Merton, meditation and Dzogchen Beara, and the many different roads to silence.

When we first met at UCC he was highly suspicious of me, though I too had come from a family in a council terrace. We were both working-class imposters in a bourgeois University campus, poor kids who'd over-achieved through Donogh O'Malley's 1967 Free Secondary Education. But he saw me as a Cappoquin culchie from a Fianna Fáil milieu and, intellectually, that was unforgivable. But when I took him home to meet my mother who read his tea leaves he was intrigued. My mother blessed herself when he came into the house because he looked like the Christ as revealed on the Turin Shroud, and he was as emaciated looking as a martyr. It was a look he cultivated to great effect. My mother loved him even more because of his surname 'Dunne', a name she associated with two glamorous sisters from her own childhood in Dungarvan. My mother was no different from the bustling women who climbed into the Mobile Library van in Bishopstown, Cork, who stared at him in awe, wondering whether they should pray or flirt with him. The City Librarian, Seán Bohan, used to refer to our Mobile Service as 'Wanderly Wagon', as it was staffed by myself, Seán Dunne, the actor Eamon Maguire and the great Clare musician, Noel Shine. Management were never quite sure if our doors would open. Each day at work was a rollicking adventure, yet we managed on some afternoons to lend over a thousand books. The book cards may not have been kept in strict alphabetical order but every borrower went home roaring with laughter.

That's how it was with Seán Dunne, the day lit up in his

Seán Dunne, A Memory

company. After he entered journalism, and his new life at the heart of the *Examiner*, his work rate became astonishing: wonderful 'Weekend' newspaper editing, collections of sublime poetry, irreplaceable anthologies and heartrending memoirs and self-scrutiny. If you haven't looked at his work for some time go back again: read his *Collected* from Gallery, read *The Road to Silence* and dive into his immortal *Cork Anthology*.

*Irish Examiner,
2019*

Selected Poems: Seán Ó Ríordáin
Preface by Frank Sewell (ed). Foreword by Paul Muldoon

The brief author's note to this impressive and important book tells us that Seán Ó Ríordáin was born in County Cork and lived his entire life in Ireland. In a way that note tells us everything for this is a new kind of publication, a new moment in the immortal life of Munster's greatest poet since Brian Merriman. This edition is part of Yale University's 'World Republic of Letters' series, beautifully edited and designed, with Martin Sipa's haunting and resonant image of a moth at night caught in an overhead light. Those who know the work of Ó Ríordáin will know how central and private that image really is:

Ach dhoirteas-sa an púdar beannaithe
'Bhí spréite ar gach sciathán.

(How I sprayed the holy powders
Broadcast upon each wing.)

Here is a poet whose life force was a moth membrane in ruins, who was robbed of the vigour of masculinity by the ravages of tuberculosis. Here was a Cork genius as hermetic as Cavafy and as gloriously patriotic as Éluard. Ó Ríordáin was not a one-dimensional poet; his life was not simply a monologue of suffering. Sewell's fine editing and trenchant Preface reminds us that while suffering and slow physical decline are constant themes in the work this poet also had a playful, mischievous side. The 'unremittingly dark impression of the poet' created by the repeated anthologizing of a limited group of poems has, in Sewell's opinion, limited our view of Ó Ríordáin, a poet of striking images and haunting phrases. The fact is that in keeping with his mid-century contemporaries in other countries Ó Ríordáin read widely, hungrily absorbing influences from other cultures, in the manner of his exact contemporaries like Theodore Roethke or Dylan Thomas. He made use of the same tricks of word-music and irrational association. His accretion of word fragments and fabrications, of a linguistic outlook that saw language as something liquid and malleable can best be seen in Theodore Roethke's 'I am, says the Lamb', Thomas's 'Fern Hill' or, indeed, Delmore Schwartz's 'Summer Knowledge'. He is their kind of mid-century poet, and in worldly terms they could have been his soul companions as he moved from the Motor Licensing office at City Hall to Heatherside T B Clinic and Sarsfield Court Hospital.

Ó Ríordáin was a poet who stretched the auditory muscle of a language. His earliest material would famously crash against the critical rock of Máire Mhac an tSaoi's learning and grammar, but over time even that gifted scholar-poet would be won over. One of his favourite words was '*blas*/taste', as Sewell points out in his Preface, a word that would be even more famously colonized by another Cork wordsmith, Rory Gallagher. Ó Ríordáin was a poet of ambiguity, humour, satire, and with an acute awareness of the plurality of selves that can be harvested by any writer:

> *Lean na pianta ag argóint,*
>   *Mise an t-abhar,*
> *Focal níl sa phianfhoclóir*
>   *Ná rabhas ann./*

> *The pains kept on arguing,*
>   *with me as their subject.*
> *In the lexicon of pain,*
>   *I've gone through every word.*
>
>   (trans. Mary O'Malley)

Thomas McCarthy

This plurality gave his art a multitude of entrances and exits, from the satire of 'Tulyar', where the Aga Khan's stallion was now providing sexual service in the interests of our Jansenist state, to the gallows humour of 'Rian na gCos' with its sharp 'Níor saolaíodh mé gur cailleadh é' or, in Francis O'Hare's fine translation:

> *I never was born till he was dead —*
>   *there's many a me in myself,*
> *one lost with every word uttered*
>   *rising with every breath.*

Ó Ríordáin's poetry also forms a strange but purposeful menagerie, a veritable cage of birds and 'lucht ceithre chos', a Ted Hughes kingdom where communication occurs beneath language or beyond it. Here the black dog and the unsophisticated duck are the wry constituents who cannot be moved by mere comment. The poet is the Aesop of this kingdom who receives timeless fables from ducks, moths and cats. In 'Catchollú' you know you are in the presence of a cat person, one of those beings who understand and love cats for their shape-shifting integrity. Only a true cat person could write, 'Téann sé ó chat go cat', understanding that a cat can change personality at the stir of a paw. There is a comment on the nature of poets in this also, for poets like cats survive through at least nine imagined deaths.

To Paul Muldoon falls the task of translating two of Ó Ríordáin's greatest poems, 'Adhlacadh mo Mháthar' and 'Cnoc Mellerí'. Needless to say the task is carried out adroitly. But it is interesting to contrast a line or two of Muldoon with the translation of Greg Delanty, a Cork poet who translated a selection of Ó Ríordáin while he was working on his own tremendous anthology of Anglo-Saxon poems for W W Norton. None of Delanty's translations appear in this Yale *Selected*. This is a pity. Here are two versions of lines from 'Adhlacadh mo Mháthar':

> '*a rustle in the silk of gloaming, the interminable hymn*
> *of an irritable bumblebee*
> *piercing the evening's scrim*'
>   (Muldoon)

and

> '*the silksusurrus of afternoon,*
> *a damn bee droning,*
> *ululatearing afternoon's gown*'
>   (Delanty)

Both translations are superb, both much more than adequate, but they do remind us that poetry is translated not into mere language but into a personal language. Muldoon creates a sharp and unfussy version of 'Cnoc Mellerí' — compressing 'd'fhéachas go fiosrach gan taise gan trua' to 'a pitiless gaze' and 'M'aigne cromtha le ceist' to 'my mind still laden with qualms'. A translator of poetry must be a poet, otherwise too much pedantry gets to represent art. Luckily, Sewell has made some good choices here — there's Theo Dorgan, Paddy Bushe and Colm Breathnach, Nuala Ní Dhomhnaill and Celia de Fréine. Dorgan's versions of 'Ifreann', 'Oíche Nollaig na mBan', 'Tost' and 'Solas' are perfect poems in the host language — a line from 'Solas' goes like this, 'Do dhein comhdhubh de dubh is geal / what has been black or bright one equal dark'. Paddy Bushe, also — a rare diglottic poet of stern elegance — produces gems in English out of 'Gaoth an Fhocail' and 'Ní Raibh Sí Dílis:'

> *The Lee flows east like an old prayer,*
>   *an unbending psalm,*
> *and a harvest moon is imprinted*
>   *on the wide stretched calm*
> *of the firmament . . .*

Thomas McCarthy

Reading these versions by all the poet-translators reminds me of the Greek poet George Seferis's remark to a friend who'd complained that Rex Warner, a poet with uncertain Greek, had been chosen as his translator: 'Ah, but he has an exquisite command of his own language!' This is what one hopes for in every translator of poems.

Hopefully this selection will go far, penetrating, with luck, the American academic library market. In our chilly climate after the death of Heaney I hope this book leaps beyond the wall of a self-limiting US Irish Studies to capture a new readership among the two thousand or so writing programmes in a largely indifferent Waspish world. Yale University Press and Frank Sewell have created a serious memorial to a great Irish soul of unbridled imagination. Though a poet may be politically timid, silenced by deprivation and illness, the poetry still soars like an eagle. This truth of imagination, that it is as strong as death, was never more radiant than in the poems of Ó Ríordáin who broke free from the limits of his generation: 'Tá fairsingeacht smaointe / San abairt is lú.' (There's grandeur of thought / in the shortest sentence.)

Irish Examiner,
2014

Nine Bright Shiners by Theo Dorgan

This is a very substantial new collection of poems from Theo Dorgan, almost a personal anthology compared to the spare and thematically tight previous work, *Greek*. The nine bright stars are remembered heroes, family and friends, all now deceased, but all acting, as well, as nine radical calls to communal remembrance. Dorgan belongs to a very particular generation of writers — novelist Roddy Doyle and playwright Billy Roche would be his companions — who see the earth through unapologetic and unreconstructed left-wing spectacles. There is a strong political sense in these poems that the poor shall inherit the earth and that poets, somehow, will one day own all the means of production. Dorgan's is a generation of intellectuals radicalized by Marcuse and Sartre, illuminated by Costa Gavras and bewitched by Neruda and Gabriel García Márquez. Newer generations of Irish writers, those reared in a private, ironic world (so private that they are outraged by the free gift of a U2 album) could never understand the massive optimism contained within Dorgan's unbroken sense of community. Such a belief in political community is, in a very real sense, an affront to the modern. Frankly, my modern dears, Dorgan does not give a damn:

> *I saw his last matches for the Glen, the young bucks*
> *already impatient to sweep him to the heavens*
> *where blood and raw knuckles, mud and defeat*
>
> *or victory would fade into remembered youth —*
> *A child myself, I sensed their insensate cruelty,*
> *the watchful precise impatience of the young.*

Thomas McCarthy

The poem here is 'Learning My Father's Memories' and the remembrance is of Christy Ring, the greatest of them all, it could be said, who when he rose to catch a *sliotar* was pushed sky-high by several adoring townlands, from Cloyne to Blackpool. It is that sense of community that Theo Dorgan captures in order to describe and praise life. His method is to photograph each hero in the gap of danger and to track him or her all the way to the winning post. It is a poetry calculated to infuriate sociophobes of every persuasion. Thus the much-loved Charlie Hennessy is imagined surviving the treachery of the violent ocean with the help of friends, the beautiful artist Deirdre Meaney is captured ascending to a chateau, a public servant whispers in the poet's ear of the death of Michael Hartnett, a mysterious sailor accompanies them on a voyage between the Sovereigns and Oysterhaven; all harbours are reached through the chugging diesels and slopping bilge tanks. Mysterious strangers attend at ocean voyages and watch the Houses of the Oireachtas at night. Crisis is shared and, though Lar Cassidy is dead, the light still burns in the Arts Council windows — the last light of public funding is not quite extinguished. We may yet survive: this is Dorgan's personal weather, his outlook, his irrepressible poetic optimism that shines through all crisis and hopelessness. Among the persistent medallions of optimism that glitter in poem after poem are cups of tea and cigarettes.

No other Irish poet has made so many references to tea and cigarettes in his work. Firstly, let's deal with the tea aspect of the poetry. In 'Times on the River' he comes up with 'tea for the helm', in 'Skelligs: Sailing to the Edge' he settles to 'unscrew the thermos drink', in 'Nine Instances of Grace' he pours tea in two different sections, while 'tea leaves swelling in the pot' feature in 'Five Haiku for You' and there is a full pot of tea in 'The Shelf' as well as tea made in 'The Gifted Life' and 'Tea, I think, temper the work' in, again, 'Nine Instances of Grace' where, incidentally, he pours 'tea into your favourite blue mug'. Tea is a companion, but also a technical assistant, a kind of spiritual enjambment, working in the same way as the number of apparitions, ghosts, strangers, and the number of refrains, both in Irish and English, with which this work is punctuated. Each of these is a companion in the work, part of that assured community working like a *meitheal* to help the poet complete his thought or canvass the reader's attention.

'I had paused to light up a cigarette,' the poet announces in that mysterious early poem 'The Angel of History'. Later, he sees Deirdre Meaney 'draw on a cigarette, taking me in' while in 'Gaffer' he says, 'I sat there smoking.' The number of references to breath, breathing, air and wind is simply extraordinary and a medical practitioner reading his book would have a panic attack, and for very good reason, for the book is full of clinical signs. 'Stopping to catch my breath, I heard a voice' is the title of his poem after Jean Berger, while in 'Learning Death' he writes of 'that unmistakable catch in the breath' and in 'Insomnia' he says, 'Because I could not catch my breath.' In 'The Love Poems of Lena Stakheyeva, part 6' he explains that 'There is a way to walk and breathe' and in 'Nine Instances of Grace' he reassures us of 'How lucky we've been / to drink the air.' In 'Setting Out' he uses the phrase 'night is breathing soft and dark' twice, while in the brilliant poem of domestic love, 'Watercolour', he remarks upon that 'quiet weight / of breath and gesture'. In 'Aftermath' the protagonist takes 'a deep, cold breath' and in 'Nine Bright Shiners' the poet describes 'our breath staggered and wispy in the air' as well as 'your first breath drawn in these dark waters'. There are other instances, but 'The Look Again' probably sums up both the description and the implicit alarm:

> *The pressure in my chest now so intense*
> *That I am half afraid to breathe.*

Smoking and the yearning for air are constant themes, however understated. Dorgan's recent past as a sailor could be

Thomas McCarthy

seen, from the evidence here, in an entirely different light: as an effort to breathe freely. The metaphor is both central and powerful in his work, for, to breathe freely is to be at one with his past, to be united with parents and grandparents. All of his work has been a great voyage south, to the full health of an encounter with 'Cape Horn' where 'I open my arms / to this wind from the icebound south.' This is another exquisite log book in the long voyage of Dorgan's nimble ketch of poetry.

Irish Examiner,
2014

Quarryman: A New Generation Takes Control

Editing *Quarryman*, distributing *Quarryman*, selling advertising space in *Quarryman*: all were core validating activities for several generations of UCC literati. The physical 'Quarry' itself, from which many an undergraduate Neanderthal man emerged, covered in muck and blood, is now long gone. I can recall the supreme efforts of Arts students as they tried to overcome the rugby-honed ball skills of Engineering students during those riots called soccer matches in that hole in the ground in the early 70s. A fine and refined Library building now covers the blood and the memory of those years. But let's move from muck to poetry: originally begun as the Q.C.C. the student magazine then became *The Quarryman* for a time, before the name was abandoned in favour of *The Chronic* of 1919/1920, but this was dropped yet again for *The Locker* in 1924. Then, it seems, due to the War and a 'deplorable laxness' there was no magazine until March 1929 when the students of UCC revived the old *Quarryman* name. This new *Quarryman*, which continued well into the 1970s, is a gem among student publications. In my day the editors, from Patrick Crotty to Greg Delanty, were energetic, well motivated and extremely opinionated, all qualities highly desirable in leaders in any walk of life. Both editors, incidentally, were influential student-poets who went on to become Professors of Literature in Aberdeen and Vermont and influential editors on a world scale: one thinks of Crotty's monumental *Penguin Book of Irish Poetry* (2010) and Delanty's superb Norton anthology, *The Word Exchange* (2011). UCC has never failed to produce writers and editors of the first rank. As the thriving metropolis of Munster, 'the undisputed Queen of the South' as Micheál Mac Liammóir once described Cork, without irony, Cork and UCC should always be the first and final refuge for high-level discourse and freedom of imagination in the South. It is the primary function of a university to act as a sanctuary, a safe haven for poets and dissident voices. A university campus should always be in a state of dialogue with its hinterland, like a great theatre company or a centre of broadcasting. It would be impossible to overstate how important freedom of expression and imagination must remain in a world of increasing religious fanaticism, standardized corporate responses and insatiable PR commentaries. A writer must be free to speak from the heart and *Quarryman* is one of the platforms from which a personal, artistic statement can be made. The most permanent statements find their form in literature, and such statements of freedom will be found in *Quarryman* as poetry and fiction. There the work begins for the editors of today and of the future: in the cacophony of a wireless world how can distinct and dissident voices be protected and sustained? When print was propeller-driven the world was more easily controlled.

College magazines don't occur in a vacuum; they breathe off the sense of creativity in the space around them. There were days in February and March of 1975 when things were really moving fast in terms of poetry at UCC. The narrow stairs of 'Brighton Villas', the English Department home, were snarled in a traffic jam of poets. In one office Professor Lucy was polishing the work that would be published as *Unfinished Sequence*, while in another the great Ulster poet, John Montague, was collating the lyrics that would become *A Slow Dance*. Twenty students attended our first student-led workshop. Five new poets read their poems and discussed the formal structures and the established tones, rather than any philosophy, behind the work. This is *exactly* what a workshop should be. The poets John Montague and Gregory O'Donoghue attended our second workshop that year. I remember Montague saying that 'something big' could happen out of the work of our group. He talked to us about the original Queen's University workshop that Heaney and others had attended in the 60s. Montague felt then that the time was ripe for a new Munster movement in poetry. I recall him saying that we all needed to look at ourselves coldly and objectively because within our new workshop there was enough latent talent to form a whole new school of poetry. We already had a venue and platform on campus and in the Old Presbyterian Church in Prince's Street. We planned to start a second magazine to add to *Quarryman*, and we now had a new University Theatre that would, we were convinced, link the poets of the city, Robert O'Donoghue, Anthony Blinco, Seán Ó Criadáin, with the poets of the college like Liam de Bhall (William Wall) and Theo Dorgan. And Gerry Fitzgibbon of the English Department began his encouraging poetry feature in the daily *Examiner*: eventually he would publish many of the UCC poets of that era. Liam de Bhall also set up a creative partnership with the artist John McHarg, publishing UCC poets in his beautiful, elaborately designed *First Issue*. Most of my spare time — and time I couldn't spare — was taken up in organizing the Poetry Workshop. The principles we developed merely by practice were the same as the ones I found in operation at the professional Iowa Writing Program fifteen years later.

That semester in 1975 the publisher-poet Peter Fallon came to UCC for a reading with Seán Dunne, Gregory O'Donoghue and Theo Dorgan. I did the introductions for that reading and talked for hours about publishing with Fallon and Montague. Fallon spoke to us, I remember, about The Gallery Press, its operation and its future. It was through him that we learned about Pearse Hutchinson and Eiléan Ní Chuilleanáin and their new magazine, *Cyphers*. 'Keep in touch,' Fallon said to us all as he departed (probably the nicest thing a publisher can say to a bunch of new poets).

Later that same year, it was May 5th, Robert Graves, an almost mythical poetic figure, gave a wonderful English

Thomas McCarthy

Literature Society reading. Graves came to visit us from Majorca. I sat beside him and Mrs Graves at the Oyster Tavern dinner. He said to me that Rupert Brooke was the nicest of the Georgian poets. He also said that 'of that lot' Winston Churchill was the only gentleman. He said that poetry is no longer being written in England but that he got 'the sense of poetry' when he came to Cork. At the reception he was, of course, besieged by people, becoming very fatigued, but we got him away to the Oyster for dinner. He was an old devil and a scoundrel (and grossly irresponsible, it must be said), but a master in the craft of poetry, and one of poetry's greatest theorists in *The White Goddess*. Earlier in the day, at a seminar in the English Department, Graves was asked if he had any advice for budding poets. He answered, without hesitating: 'Poets! If you are budding come into bloom!'

That would be my advice also to the new generation of poets and fiction writers who will dominate College life and make a stir for literature in the cauldron of activity that is now the university campus. Be of great determination and hope; be of unbridled hope for your work. It is the most important thing in the world; it will become a lifelong mirror held up to the soul. *Quarryman* is an important part of the structure of the new wave of literary voices, voices we will hear more and more in the coming decade. The voices in the current issue, the pathos and anguish, the warmth and desolation, all speak of the permanence of the human situation. They speak of a personal being that is universal, in voices that are instantly recognizable in any cultural space occupied by the young.

I wonder about — and I marvel at — these new hipster poets and fiction writers. I love the attitude, the individual viewpoint, the integrity of the personal worlds described. I've just been reading about the most popular hipster baby names in Santa Monica, Austin, Texas and Madison: names like August, Daisy, Dexter, Dixie and Flora, Hazel, Hugo, Ione, Kai, Luka, Millie, Poppy and Romy and then I realize that

Quarryman: A New Generation Takes Control

there's been a localized hipster baby-naming going on in Cork, in Schull, Dingle, Kinsale, old Montenotte and Gardiner's Hill/St Luke's and other places where the uber-cool book-lovers congregate. We will have poets named Aoife, Oisín, Sorcha, Doireann, Darragh, Dearann. Naming such persons, our newborn, is the most powerful first use of language. It is the first familial act of poetry in our lives. The names remind us, also, that our personal lives are our best imaginative resources as we settle down to write a poem or a screenplay. A generation hence, in UCC, a Sorcha will be writing a poem for Dexter, a Romy will be writing love letters to her hipster kid, Darragh. The future unfolds before us and *Quarryman* will be the first witness documents containing, as it always has, the first fruits of new love and the first successes of a new editor's reign.

Quarryman, UCC,
2020

Gerald Y Goldberg and Cork

Happy St Patrick's Day to all my FB Friends, especially those very dear and much-loved friends who spend their lives handling Irish books in American cities. It is always a time of year when I go back and read old books, Joseph Brady's *The Big Sycamore*, for example, or Daniel Corkery's *The Threshold of Quiet*. There are so many good old books to revisit, books that illuminate one tiny corner of Irish life so well that they stay in the mind forever.

The other day I sat all morning in the Library reading Gerald Y Goldberg's rare and brilliant book, *Jonathan Swift and Contemporary Cork*. It must be over forty years since I first read it. It is a masterpiece, a lawyer's masterpiece, telling the story of Swift's fractious and unfinished relationship with the Corporation of Cork after the city had granted him its Freedom, as well as the great Dean's hopeless attempts to have his candidate appointed to the Church of Ireland living of Kinsale (Rincurran). I can hear Lord Mayor Goldberg's voice on every page, the cautious and considered opinions, the adamant tone of his perceptions and pronouncements, and his lethal choice of quotations. Gerald Y Goldberg had a marvellous speaking voice and the poet Seán Dunne and I used to stop him in his tracks as he rushed from the South Mall to City Hall or from the Crawford Gallery, where he might have dropped his wife Sheila on Cork Orchestral Society business, to Patrick's Bridge as he bustled across with his windswept papers. We wanted to hear his vexed opinions and to listen to his voice as it boomed above the din of Cork traffic. It was music to our ears and Seán who had a natural ear for music would listen and relish every Goldberg phrase.

Gerald Y Goldberg and Cork

Like an aristocratic Warburg in old Hamburg the tall Gerald Y would halt for us in mid gallop because we were poets. An uncle of the literary Marcus family, of the novelist and editor David and the scriptwriter and film maker Louis, he loved that deep and instant dive into literary things. He collected poetry books and poetry journals assiduously, sometimes coming into the City Library in search of the poets who worked there, wanting us to sign our latest collections, wanting to extend the moment of signing so that he could make a major point about poetry that had been unsettling his mind for days. He would want us to consider the matter and offer advice. The advice might often be rejected but it was noted with respect, though we were only young poets and clerks in the Library while he was a Lord Mayor, a lawyer and a man of property with one of the most famous addresses in Cork — every sculptor and poet in Cork knew it by heart — 'Ben-Truda' on the Rochestown Road.

It was Gerald who first suggested that in Munster poetry we should all try to give expression to a new age in Irish life, to a looser kind of Irishness. And this was in the late 70s when the oil crisis had taken the wind out of the sails of the Lemass 1960s Irish optimism and openness. Each one of us has to work, he said, towards a much wider definition of what it means to be Irish. He knew that the Ulster Troubles had narrowed our vision again and made Ireland more Nationalistic and regressive. Here was a man whose family had been bullied out of Limerick City and fled to Cork in that infamous Pogrom, his father's damaged business premises being taken over by a family called 'South'. How strange are the ironies in Irish life, Gerald would say, as he ironically recited the words of 'Seán South of Garryowen', and then: 'well, poets, continue reading those Irving Howe books in the Library, he'll teach ye a thing or two about all that.' He laughed when I showed him the Gaelic League advertisement from the 1900s that reassured patriotic Irish-speaking customers that no Jews were employed in the stitching of their Irish garments. Like him I was alert to the anti-Semitism in all bourgeois Catholic cultures. Bless you poets, he'd say, you're always alert to these things and you're never afraid to speak up. Don't ever fear unpopularity; popularity is completely overrated. Then he reminded me, knowing that I was from Cappoquin, that to hear Sir Richard Keane of Cappoquin House proclaim in a voice and accent like the Duke of Edinburgh or Sir Anthony Eden that he feels completely Irish is to have one's views of nationality severely challenged. Politically one might not accept Sir Richard's proclamation, explained Gerald Y, but socially and historically he was completely entitled to his Irishness: he was a Cappoquin Keane, after all, Gerald Y said, and one of the original Gaelic families of County Derry, the O'Catháins, who had fought for King James at the Battle of the Boyne. How many Irishmen still in Ireland can claim their family fought with King James? Not many, I can tell you, because they all hightailed it out of Ireland with all their possessions, leaving wives and children behind. They couldn't wait to flee, leaving their poor foot soldiers behind to suffer under the Penal Laws. And what did Ireland do? It trained its historians to make heroes of them, Wild Geese and all that nonsense, the people left behind were the real geese. Just one Keane survivor of the Jacobite Wars had changed his religion and begun to practise law. You do things to survive, Gerald Y said. History teaches us that. Keep up with the poetry now, don't let me down.

Swift's eighteenth century: this was where complications always began in any Irish discussion, in discussions centred upon identity and race and authenticity. The Lord Mayor was convinced, he said, as the wind whipped his papers on Patrick's Bridge, that only literature and art can reconcile these impossible tensions of identity. Only literature has that capacity for stretch. 'Think,' said Lord Mayor Goldberg, 'if we lived in Cork in 1720 we'd all be getting on much better with each other than we do today. Our understanding of our common humanity has gone backwards, I'm telling you.'

Gerald Y Goldberg and Cork

And, as poets, it is literature we proclaim. But as poets we must see Munster, and Cork, its capital city, as the very epicentre of a more open Irishness. If we could achieve this, if we could enlarge the Munster discourse politically, culturally, religiously, we would not have wasted our lives. How often did we talk about our dream province, our dream Munster: a vibrant province of three powerful cities, Cork, Limerick, Waterford, with a population of two million persons, including half a million Presbyterians and quarter of a million Jews, all prospering, all feeling completely at home. So many Presbyterians would ensure a constant traffic between Munster, Ulster and the States south of the Mason-Dixon line and so many Jews would ensure a hugely cosmopolitan traffic between Munster, New York and Israel. What a province Munster would be, a prospering Catalonia of the Atlantic, a land not just of fine Jameson but of Bushmills and kosher dinner parties. This is the kind of Munster that Gerald Goldberg dreamt of, along with me and dreaming Seán Dunne; that's why there was so much warmth in our brief encounters. Goldberg was so like myself in those days; our brief encounters were set in the eighteenth century, in the golden Cork of Lord Orrery's and Swift's correspondence. The first time I met Lord Mayor Goldberg in the City Library I'd quoted Orrery's letter to Swift that describes the showering of Cork's citizens with oat bran and flour on the day a Lord Mayor is elected (I think I must have found that reference in Seán Pettit's book, *This City of Cork 1700-1900*), and Windele's description of the older custom of showering the new Lord Mayor with oat bran as the Mayor moved in procession from Christ Church to St Peter's Church in North Main Street . . . hence the origin of the expression 'bran-new' (not 'brand new' as is commonly used). These were the small details Gerald Y loved.

I've been trying to get my hands on a copy of Goldberg's *Jonathan Swift and Contemporary Cork* but it's impossible to find. Even Ger Sweeney in the Lee Bookstore long ago couldn't find a copy for me. Not that I could afford it. But that has never stopped me. But because we have a good public library service, because there's still a place in this State where an ordinary person can spend hours enjoying something rare — long may our politicians protect the enriched public realm of our libraries — I was there for hours reading Gerald Y Goldberg's marvellous writing, its descriptions of Swift's efforts to better himself and his friends every bit as frantic as Antoinette Quinn's description of Patrick Kavanagh's 1940s attempts to land a decent job. Here is the Cork lawyer Gerald Y Goldberg at the height of his information giving:

> 'Swift's failure to win preferment was attributed by him to the opposition of the Archbishop of York, Dr John Sharp, and to the hatred which the Duchess of Somerset had for him. It is noteworthy that in August 1711, when Oxford and St John talked about Swift to Queen Anne she said she 'had never heard of him'. The Archbishop made it clear to the Queen, following upon publication of A Tale of a Tub, that in his opinion the author, Swift, was unfit for a seat on the episcopal bench. The Duchess was enraged by the Windsor Prophecy. The Duchess was Queen Anne's Mistress of the Robes and, because of her Whig loyalties, Swift and his friends wished to have her removed from office. Mrs Hasham, formerly Abigail Hill, a close friend of Swift, asked him not to publish it because, as proved right, she feared it would anger the Queen. It was, however, published. When Swift wrote The Author Upon Himself he attributed his failure to obtain preferment to: 'A crazy Prelate, and a Royal Prude, / By dull Divines, who look with envious eyes, / On ev'ry Genius that attempts to rise.'

Facebook,
St Patrick's Eve 2017

Memoir of an Irish Jew by Lionel Cohen
Preface by Yvonne Cohen. Foreword by Alannah Hopkin

'And here I will digress a little and tell you my opinions of drapers in general. With a few exceptions, I considered them to be the meanest money-grabbing types it has ever been my misfortune to come across,' writes the exasperated Lionel Cohen in this thrilling, trenchant and hilarious Cork memoir. He had just turned down a sudden offer from the new Israeli government, an offer that would have made him Chief Officer of the first Israeli Coastal Radio Station. He was longing for the sea, for his salty 'Sparks' cabin aboard the 6,000 tonne *Kedmah* as she plied between Marseilles and Haifa under the Star of David. Trained at the old Cork Radio School the style of his Morse-code signalling had become an instantly recognized personal signature from Tilbury Docks to Parramatta Docks. In 1940 he had run away from home and joined the Irish Army in response to de Valera's appeal for men to defend their country against invasion. It was the first of his many responses to appeals for help, a character trait that would determine the course of his entire life. As army recruit No. 213032 he was present to enjoy Major General Costello's pithy speech to the Coastal Artillery unit: 'His message was that if there was an invasion of Ireland, we would never get off Spike Island alive, so make sure we died like soldiers.' This part of his memoir must constitute the best personal record of Cork Harbour's Coastal Defence units ever written, or ever likely to be written. After the Emergency he set sail on various tramp steamers and cargo vessels, eventually serving on a homeward voyage as Radio Officer aboard a luxury P&O liner. Then the foundation of

Israel intervened.

Then his Uncle Dave died and his father needed him to come back to Cork to run the business, a life he dreaded. He was soon shackled to the family garment factory, a business surviving on a pitiful margin of five per cent while selling to Munster drapers who demanded forty per cent discount. The business was viable only as long as Lemass's import tariffs protected the little enterprise. Lionel's consolation was motor-cycle racing and he became a crack scrambler and, for twenty-five years, secretary of the Munster Cycle and Car Club. But running a business with sixty employees was no easy task, especially after he ended up in Sarsfield Court Hospital with TB. By the time he recovered the Cohen business was doomed: 'The bank overdraft was creeping up again. I knew I had to make some decision or else I would be back in hospital . . . This was really one hell of a time and I walked and walked the streets trying to reason it all out.'

The fact was he had no head for business, no instinct for profit. What happened next was as extraordinary as any other unexpected turn in his life. He took a job with the Brothers of Charity at their boys' care home in Lota, Cork. This inspired him to attend the Kilkenny Diploma Course in Residential Childcare, run by his hero, Sister Stan. The knowledge gained in Kilkenny transformed his life, bringing joy and fulfilment as he now worked with empathy and renewed stamina. Even his Morse-code skills came into their own as he learned the special sign language, 'Lámh', that was used to communicate with deaf special needs children. Inspired by Eunice Kennedy Shriver he became involved in the Special Olympics and he would meet her in Dublin in 1985. Those late years were wonderful ones and this memoir, written only for family reading, is one of the best Cork memoirs ever, a worthy companion to O'Connor's *An Only Child*, Galvin's *Song for a Poor Boy* and Ó Murchú's *Black Cat at the Window*. The book is enhanced by marvellous photographs: Lionel in uniform at his sister's wedding, Lionel with his belovèd May

Memoir of an Irish Jew by Lionel Cohen

at the Victoria Hospital dance in 1952, Lionel with his granddaughter Ruth walking by the sea at Ballinskelligs — all of it part of one of the most colourful lives lived by a member of that serious and mainly literary community of mid-century Cork Jews.

The Irish Times,
December 2021

Preface to a Planning Document

On May 2nd, 1917, nearly a century ago, the Cork Improvement Bill passed the Report Stage in the House of Commons, London. The Bill had been brilliantly shepherded through its Parliamentary votes by the determined County Cork MPs, Maurice and Tim Healy, whose great fear had been the opposition of Ulster Unionist MPs worried by the setting up of the Ford Motor Works at Cork. But Tim Healy's advocacy won the support of Captain Craig, Sharman Crawford and Bonar Law. The Ford assembly works, the beating heart of Cork's industrial might for the next sixty years, had come into being. The approaching centenary of this Bill in 2017 should remind us of how well the interests of Cork were protected by the old and now forgotten Irish Party at Westminster. The care of this second city of the State, and its interests, is one of the highest duties of Irish public life, and members of the old Irish Party were keenly aware of this. We would do well to remember them, to understand how the interests of cities need to be protected at the highest political level. Cities are massive human and economic constructs and we should plan their fate with great political care.

And why should we protect the interests of our cities? Can't cities with their population density and commercial imperatives look after themselves? The answer is, no, they can't. More than ever cities are subject to planning regulations as well as transport and housing limitations. The future of the world lies in its cities. A city can be choked by deliberate political acts, just as a city can spring to life after seventy years of inertia by a Bill such as the Cork Harbour Act of 1820 and the Cork Improvement Act of 1917. To watch a city

Preface to a Planning Document

rising is a beautiful thing. A city is a living organism and the purring sound of this organism as it thrives and grows is the sound of people assembling and dispersing, on buses, bicycles, trains and cars. There is a poetry in city life that's beautiful. Writers like Frank O'Connor and Mary Leland, or Conal Creedon and Kevin Barry, have captured the essence of Cork life in their books. They are our eternal witnesses, their works giving us glimpses of a deep urban soul. Reading them, and others, should centre our sense of recognition, as well as giving us huge hope for the human permanence and future of local urban life.

And this life is such a critical thing, such a lived reality within the politics of our modern era. Nowadays Cork City Council has become a crucial enabler and supporter of this expanding human landscape, providing sports facilities and community playgrounds and meeting spaces. In terms of this active creative city the Council, again, supports the internationally acclaimed Lifelong Learning Festival, the hugely popular Marathon, the *Céilí Mór*, and many other mass participation events where the city as a humane, living landscape comes forward to reveal its great bold strength. A city, yes, is its buildings and physical infrastructure, but it is also that vital historical, living network of loyal communities working together, inspiring and enabling networks such as our Faith community and our Gay community, our Arts, Libraries and Theatre organisations. All fold together into a single prodigious affirmation of life by the Lee.

I'll always remember the day when I became conscious of this urban power of Cork. It was during the closing days of Cork's reign as a European Capital of Culture in 2005. I was taking an official from the Ministry of Culture in Budapest on a fact-finding and historical tour of the city, something I loved to do. This highly placed official was an historian by profession and she wanted to absorb the atmosphere of an Atlantic city. She was impressed by the total package of Cork, the beautiful winter city, the energy of Patrick Street

Thomas McCarthy

on Friday morning, the aromas of the English Market, the burning candles in Ss Peter and Paul's Church, the Crawford and Glucksman galleries, the great James Barry exhibition, the young European engineers she met drinking at café tables. At such moments, on days like that, Cork City makes a deep impression upon an educated stranger. This impression is not false, it is pure gold, and it is what good planning strives for. It is why hours and hours are spent researching, developing and resourcing the City Council's strategies and reports. It is why planners and ambitious local politicians try to create the most intelligent city possible, a city that shares the burden of the nation, not just a region. Urban culture is what you grow highly alert and intelligent citizens in: Cork has a great deal to offer Ireland, not just Cork. As the city demonstrated during its pulsating year as European Capital of Culture, or when hosting Queen Elizabeth II, the city responds to any national challenge with a generous sincerity and confidence. Cork is ready to put its shoulder to the wheel, to do some heavy lifting for Ireland as well as for itself. This is how it should be.

Cork City Planning Department Document, 2016

The Lonely Voice by Frank O'Connor

There is a well-known photograph of Frank O'Connor taken by the librarian Dermot Foley in 1930: Foley has captured the young adult O'Connor in the doorway of Pembroke Library. O'Connor was a librarian too, a custodian and keeper of the printed word, a bookish young man leaning against his newly painted, freshly pointed branch library. He was, by all accounts, a proactive and imaginative librarian, organizing readings and gramophone recitals to extend the reach of the library and to embed the new service within the community. Gifted, musical, a self-educated ex-IRA man who worshipped the memory of Michael Collins, on that day in 1930 O'Connor was already a published poet and fiction writer. At that moment, in the long boring pause after the Irish Revolution, he seemed to be gazing into the future. He can hardly have foreseen then all the literary immensity and pain that lay before him, all the rhetoric, betrayal and fame.

It is fitting that another library — in this case, Cork City Library — should republish this seminal work in the city where O'Connor began his career in the County Library Service whose headquarters was for many years in and around Cork's city centre. *The Lonely Voice* is now reissued to mark the centenary of the writer's birth. It is a matter of historical fact (to borrow an O'Connor phrase) that he was born as Michael O'Donovan on the 17th of September, 1903, in Douglas Street, Cork, just across the River Lee from the current City Library building. His father was a Sergeant of the Munster Fusiliers who had fought in South Africa, while his mother, Minnie O'Connor, had been sent into the wide world from the Good Shepherd Convent at the age of fourteen.

Thomas McCarthy

With a father who was a martyr to the drink his family lived the peripatetic existence of the loosely employed urban poor, moving from Douglas Street to Blarney Street to Harrington Square off Ballyhooly Road, close to the attractive and cultured quarter of St Luke's Cross. It was in this district that O'Connor's imagination caught fire. Harrington Square is no Mayfair or Ballsbridge, but it is an airy, intimate and atmospheric quarter. It is within easy walking distance of Cork City centre. It collects and amplifies the cacophony of exquisite sounds so particular to Cork. Halfway up the stairs of Cork life it mixes the rhetoric of the flat of the city with the whispering wicket gates of bourgeois Gardiner's Hill and Montenotte. If O'Connor's childhood home had been happier it would have been an almost perfect place for a social realist to begin his writing career.

Like many an only child O'Connor was a great collector of father figures. One thinks immediately of AE (George Russell) and W B Yeats. But the most powerful early influence on O'Connor, his first great father-love, if you like, was Daniel Corkery. The young Corkery arrived as a teacher at St Patrick's National School at a moment of high hopes and fierce literary energy in his own life. From him O'Connor learned Irish, as well as the rudiments of classical music, of Irish folklore, of visual art and reading. A highly motivated National Teacher, Corkery brought to the classroom not merely education but civilization. O'Connor thirsted for knowledge, for detailed explanations. Through those teenage years, through excitement and humiliation, through the Trade School of the North Monastery and a GSWR clerkship, Corkery provided a lifeline of books and gramophone records to the floundering author. But most assuredly, powerfully, preeminently, it was the gift of fiction that was the primary inheritance O'Connor received from Corkery. Walking through Cork City one day in 1916 O'Connor came upon a copy of *A Munster Twilight*, his teacher's first collection of stories. Containing elemental work like 'The Ploughing of Leaca-Na-Naomh' and 'Vanity', as well the uncompromising urban landscape of 'The Return' and 'The Cobbler's Den', this work was the spark that would propel two great Cork short-story writers, O'Connor and Ó Faoláin, into imaginative life. The young O'Connor saved a shilling to buy his own copy of the book. Ownership of the book became a ticket to adult adventure: it was entry into the world of Tolstoy, Chekhov and Turgenev. After *A Munster Twilight* O'Connor could never return to the comforts of childhood stories and English comic books. From then on he would be a disciple of Turgenev, like Corkery, of that social realism in marginalized worlds.

Which brings us to this book, *The Lonely Voice*. It is the work of a writer at the height of his powers, a writer who had just sold ten thousand hardback copies of his Knopf autobiography, lines from which would be quoted by John F Kennedy in his famous NASA moonshot speech. O'Connor was then a visiting professor at Stanford University, teaching students like Ken Kesey and Larry McMurtry — yet still a disciple of Corkery and Turgenev. This is a writer's book, entirely free of the critical jargon that suffocates personal insight and creativity throughout the world. Here there is none of that postgraduate quackery that disables young ambitions, nothing that turns the really gifted into lackeys of lecturers who should know better. What is so impressive still about *The Lonely Voice* is its very personal voice: oracular, passionate, Byronic. The writers Malcolm Cowley and Wallace Stegner who had invited O'Connor to Stanford in 1961 must have felt completely vindicated by this book. In place of dull criticism they got the gifted anecdotes that fill the margins of a writing life. They got a mature writer's viewpoint, the full blast escaping from the close custody of endless working hours.

O'Connor, who began as a poet, was never a prisoner to any kind of mysticism, Catholic or Celtic. Unhappiness in Harrington Square and hunger in a 1920s Republican prison camp would turn any young man into a Russian realist.

Thomas McCarthy

Appropriately his lecture series opened with an analysis of Turgenev's *A Sportsman's Sketches*. In discussing 'Khor and Kalinitch' he says, 'The device which Turgenev uses instead of old-fashioned narrative is antithesis — and, however that device may have been used by later writers, Turgenev always uses it with artistry.' But it is the story 'Yermolai and the Miller's Wife' that contains the essence of the modern short story. O'Connor identifies this essence as the 'telescoping of a whole life story into the experiences and comments of a couple of supernumeries'. And the four boys telling ghost stories in 'Byezhin Prairie' with its recollected sounds made by a drowning comrade immediately undermined by this information: 'He was not drowned; he was killed by a fall from his horse' — all of this reinforces Turgenev's anti-sentimental, point-counterpoint method so admired by O'Connor. There are few writers, according to O'Connor, who had as much of the essential stuff of humanity in them as Turgenev.

O'Connor is tougher on Maupassant, more withering and critical. He is 'repelled' by the 'skimpiness' of the later writing when the powerful influence of Flaubert (so evident in 'The Tellier House') begins to wane and the characters remain unrealized. 'The surface of a great story is like a sponge: it sucks up hundreds of impressions that have nothing to do with the anecdote,' says O'Connor. Spoken like a true poet. When he moves on to the subject of Chekhov O'Connor is even more expansive, admiring, and responsive in the face of the Russian's brilliant exposition of the moral slavery that entraps ordinary human lives. Laevsky, that despicable character in 'The Duel' is the one who establishes the best aesthetic for short fiction: 'he would have to bring himself to stern, uncompromising action.'

It is while discussing the stories of Rudyard Kipling that O'Connor moves closest to a clear definition of good writing. Kipling seemed to write out of a submerged population, the British soldiers and imperial servants in India, who could be compared to the submerged populations of prostitutes in

The Lonely Voice by Frank O'Connor

Maupassant or harsh countrymen in Chekhov. But Kipling's weakness of characterization and narrative inability betrays a deeper political falsehood: Europeans in India were not submerged in any real sense; like the Anglo-Irish they were an Ascendancy. In describing them as submerged Kipling embodies hysteria rather than loneliness. Kipling's is an oratorical approach, 'a consciousness of the individual reader as an audience who, at whatever cost to artistic properties, must be reduced to tears or laughter or rage'. Kipling's flaw, according to O'Connor, is his inability to speak with a lonely voice: 'Kipling always speaks as though he himself were one of a gang.'

Why did James Joyce not write another short story after 'The Dead'? In a brilliant reading of *Dubliners* O'Connor sketches the decline of imaginative autonomy in one writer's submerged population. A degenerate Ireland pops a few bottles of stout for Parnell; they form the three volleys of Joyce's farewell to the short story. The fictional journey from 'The Sisters' to 'The Dead' is a journey from social experience to incantatory writing. In Joyce one finds a gradual ascendancy of grammar, an escape from narrative into 'intolerably self-conscious' moods: 'Joyce's submerged population is no longer being submerged by circumstances but by Joyce's irony.'

O'Connor goes on to identify and catalogue each submerged population, from Mansfield to Hemingway, from Isaac Babel to D H Lawrence. In Mansfield he sees intelligence and brilliance at work; in Hemingway he sees the danger that storytelling could become a minor art where 'It is all too abstract.' In Babel's *Red Cavalry* (1926) he names a book that 'influenced me very deeply when it appeared in English'. Here in the narratives of Civil War, of quick movement in the region of Odessa, of brother against brother, O'Connor must have found the social and political harshness that was a counterpoint to Corkery's *A Munster Twilight*. In reading it he must have recognized the writer in himself and the

Thomas McCarthy

materials of fiction in his own lived experience. The price of freedom, in the widest sense, is to have to experience epiphanies of human nature. 'The saddest thing about the short-story,' he says, 'is the eagerness with which those who write it best try to escape from it. It is a lonely art, and they too are lonely.'

But *The Lonely Voice* is the product of a crowded companionship. It is written with the trenchant eagerness of a master, an Irish writer in the prime of life. It is offered now, in this centenary of O'Connor's birth, as a gift from a Cork Library Service that serves his own region, his own submerged community. We should treasure these trenchant opinions. They remind us of the strength of Frank O'Connor's character and they restore to us some of the tone of his wonderful voice.

Cork City Libraries,
2003

University College Cork Conferring Address

President of UCC, Professors, Reverends, graduates and distinguished guests:

I spent most of my undergraduate hours at University College Cork writing poetry in an armchair that was placed against the window on the third floor of the New Science Building. In that armchair I wrote at least six of the poems that won the Patrick Kavanagh Award in 1977, an award that turned my head away from academe towards the peculiar world of literature. As one of the worst students ever to pass through the gates of UCC, floating along poetically on a summer Pass in Archaeology and Geography, allowed to do the Honours English papers by grace of the College authorities before doing the MA Qual in English, it's a particularly poignant honour for me to be invited by UCC's President Murphy and Professor Caroline Fennell, to attend an actual *Honours* conferring ceremony. So, I am very moved to be here, and I am equally conscious of how wonderful you are, today's Honours graduates, to have kept to your studies, to have handed up all your assignments, to have fulfilled the hopes of your professors and your families. I congratulate you. Well done. You are now graduates of one of the most beautiful and one of the most highly regarded universities on this side of the Atlantic. I know you will mark this day by allowing at least six weeks to elapse before asking your parents or your bank manager for more money.

But before talking any more about you and how terrific you are, and you are terrific scholars: let me say a few words about UCC, this academy, establishment and campus. It is forty years almost to the day since I walked between the laurels, rhododendrons and tricuspidarias, past the tennis courts, on into the galleried lecture rooms of the old West Wing. I was one of the O'Malley generation caught by the rising tide. I was the first person in my family to go to university. My brother Kevin followed me six years later and he redeemed the academic honour of the family by becoming a Kelleher Scholar in Engineering all the way through.

What struck me forty years ago as a youth who understood trees and flowers, and it is as true today as it was in 1972, was how well managed the entire establishment of UCC really is. It is impeccably managed. Look at the maintenance of the fabric, the shrewd, long-term planting, the condition of paintwork and door frames, as well as of glass and steel. We tend to forget that a university has to self-govern; it has to find willing staff who will support committees and write administrative reports in addition to their teaching and research duties. How lucky we are in Munster to share the fruit of all their administration and all their teaching in this lovely place.

But this day is about you. About how wonderful you are. How gifted you are. And what a future lies before you. You would never think it, would you, the way things have been, that there is any future at all? You and your parents have lived through half a decade of relentless decline. In fact my guess would be that your families have frightened the lives out of you at this stage; my honest guess is that a more anxious generation of university graduates hasn't assembled in this place since October of 1939. Our economists and the bankers seem to have got everything wrong. We have inherited a new Congested District, the useless and sterile carcass of our Celtic Tiger. It is all a genuine source of anxiety, and even despair. My economist friends, all of whom wished they'd gone into poetry, or at least stayed in the Long Valley or Bill Ludgate's bar with the poets, tell me that we need about another ten per cent. Ten per cent of what, I ask them. Ten per cent further

University College Cork Conferring Address

decline, they say, of wages and costs; and then we can start all over again.

I don't know. But I can tell you this, as a poet, and as one of the O'Malley generation, the future will be much better than anyone in this hall can ever imagine. There is nothing in the public discourse, nothing in the media, nothing in any political programme presented to us, that can give us the equipment of hope. Hope, as the poet Máire Mhac an tSaoi once explained to me, hope is not a feeling, it is much more powerful than that: it is a virtue. It moves things. It drives enterprise, it forms companies, it assembles community workshops and community-based action groups. Hope inoculates us against inertia. It makes us turn our faces to the sun, despite the stiff breeze.

Why do I tell you that the future will be much better than anyone in this hall can imagine? And I tell you this with complete confidence in Ireland and its people. I tell you because I've worked in a library all my life: I've stayed close to the archives, the papers, the microfilms, the biographies, the reports, the registers of electors, the constant readers. I've handled a book by experts, published by W H Allen in 1954, that predicted there would be no one left living in Ireland by the early twenty-first century, such was the pattern of migration and population decline: 'many sober students think that the Irish are already far along on the path to extinction', the learned editor wrote. I've handled Colman O Mahony's masterful book, *In The Shadows: Life in Cork, 1750-1930*, a book that will tell you what real Cork slums were like: how, in the summer of 1847, about 15,000 people each day — 15,000 souls! — were given outdoor relief at Barrack Street, St Luke's, Shandon, Blackpool and Harpur's Lane. Nowadays, as any of you who have worked with the poor will know, it is heroin as well as hunger.

As someone who works in a Public Library I hope that there is a scholar in this hall today who will give Ireland its definitive work of historic sociology. Such a sociology is desperately needed. We have had enough of hatred, outrage, disappointment: our editorial writers can't invent any more honest indignation. What we need now is to explain ourselves to ourselves, and move on.

One thing I am sure of: time is on your side. You have more time than I have. You own more of the future than I do; and not only is it your time, but it is time full of infinite possibilities. No doubt you will see people, as I do in the library every day, trying everything to heal the past, going from Reiki to chakra crystal healing, from Alexander technique to devotion to Padre Pio. How resilient, how astonishingly resilient, people are in the aftermath of trauma. Ireland is like that. As James Connolly said, 'Ireland without her people is nothing to me.' For certain you will have time to see Ireland rise again. And you, *you*, will rise with it.

My own generation, the late baby boomers, will begin to vacate the public service within the next two to seven years. Even if the public service in Ireland is shrunk back to the smallest possible number imagined by a fantasizing director of the ECB there are still quarter of a million public servants who will have to be replaced over time to run this country. Not now, perhaps not next year, but sooner than any politician thinks, your qualifications and your qualities of caring and advocacy will be needed by Ireland. And you will be ready for such national work because while others wallowed in inert self-pity you never lost faith in yourselves: you studied and you graduated. This is a brilliant personal achievement and must remain an enduring source of pride to you and to everyone associated with you.

When I look at you assembled here on this important day I am reminded of another fine day in UCC, a day years ago when the great Scottish poet, Hugh MacDiarmid, read to a capacity crowd in this campus. As MacDiarmid said to us in his great poem, 'Island Funeral', we may have only a small part to play in the great orchestra of Europe, but it is a real part and only we can play it. Listen to MacDiarmid:

University College Cork Conferring Address

*The cornet solo of our Gaelic islands
Will sound out every now and again
Through all eternity.*

I have heard it and am content forever.

Autumn 2011

PART SIX
A QUESTION OF RESPONDING

Poetry and the Memory of Fame

I once felt quite famous as a poet. Indeed, now that I think of it, I have felt famous twice. These two periods of really unsettling fame came back to me recently as I dealt with a young poet at the Lending Desk of the Public Library where I've worked for over thirty years. The young borrower had been coming into my city-centre branch for over a year, dropping grease-stained envelopes stuffed with five or six poems and then returning a few days later to listen to my responses to his raw and energetic work. There was this one morning when we'd had a very strenuous, useful exchange of ideas around his improving technique. In that pause when a conversation just ends the young man suddenly said to me: 'You know so much about poetry; you read it so closely. Have you ever thought of writing anything yourself?' At first, I didn't know what to say. Should I recite the titles of my eleven published books, including eight collections of poems? Should I be angry with this world of the young that has never seen my books? What the hell was he doing, handing me these regular tasks in poetry if he didn't know that I was already a published poet, that I was at least one step ahead of him? He explained that one of my library colleagues told him that I was interested in poetry, that he should show me his work. He turned away and left. Soon after, I was transferred to another branch library in a faraway suburb — my last posting before I retired early to write full-time — so that we've never met again. Hopefully we will meet again, long enough for him to sign his first published book.

But his lack of recognition or, rather, my umbrage at not being recognized, has made me think of the way our names ebb and flow, in and out of 'fame', over a lifetime. What does it feel like to be recognized, to be made famous by persistent attention? Yes, I do remember very clearly the first time that I felt carried away, catapulted onward by a force larger than my own life. I was just sixteen years old at the time. It was in the spring of 1970 and I'd had my first poems published in the local high school magazine. I received a letter, sent to me through my English teacher, from a mysterious Anglo-Irish aristocrat who lived in a grand mansion just three miles from my school. The letter praised my poems and invited me to take tea in this gentleman's library. A chauffeur-driven Mercedes was dispatched to the school gate and I was driven off to my first encounter with the aristocracy, chauffeured by Tommy, who was once a rear-gunner in a Lancaster bomber. 'The master thinks yer poems are grand,' Tommy said to me, 'he's mighty interested in meetin' a fellow writer from the neighbourhood.' I can see now that he was trying not to burst out laughing. I was met at the door of the eighteenth-century mansion by a formally attired butler and led into a magnificent library that contained 20,000 volumes of mainly Slavic texts. The literary gentleman was W E D Allen, a former British diplomat and spy catcher, former Unionist-Conservative Member for West Belfast in the Imperial Parliament of the 1920s, former editor of the 1930s Fascist magazine, *The Blackshirt*, author of the best history of the Georgian people published in the English language (according to Laurens van der Post in his autobiography, *Yet Being Someone Other*), author of *Caucasian Battlefields*, *The Ukraine* and *Problems of Turkish Power in the Sixteenth Century*. This seventy-year-old aristocratic scholar climbed down from the gallery of his two-storey-high bookshelves and introduced me to his fourth wife, a quiet Australian nurse who'd come to take care of his dying third wife, Natasha Maximovna, who had been the ikon-restorer daughter of a Moscow lawyer. Mr Allen's first wife had been the debutante daughter of the Earl of Lovelace, a woman who'd probably been the basis for the character of the globe-trotting Amber, the love interest in Allen's pseudonymously published 1936 spy novel, *Strange Coast*. These details I discovered later.

Though the penniless son of a country postman I wasn't in the least intimidated or impressed by this ménage. After all I was a poet from a small town that was famous for its poets — 'Ah, Cappoquin of the poets,' was how the venerable Máire Mhac an tSaoi addressed me when we were first introduced. I assumed instinctively all the social status that the title 'poet' confers in Ireland. I argued furiously about Irish history and poetry with the assembled company that included two Russian scholars and two directors from Barings merchant bank in London (my Mr Allen, as I discovered from various editions of *Who's Who* in the local library, was a director of several public corporations and a member of Gentlemen's clubs, including Bucks and Cavendish in London, the Kildare Street Club in Dublin and Cercle d'Orient in Istanbul). After several lively hours I left the house with a borrowed leather-bound copy of Lermontov's poems. In the years that followed I was chauffeured back and forth across the Irish countryside, carrying manila folders full of handwritten poems, as if to the manor born. Although I didn't even possess a typewriter I thought it the most natural thing in the world for a poet to be chauffeur driven, pampered by butlers and petted by elderly aristocratic ladies with bald Chihuahuas in their handbags. The novelist Muriel Spark, a house guest, set fire to one of my execrable poems with her long cigarette. She kissed me and begged forgiveness. A few years later she had a falling-out with her publisher over the ownership of a horse. At the dinner table a director of the National Gallery sought my opinion on Paul Henry's paintings. I informed him that Mr Henry was colour-blind. The daughter of a former British Ambassador to Moscow presented me with a copy of Ginsberg's *Howl*: it was a most singular introduction to American culture. All assembled agreed that America under Nixon had gone to the dogs, that Vietnam would fall to the friends of Claud Cockburn, a Communist gentleman who lived in another mansion in a little village nearby, and that Russian tanks would reach the outskirts of Paris before the winter of 1974. All were convinced that the future of civilization lay in some small tax-efficient European principality like Monaco or, perhaps (if Tito could become agreeable) in the apartment of some exiled princess in Montenegro. Dry Martinis and Old-fashioneds, peach champagne and Hennessy Cognac, all floated around the lacquered Russian antiques and Ottoman prints: this was certainly the life for a poet. My imagination became saturated with the materials of their cosmopolitan politics. If this was the life of a writer I was signed up for the duration.

Also a house guest in this lovely, not at all crumbling, Anglo-Irish mansion was Terence de Vere White, Literary Editor of *The Irish Times*. By the time I was seventeen years old I had my first poem published in the *Irish Times* famous Saturday Page. After that I became insufferable and unteachable with vanity. My school grades went slowly downhill as I studied less and less — I was simply too busy in the high society now offered by the life of a poet. A drying wind of fame blew and blew and blew: my name was called again and again in the most seductive aristocratic voices. I was a poet who had risen from the serfs and they were all smitten like Moscow boyars. To be petted continuously was simply adorable and I fell languidly into undergraduate life in the nearest city, Cork. I tried to do as little as possible and succeeded. But Mr Allen died suddenly while I was at college and his house and library were auctioned off to strangers before I could claim back the two books I'd lent him. By then I'd found another poet-adoring aristocrat, the grandson of Ireland's premier peer, the Duke of Leinster. I moved my books into a wing of his beautiful shooting lodge inside thirty acres of woodland, organized the garden, the kitchen, the rental payments from a tenant farmer, the hanging and lighting of priceless Jakob Bogdani paintings. I held my own court for poet-friends by the Adam chimneypiece, beneath the beautiful portrait of his mother, Inez, Lady FitzGerald. My poems were dispatched regularly to the London offices of the exclusive stockbroking firm of Panmure Gordon where he was a Partner. They were typed in triplicate by a secretary called Miss Kent and returned to me. Lloyd's Log of underwriting names as well as the *TLS* became my weekend reading. My manuscripts, at least, were having an international life. All went well. I tended the gentleman's acres and wrote poems.

Then, in late 1977, the second blessed wind of fame blew open the windows of my writing life that had become more settled and routine. It was a phone call, as often happens. My parents, like many working-class couples in 1970s Ireland, couldn't afford a phone, so that the call came to me through a neighbour who was the local fire chief. I jumped over three garden walls to reach his hallway and heard, for the first time, the voice of an excited journalist. 'Congratulations! You've won the Patrick Kavanagh Award. The judges, Seamus Heaney, John McGahern and John Ryan, loved your work. We need to get a photographer to you straight away. Would you be prepared for interviews before five this evening? We want to run it in the Sunday papers, in all editions.' A full-page broadsheet feature interview with me on my twenty-seven poems was published in that week's *Sunday Independent*, followed by my photograph in every national newspaper on the Monday morning. This was the very beginning of seven years of sheer wonder, years that would be full of interviews and photographers, of invitations and introductions, of readings and wild reviews — and of three collections, *The First Convention, The Sorrow Garden* and *The Non-Aligned Storyteller* that filled my youth with undeserved honour. Less than a year after the first award I was descending the steps of a United Airlines jet into the suffocating heat of an Iowa August, a sojourn where I would share an apartment with the legendary Pakistani Lenin Prize winner, Faiz Ahmad Faiz, and the Greek short-story writer, Dimitris Nollas, and

Thomas McCarthy

walk up and down S Dubuque Street with Paul Engle as he reminisced about the Irish poets he'd hired for his famous Workshop, the gifted and unreliable, the puritan and the licentious. In Prairie Lights Books I found two American books that would set my heart ablaze with envy of their beauty, *Self-Portrait in a Convex Mirror* by John Ashbery and *Stars Which See, Stars Which Do Not See* by Marvin Bell. I came back to Ireland to write the poems that only Ireland can force one to write: the grandson of the Duke of Leinster sent a car to Shannon to collect me. But in Iowa, at the International Writing Program, I had encountered the modern and this had punctured the balloon of the hermetic aristocracy. I tried to settle down to a more modern and humiliating ordinary life in the City Library. But in those years, when I was still only in my mid-twenties, work was just an interlude of rest between flights; for when you're young and suddenly visible the world absolutely adores you. It literally wants to eat you. I fell into bed each night shredded by attention. It is truly impossible to explain but it is bigger than any personal strength that one can muster against it; one is simply carried along and constantly, youthfully, so ungrateful.

Those were my two great encounters with fame: seven glorious years that have been followed by over two decades of a productive quiet. There is a time for everything, I think, and life is generally very wise. It comforts the poet who will listen. In general most poets' lives are lived in a measured obscurity, punctuated by the brief frissons of published books. That long quiet through middle age is like the re-emergence of white space around the very first poems. That quiet brings wisdom and turns many lyric poets into novelists because they begin to see, as the late Frank O'Connor pointed out, those patterns of injustice and intrigue that fill even the most banal life. Early encounters with an aristocracy taught me that one can write poetry devoid of social purpose — that certain poetic projects can be sheer self-indulgence. Left alone, I fell into a companionship of eccentric reading, collecting every edition of a forgotten priest-writer of the nineteenth century — Francis Sylvester Mahony, or Father Prout as he styled himself in his great published work, a book of essays that was reprinted every seven years throughout the nineteenth century. This priest's most famous poem is 'The Bells of Shandon', sung by every sentimental Irish exile for over a hundred years — what the Irish exile did not know was that the work was part of a complex linguistic attack on Ireland's national poet, Thomas Moore of *Moore's Melodies*. Mahony/Prout hated Moore and hated Daniel O'Connell, the two national heroes of Ireland. Hating them, and their fame, became his life's work. 'I have been kissed by no man except dear Father Prout,' Elizabeth Barrett Browning wrote to her husband from Florence. This was the kind of company my obscure Cork balladeer and essayist kept in London, Paris and Florence. He was independently wealthy, fluent in French, Italian, Greek and Latin, and he could do what he liked — which he did, between bouts of singing and whiskey drinking. How can knowing any of this be of any use to any poet of today, to any earnest contemporary reader of Poetry? I can only answer: why, in the name of God, should everything be useful? Is it not possible for me and for you to make poems out of completely useless information? These elements of useless information, these aristocracies of self-indulgence, have filled over two decades of my quiet life in the Public Library, giving me two books of poetry that I am proud to have written, *Merchant Prince* (2005) and *The Last Geraldine Officer* (2009). 'You do realize,' my wife Catherine warned me again and again, 'that no one will understand a word of this stuff. There seems to be no purpose to it when every Irish poet is trying to address Ulster's problems.' She was right — neither book climbed to the lower reaches of a national shortlist, never mind a literary prize. Oh, but the company I kept while they were being written!

This high companionship of self-indulgence is hugely underrated in modern teaching. It needs to be taught again.

Thomas McCarthy

Poetry, the best poetry, the most purposeful poetry, arises out of the fullness of the self. It is not the result of a given programme, an agenda, a canon. The dynamic noise of a poetry workshop, its communal imperative, does compel young poets to be clear rather than complex, to be social rather than desolate. But the best education in the poetic art must oscillate between the two, between the need to dream fiercely and the need to communicate. Our personal temperament is an essential part of our technical equipment as poets: it is the one part of our equipment that we cannot teach to others, though many of us yearn to do so as we grow older. Our temperament is the thing that will die with us, leaving traces only in the best work. Technically — I mean from the standpoint of writing new poems — all the historic suffering of the Irish nation has no more moral weight than the anonymous cadaver on the dissecting table of Gottfried Benn. The materials available to a new poet are that simple, that open, that personal. Have courage, I would say to any new poet; have courage while your poem invites you into itself. This fullness of being — the vain clarity before a poem begins — must have been what the twenty-five-year-old André Gide meant when he wrote in his *Journals*: 'The most beautiful things are those that madness prompts and reason writes.' Essential to remain between the two, close to madness when you dream and close to reason when you write. In other words, the fullness of your self is available from the start: exploit it. For poetry's sake, keep dissecting the self until you find the infection that is interesting. Be open to technique, I advise younger poets; by all means, learn everything new that can be learned about a poetic effect, about what the phrases do when they are layered together on the page. Understand that a poetic tone shared and recognized across the English language is part of the Esperanto of our modern era — we search for a tone that reassures us of the author's modernity. Far from avoiding new work from young writers most editors yearn to find something new, yet something with an assured

Poetry and the Memory of Fame

and seriously polished tone. But temperament, the personal atmosphere of your life as a poet, that is something the gods have given you at birth: throw a security cordon around it, it is yours for life, through all the fame and, more usually, the persistent absence of fame.

These matters of poetry and fame, of indulgence and wilful obscurity, seem to be in the air again as I travel throughout Ireland. This year, 2015, has been designated by our government as the year to celebrate William Butler Yeats on the 150th anniversary of his birth — 'Oho, noho,' as Samuel Beckett said to the Cork beggar who'd promised to say a prayer for him. Not that again. Not that there's anything wrong with Yeats: his work is exquisite and his fame is legendary. It's just, well, you know . . . What about encouraging a few people to read living poets, to buy books by the living? Yeats's death in a bleak year (1939) reminds me not of Yeats, but of another Irish poet who was wandering around the East Coast of the US at that time — the Ulster poet, Louis MacNeice. I've been carrying a copy of MacNeice's collection of that time, *Plant and Phantom,* in my satchel these last few months. I love his plain company. I love that he was wandering. I love that he wrote this, in 'Plain Speaking' — 'Definition is tautology: man is man, / Woman woman, and tree tree, and world world.' At a time when Yeats died, when Ireland and Europe were falling apart, it was important to state plain facts. MacNeice would elaborate further just a few months later in his magnificent critical study, *The Poetry of W B Yeats.* Here he is on the art of Yeats's poetry:

> *The thought taken from its context is esoteric and, indeed, unsound, but that does not matter for it is perfectly fused into the poetry. Diction and rhythm are happily wedded to their subject. Yeats was a great trickster with words, but now there is something more solid beneath the gilding.*

MacNeice had arrived at his chapter on Yeats's masterpieces, *The Winding Stair* and *The Tower*. MacNeice overcame his and Yeats's melancholy by studying it. Overcoming it gave him prodigious moral strength, enough strength for him to return to England and engage in the great war against Fascism, a war that was, at that moment, being fought for the very survival of English civilization. Morally poets seem to wander from moments of dread to moments of dread.

For many months after Seamus Heaney's death in Dublin I felt a catatonic sense of melancholy. It's no exaggeration to say that many poets felt that a second Yeats had died, that Ireland, once more, would struggle on in that long, familiar Yeatsian shadow. An atmosphere of foreboding had already been in the air, in the very bones of poetry, after the death of Dennis O'Driscoll less than a year earlier — Dennis, so loved and such a lover of every kind of poetry, had been both a superb poet and Irish poetry's number one cheerleader. Their deaths have created a singular, catastrophic sense of absence. That anything else might get written seems like a miracle. Heaney's fame displaced so many other 1960s brilliant careers in the public imagination of Ireland — Kinsella, Mhac an tSaoi, Montague, Mahon — that many Irish endings seemed to fold into his spectacular trajectory. The funeral itself, broadcast live on national television, with Presidents, Ambassadors, Nuncios, actors and rock stars, was as close as a non-President might ever get to a State Funeral. And, in typical Irish fashion, it was a funeral of two parts: the Dublin part and the Ulster part. In Ireland the integrity of our historic quarrel is always captured at a burial.

I miss Seamus Heaney's voice on Irish radio and television, and I miss those distinctive, bold black-inked letters and postcards from Dennis O'Driscoll. A poem published in some far-off place or a poem broadcast on radio was sure to elicit a postcard from Dennis; it was as if one was being minded. Now there is no big-hearted creature left to watch over us and to praise us so intimately. Was Ireland ever so silent? In

Poetry and the Memory of Fame

truth, for my own generation at least, the deaths of these poets may mean the end of greatness. While they lived the plot of poetry thickened: poetry had an urgently visible, public, even political, role. While they lived we were all attending at their extraordinary poetry workshop invented by Yeats and directed adroitly by Heaney, a workshop called Irish life. Leaving Dublin after the funeral cortège headed north I felt as I felt when I was a twenty-four-year-old boarding the plane at Cedar Rapids airport, leaving Iowa and the companionship of serious mentors and literary scholars. A sense of hope or political intensity is always left behind on the hot tarmac of experience. Now poetry has become very private again, very urban and European, as hermetic as the private life in Samuel Beckett's letters or in the lyrics of Gottfried Benn. Instead of catching the fruits of an outdoor Ulster poetry in Heaney's profuse orchard we must now scurry like true Europeans along the backstreet pavements and hard cobblestones, like refugees clutching our little green ration books. We must write with the guilt of ordinary survivors.

Yet the idea that in poetry there is only so much oxygen to go around is a mistaken one, an erroneous proprietorial and peasant point of view, as if Irish poets had to draw lots to divide the Encumbered Estate of a dead landlord. Poetry is truly an anaerobic creature, creating the atmosphere to sustain itself from the very atmosphere of itself that it creates. It is foolish to look outside the act of making poetry for that oxygen. One's personal poetry, the fruit of one's temperament, is an unassailable realm. Its success or failure has hardly anything to do with anyone else in the deepest sense. There is, of course, the post-facto politics of published texts, the world of reviews and awards, yet this world is but a distant rumble of thunder barely audible in the realm where poems get written. So often one meets new poets who are obsessed with the 'politics' of poetry and its trivia: they make the heart sink because you feel that they may never arrive at that point of repose where their deepest work will get written. The place

Thomas McCarthy

where poems get made is much quieter than the place of fame. You want to tell these youngsters to slow down, not to rush at that first rung of Cavafy's ladder or they may miss it. In the Irish context it is important to recall not just the illustrious career of our lost Nobel Laureate and the 1960s careers in poetry that may have been pushed sideways by the force of Heaney's fame, but those other talents and careers that flourished in the long Heaney era during the 1980s and 1990s. There have been significant, even illustrious, other careers in contemporary Irish poetry — think of the work of Eavan Boland and Paul Durcan, of Nuala Ní Dhomhnaill and Paul Muldoon. While the greater public realm rained Heaney achievements upon us all these other Irish poets went out into the sodden garden and grew a harvest of their own making. In their now long careers they have been exemplary. Beyond them, in the 2000s and 2010s, another generation flourishes, youthful, exotic, dramatic, filled with purpose and uncanny professionalism. Names like Alan Gillis and Leontia Flynn, Leanne O'Sullivan and Ailbhe Ní Ghearbhuigh come to mind: their newness and exuberance is simply magical. These poets endure both inside and outside fame: their permanence is already an inner permanence. Fame may come up noisily to meet them, but if it doesn't, what matter: their work is a thing of beauty. When you meet poets who are so young and so patently gifted, really burnished for fame, you want to do something — to push them on, to shove them into the arms of excited reporters, photographers, award givers. You want them to have that lovely feeling of being carried away by fame, if only for the first few years. After that, when the chauffeur-driven Mercedes and butlers carrying Dry Martinis have disappeared, when things become calm in that long inertia of mid-career, they can reap a more mediated harvest, in the manner of Norman MacCaig or Stanley Kunitz, of desolately beautiful later poems.

Poetry,
2012

Praise in Which I Live and Move and Have My Being by Paul Durcan

Veteran readers of the *Examiner* will remember the marvellous contributions of UCC graduate, Paul Durcan, published regularly in this paper some years ago. On many a grey morning in O'Connell Street, Dungarvan, I boarded the bus that once nearly killed me in 1978 only to read his words while we trundled across the Southern regions between Grange, Youghal, Killeagh and Castlemartyr. By the time I'd reached a fresh cup of tea and a curranty bun in the Glandore Café of Cork's Parnell Bus Station I'd absorbed every word of Durcan for that day. In what now seems a Cork golden era of Patrick Galvin and Bobby O'Donoghue, of Lucy and Montague, Durcan contributed his generous, unique thoughts on poets and poetry, on art and life. He was already a published poet, having seen *Endsville* through the press in 1967. But within years of those *Examiner* columns Durcan would rise to Parnassian greatness with crucially important books, *The Berlin Wall Café* and *Going Home to Russia*. In those later years Poetry Book Society Choice, Whitbread and Cholmondeley Prizes as well as a massive reading public attended to his unique fame and public persona. But this was a fame that came to an intensely private man whose terror of having attention drawn to himself is cleverly admitted in the first poem of this new collection. He watches the popular novelist, Amanda Brunker, signing her books in Hodges Figgis:

> 'The third thing I think is: Roll over Jane Austen!
> What cunning, what audacity, what breezy, cool arrogance!'

Thomas McCarthy

Marvelling at the confidence of the very young and the very beautiful he writes, 'Methinks I tick too much.' In later poems, such as 'The Lady in Weirs' or 'To Dympna Who Taught Me Online Banking', he comes face to face with an older, less competent self, a spirit that lives alone. Those who live alone, the homeless, the imprisoned, the maternal and the saintly, all populate this book of praise and elegy. In 'Post-haste to John Moriarty, Easter Sunday, 2007' he captures that sense of spiritual journeying, a peace in being near someone holy who leads the Stations of the Cross beyond Westport:

> *And I could hear you, John,*
> *Among their cadences,*
> *Their luscious crevices,*
> *Your torrential whispers,*
>   *Et egressus est Jesus cum discipulus suis trans torrentem Cedron.*

The spiritual formation of the poet, those preambles and prayers that punctuate a devout Christian life, are an essential part of Durcan's texture and textile. The title of his latest book is taken from the liturgical world, coming as it does from Acts 17:28 — 'For in Him we live and move and have our being —' though Paul Durcan must have derived more specific comfort from the apostle's subsequent phrase 'as also some of your own poets have said, "For we are also His offspring."'

Durcan was born during the Emergency into a privileged legal family with strong Mayo Fine Gael connections. There is no doubt, both socially and spiritually, that one can take the Jesuit boy from Gonzaga but one cannot remove Gonzaga from the learned poet. His fall out of heaven has been a steeper fall precisely because of the heights from which haut bourgeois Ireland has fallen. For decades Durcan has mapped our country as it descended into hell. No other poet was so well prepared for this prolonged and bitter cartography. In our own lifetimes we lost not only a system of faith but an elaborate context out of which we moulded our marriages, businesses and political loyalties. Durcan's childhood was spent in the abundant Irish Catholic world that is now almost completely forgotten, misconstrued and misrepresented. Durcan in his poetry and commentary has interrogated all of these matters, pre-dating Dermot Morgan in his satirical humour, anticipating Eoghan Harris in his ecumenical politics and Nuala O'Faolain or Nell McCafferty in his companionable praise of strong women. He is pre-eminently the poet of the strong woman, whether it's the Limerick PhD candidate in 'Petit Déjeuner with Breda', the Bosnian beggar in 'Mother and Child, Merrion Square West' or the artist in 'Stage Four':

There was a kind of nobleness about Helen Barry Moloney —

Of indomitable gaiety, of gritty integrity.
Of uncompromisable spirit, a rebel artist.

Each poet belongs to his or her own generation. An identifiable generation accumulates around an artist the way mussels grow around an old rope immersed in seawater. Generations do follow and new readers are born but the first readership clings to a writer like a family. Durcan's readership was that first generation of our Catholic decline. In his work one can see the disintegration of an entire bourgeois Ireland: imaginatively he was the first to grab Ireland as it fell from grace. His poems accumulate on the seashore of the publishing world, glittering shards and deeply gouged jewels of educated sensibility. If Ireland ever became lost to history the decades between 1968 and 2008 might be reconstructed from the narratives found in Paul Durcan's reimagined world. People have awaited his books the way another readership awaited a new collection by Auden or Seamus Heaney. Durcan's themes speak intensely and emotionally of a grief-stricken

Thomas McCarthy

afterglow in Irish life. This new collection is both a witness document and a beautiful work of art. His work has a constantly prophetic feel to it: in truth, he consoles us:

> *By resorting to the ancient rite of lighting a fire*
> *In a public place under a tree to placate the gods . . .*

Irish Examiner,
2012

Collected Poems of Dennis O'Driscoll

Where to begin with Dennis O'Driscoll? His untimely death in 2012 was tragic, not just for his belovèd family but for hundreds of readers and followers of poetry. His was a prodigious talent, witty, ironic, sardonic, prophetic, but his influence as commentator, editor and general 'cheerer-upper' of the entire Irish poetic scene was priceless and irreplaceable. He was on first-name terms with scores of writers across the world. He had read the works of hundreds of poets thoroughly and he had formed a very settled and definite opinion on their value as artists. He shared these opinions in published commentary and edited editions, as well as upon hastily written postcards and lengthy early evening phone calls. An Irish poet might be published in the most obscure small journal, but Dennis would unearth the work and make a comment. A goodly portion of this bustling energy and commentary is captured in *Troubled Thoughts, Majestic Dreams* and *The Outnumbered Poet*, his two prose books published by The Gallery Press. A senior public servant like C H Sisson or Archibald MacLeish, O'Driscoll adored the world created by poets and poetry. He trusted this world and all its reversals and reverberations: he would have had no other world. He published nine collections of well-crafted and fully premeditated poetry. His last collection, *Update*, published posthumously in 2014 and a PBS Special Commendation, was also the swansong of Peter Jay's Anvil Press Poetry in London. O'Driscoll's posthumous future now lies with that great Manchester mothership of poetry, Carcanet Press, and with Copper Canyon Press in the United States. Yes, he was a distinctly Irish poet, that need hardly be said, but his world contained Michael Hamburger and Miroslav Holub — he was as involved in their tones and biographies as if they were also from a busy town in County Tipperary.

The first time I heard Dennis O'Driscoll's name mentioned it was mentioned with alarm. The voice calling his name on the stairs of 6 Sidney Place, Cork, was that of the young Waterford poet, Seán Dunne: 'Shit, McCarthy, did you know that Dennis O'Driscoll is a Munster-man?'

'He's not,' I explained, 'doesn't he write for *Hibernia* and isn't he a civil servant in Dublin? He's a Dubliner.'

'No, he's not. He's from Tipperary and he's just written to me. His poems are amazing. He should be in my anthology.'

That was more than thirty years ago when Seán was editing his *Poets of Munster,* the first such anthology since O'Daly's *The Poets and Poetry of Munster* in 1849. What worried the young Waterford editor was that the ink was nearly dry on his selection and he held in his hand a sheaf of a Tipperary man's work that couldn't be omitted because it was so good. Swift revisions were made and poems were shunted overboard to make space for poems like this:

'After Vinokurov'

Objects speak louder than words.

or

And here is the stone that made the river dance . . .

'Being', a poem for Julie O'Callaghan, would contain sections titled 'Entropy', 'Skeleton', and 'Death' — which contained the lines 'what will be our certified cause of death / will we expire with the lost memory of arteriosclerosis / dissolving in alcohol. Crumbling with pain / basted in our own body fat, shivering with old age . . . ' He was still in his twenties when he wrote those lines.

Collected Poems of Dennis O'Driscoll

That was in the early 1980s: the poet of *Kist* from Dolmen Press had been located correctly and a distinctive voice in Irish poetry had announced itself. Such flinty darkness in a poet so young was both impressive and strangely attractive. 'What'll I say about a fella like this?' Seán continued, balancing on the dodgy stairs, 'he must be dying or something. I'll have a chat with John Ennis about him.' More than thirty years later, in *Update*, O'Driscoll would continue to provoke us in that tone he established so early:

> *And did his warriors not go on*
> *to ask Fionn what the saddest music is?*
>
> *I catch an old-style sing-song from*
> *my Alzheimer neighbour's house . . .*
> ('The Good Old Days')

This *Collected Poems* is a magisterial book with an apt and haunting cover design from a painting by the equally enigmatic Martin Gale. It allows the prosecutor O'Driscoll to rest his case. He has collected all the capital taxes owed to life and handed them over to that universal Revenue of posterity. The sustained tones are impressive, reassuring, shocking. We see his topical commentary, his would-be editorials written at the last minute to midnight. His sense of humour is dominant and persuasive, but we know from the biographies of many comedians how a compelling sense of humour can be a carefully basted crust above a deeper darkness:

> *Out of the dung heap of chemical spills,*
> *a thornless mutant rose will sprout.*
> ('Looking Forward')

A sensory darkness, a persistent habit of cataloguing and categorizing, an understanding of processes of disease, decay and rebirth in both plants and humans, all form part of the architecture of O'Driscoll's literary biography. 'My brain is crammed with / transient knowledge,' he writes in 'The Bottom Line', but what actually distinguishes his voice is the recurrent, persistent knowingness of his statements and confessions. His thoughts are rooted in insight and learning: it is this life that's transient. He got better, darker, funnier, as he went on. *Reality Check* (2007) and *Dear Life* (2012) are arguably his best books. In 'Skywriting' he could meditate in a complex weave like this:

> *A laburnum resurgence sighted through a pergola.*
> *Unimpeded light — every pore translucent — recalling*
> *an age when the sun looked indulgently on a world*
> *in its prime, a planet slanted in favour of its rays*
> *yet unable to absorb so much illumination at one time.*

In *Dear Life* the urgency of life becomes more intense, the poet becomes impatient for knowledge and impatient to teach it:

> *And spare us the dawn chorus*
> *that outwears its welcome*
> *like a loquacious breakfast guest.*
>
> *Spare us, therefore, the spring,*
> *its fake sincerity, its unethical*
> *marketing strategies, its deceptive*
> *pledges, its built-in obsolescence,*
> *its weeds breeding like flies.*
>
> ('Spare Us')

Where did the poet find such a tone? In which part of Irish life did it become available to him? His was a humanist unhappiness, not an Irish Catholic one. The anxieties of an Austin Clarke, a John Montague, a Máirtín Ó Direáin, were irrelevant to him. His anxieties had a Scandinavian quality. His ironic good humour in the face of unknowing, in the face of a Christ-less truth, is European; it is Tranströmer-like. His poetic ancestors come from very far away, further East, maybe, from the heartland of what was the Slavic-grey land beyond the Berlin Wall. He invokes not Yeats, not AE, not some reconstructed Celtic myth-maker, but Zbigniew Herbert, Wislawa Szymborska and Miroslav Holub. He wanted to be as sardonic as Holub, as Berlin-sounding as Michael Hamburger, as decentralized and improvisational as George Szirtes. He wanted to be nowhere and therefore everywhere: in this he succeeded brilliantly. In this he had a courage not available to any other Irish poet. Even his memory of his own Thurles is 'after Zbigniew Herbert'. In book upon book he gave us an earful of this courage and, as if to drive his message home, he placed this epigraph from Paul Valéry at the beginning of the last collection he assembled, *Dear Life*: 'God made everything out of nothing, / but the nothingness shows through.' For all their pyrotechnics and radical beginnings most Irish poets will eventually settle under the cultural-political umbrellas of either Patrick Kavanagh or John Hewitt, but O'Driscoll's imagination and aesthetic was radically, incorrigibly, unconventional to the end:

> No one can look at death or the sun
> without being left entirely in the dark.
> Nor, with impunity, may the sun
> expect to gaze directly at the moon.
> Awestruck birds, fallen silent
> before totality, know this when
> the sun, corona blazing, is deposed.

The above words are, again, from 'Skywriting', one of his finest poems. That Slavic despair, rescued by irony, is always there. Szymborska's 'The One Twenty Pub' and Holub's 'Experimental Animals', as well as the epigraph to O'Driscoll's

Thomas McCarthy

own 'Crowd Scene' that is also taken from Szymborska, all act as signposts to direct us away from Irish commentary, away from ourselves and the place where O'Driscoll might be judged too narrowly. His brain may have been crammed with transient knowledge but he knew what he was doing as an artist. He never deviated from his determined projects. Even his great Heaney interview project, *Stepping Stones*, gives us a considered view of O'Driscoll as much as the view of Heaney — his obsessive, curious autopsy of the Nobel Laureate is really the most unguarded and valuable portrait of O'Driscoll at work. This *Collected Poems* also creates the last major portrait of the poet at his desk, in his office at Dublin Castle and working, thinking, obsessing, late into the night in his study at home. Here is a poet of lists ('Everyday asthma and brain tumour. / Everyday chilblains, cancers, coronaries. / Everyday depression and epilepsy...') and a poet of sequences, like 'Residuary Estates', 'Churchyard View: The New Estate' and 'Dear Life' — a poet who tried many conventional poetic forms to control his riotous impulses of despair. His was a life of awesome poetic responsibility, lived fully and lived very well. He illuminated everything he touched and challenged everyone to try harder, to do better. This great *Collected* seems less like a monument to a poet and more like a huge compression chamber from which the reader may emerge rinsed of all Irishness, struggling for breath.

Poetry Ireland Review,
2018

Blind Man's Bluff by Aidan Higgins

'In you, together with the beginner, is the old hand,' wrote Samuel Beckett of the Kinsale resident, Aidan Higgins. Truer words were never spoken, for Higgins is a dab hand at making the old new, at making fiction into a memory. *Blind Man's Bluff* is the commonplace book of a deeply embedded rather than a widely travelled sage; it is paper folding, the origami of memory. The wise cataloguer at the Library of Congress has given it the Dewey Decimal classification of fiction in English out of Ireland (823.914), but this little book is more complex than that bold classification. Beautifully arranged and printed it is more like a Beat-era book out of City Lights in San Francisco: it is memory, epiphany and rhetoric in equal measure, a project in portable *belles-lettres* that would sit easily with the pocket-sized books of Ferlinghetti and Ginsberg.

What is here has been distilled rather than assembled. Here is an installation of family snapshots, Osbert Lancaster-like drawings and poetic epiphanies, such as this:

> '*And now it was her turn to get even, when I entered the Fishy Fishy Bar with a bloodshot eye and vacillating tread, for that morning I had received no less than three injections in the left eyeball, and must have resembled Wild Bill Hickok after a good morning's buffalo-slaughtering.*'

or

> '*If I stand at the morning door a mist obscures both*

Thomas McCarthy

> ends of Higher Street. Some days it intensifies, becomes murk, out of which a figure may emerge. I can't tell male from female, the unknown from the known. The past comes closer and the present disappears. Time itself goes awry. Some days go missing. The hours are no longer consecutive, evening or morning ... morning and evening merge.'

Here is a masterful writer and a master. It is nearly forty years since I first heard the name uttered in public, from the mouth of that chronicler of the Anglo-Irish, the late Mark Bence-Jones. 'You must read *Balcony of Europe* by this man,' Bence-Jones said emphatically, 'it's the greatest book of the post-War age.' When we were at college it was all *Bornholm Night-Ferry*, all displaced, shadowy, Nordic atmosphere and relationships. And then *Langrishe, Go Down* that seemed to hit a sweet spot with the Irish intelligentsia, all pre-Banville reticence and a grandeur of characterization.

Higgins became rooted to Kinsale as his sight deteriorated. Kinsale has that strange quality of ingesting noble literary refugees, from Lady Diana Vernon to Elizabeth Bowen, from MacNeice to O'Grady, Mahon ... and Higgins. *Blind Man's Bluff* is a book of uncommon prayers, a mustering of ghosts and shadows. Restricted like Robinson Crusoe Aidan Higgins flies away with words, blindness being the mother that puts a new kind of pencil in his hand. Here are memories of childhood, of Jesuits, of Japanese men with cameras, of speech reduced to only what memory dredges up, of the blind man coming back to the child who was the writer. Page after page has the lightness of a pencil sketch, the lightness of a born writer, as Frank O'Connor described him, 'in love with language and what language can do'.

Irish Examiner,
2012

The Last Peacock by Gerald Dawe

The Ulster poet Gerald Dawe continues to exist as in an altered Longleyesque, not of childhood but of the West:

> *And who do you think should turn up next*
>   *but Professor Reynolds in her black and canary-yellow*
> *Ford Capri shooting through the highways and byways*
>
>   *to Eyrecourt amid relics of colonial pewter,*
> *the pleasure garden, the pig's foot, the rollicking wine . . .*
>   ('Land of Dreams')

Energetic, aural, playful, Dawe's *The Last Peacock* — handsomely, even luxuriously, produced by Gallery in Professor Reynolds' colours — is a dazzling reminder of this fine poet who has been constantly neglected as we in the South concentrated on other dazzlers from up North. Despite this he already has a sure persona and established reputation created by collections such as *The Lundys Letter* and *Lake Geneva* and the memoir *Looking Through You*. This new collection arrives as an assertion of that established strength and power. Memories of young adulthood in Galway, John Cheever's Dublin and Richard Ford's America, as well as an earlier sense of Sunday Schools and sects, all cohere inside this one strong collection. Everything coheres, even history, because of Dawe's adroit storytelling:

> *. . . Just down below the Mods*
> *Henry Joy McCracken sets to work*
> *on his press for a united republic,*

Thomas McCarthy

> *exposed to the open sky, the entry*
> *carries traffic from barred streets*
> *to the bookies' office, and the cry*
> *is of a furious god raised up by*
> *sombre men ...*
> ('Sects, 1984')

More of Hewitt than Longley there, methinks, more of an edge that is the edginess of Belfast harbour, of kirk and gantry, of Ulster's particularizing experience. And Dawe is the better poet for having this edge in his mental formation or world view: Belfast will always be the cultural Geneva of reformed Irish Christians. But the edge is never the whole and it would be wholly inaccurate to limit Gerald Dawe to one set of cultural attachments. He ranges widely in his poems, generous and inclusive, and with great warmth. His elegies here for Aodán Mac Póilin and Gerard Fanning are works of great beauty and deep feeling, as are the shorter but effective memorials to Milo Smith and Caroline Canning.

Ironic, colourful, worldly, Dawe's power as a poet has increased prodigiously in the last two decades, so that *The Last Peacock* is the work of a first-rate Ulster poet still at war with the world and not giving up, but at ease with his art.

Poetry Ireland Review,
August 2020

Sharp Words from Elsewhere
The Holding Centre: Selected Poems 1974-2004 *by Harry Clifton*

Harry Clifton's critical writing and statements from the academic podium have been trenchant, unequivocal, and sometimes ill-advised. It's been clear for many years that he has no conventional wish to make friends, but he is determined to influence people, especially those who intend to add their sod of turf to the damp wall that is Irish poetry. His career has not been without honour — he is both a Patrick Kavanagh Award and *Irish Times*/Poetry Now winner and recently Ireland Professor of Poetry.

Clifton returned to Ireland ten years ago after having lived that peripatetic life so well known from the biographies of Joyce or Montague, Beckett or O'Grady. Exile affected both his work and his temperament, feeding his verse with exceptional material and fuelling his mind with a missionary impatience at the Ireland, and the Irish poets, he had left behind. Yet from the beginning his poetry had a tone that was more world-weary than worldly-wise. It's as if his poetry always knew more than he did — the sure sign of a good writer. Like a cranky uncle who's spent too long in the tropics he threw insults at every poet-cousin he read, apart from one or two glorious favourites. Yet, to tell others what to write, or even how to write, is a daft ambition: if poets don't strike gold for themselves then they should move on to something else. His material, or his use of it, is unique to him. There is nothing in it for someone else:

Thomas McCarthy

> *I have a seamstress, making a shirt for me*
> *In sultry weather, in the months we are together.*
>
> *She measures my shoulders with tape, I feel on my back*
> *The cool of her wooden yardstick, and submit*
>
> *To a temporary contract, binding me*
> *To the new and the strange . . .*

In a very real sense in trying to be a teacher, a guru, a method, Clifton has wrong-footed his own work and alienated a good many readers. Not all of us are born affable, as Ben Kiely used to say, but in this world we do have to live with many fools, and with the less fortunate poetically. We were all young once, it's true, and full of religious zeal to save Irish poetry from its own limitations. But there has always been an extraordinarily presumptuous vanity in every modernist Irish project, from the self-aggrandizing propaganda of Chevalier MacGreevy to the postdoctoral insolence of Beckett's wildest pupils. The insufferable snobbery of the multilingual as they move through an asylum of provincials is never a pleasant sight: the fact is that no one kind of poetry or fiction should get permanent tenure and it is foolish to persist in a programme meant for others. Poets must save themselves. Clifton has been constantly aggravated by his impossible ambitions for us all. This concern with the inadequacy of other people's poetry, so often repeated, is really the stress caused by exile, the stress that accompanies an estrangement of great distances. The extreme cosiness of Irish poetry must seem like a dark betrayal of integrity when seen from behind the barbed wire of Mairut camp in Thailand:

> *In stateless space*
> *That frees us, somewhere between*
> *The absolute kingdoms of justice and of grace*
> *Where a birdsong intervenes . . .*

Sharp Words from Elsewhere

It was from that far distance of the East, and in the company of Thomas Mann, that Clifton first pinned the ambiguity of Western adventuring to the wall of his verse:

> *Diplomatic immunity,*
> *This is your saving grace — to restore mystery*
> *To a common weal, and resurrect from disgrace*
> *The non-political...*

This poem, 'Thomas Mann', is cool and dispassionate, complicated and exact. Its superb technique, reminiscent of mid-Richard Murphy or early Thomas Kinsella, is combined with spectacularly new material — the flames of the Tet offensive, hippies frisked for heroin, Thai girls and Buddhas — to announce a distinctive, sanguine, disinterested new voice in Irish poetry. With Clifton Ireland was away and somewhere else. The effect of this poetry was electric and inspiring, especially on other poets, such as my fellow Waterfordman, Seán Dunne. For weeks on end Seán climbed the stairs to my attic apartment in Sydney Place, Cork, with Mahon's *Courtyards in Delft* in one hand and either *The Walls of Carthage* or *Office of the Salt Merchant* in the other. 'Listen to this, McCarthy,' the young poet would shout ahead of his climbing footsteps: 'First light steals / Across the metal roofs / In silence, reveals / You sleeping, me standing aloof.' The young Dunne loved to recite in particular these lines:

> *We, in inferior reason,*
> *Travel until we fall...*

And for weeks on end a recitation of 'The Walls of Carthage' replaced Seán's usual party piece, his rendition of 'Raglan Road'.

Thirty years on, from the evidence of poems like 'Benjamin Fondane Departs for the East' and 'The Mystic Marriage', it's clear that Clifton hasn't lost his touch. 'The Mystic Marriage' is every bit as sharp, technically, as 'The Walls of Carthage' and

Thomas McCarthy

that first poem has this:

> *Unscramble the anagram*
> *Of my real name, which now is mud,*
> *And tell Jean Wahl and Bachelard,* bien peasants,
> *I forgive them as they stalk the corridors*
> *Of the Sorbonne, and the pages of the* Cahiers du Sud.

There you have it still, the prosody and information, the knowingness and the rhyme. As Colm Tóibín put it in an *Irish Times* review, Clifton's words 'glide up and out in all their hushed and controlled beauty'. The work from *Secular Eden: Paris Notebooks 1994-2004* selected here is impressive and haunting in its picture of urban endurance, displacement and night journeys. Trains are the true agents of elsewhere and disturbance in a Clifton poem, a world where the poet always arrives at 'The end of the line. A flight of metal stairs, / Surveillance cameras, walkways through the trees, / Political theatre, people at a bar / between the acts'. The earlier sonnet sequence, 'Trains East, 1991', is as impressive here as the first time it was published, chronicling as it does the oppressive grey of Europe at the winterish end of the Communist era: 'History runs through them now like a train — / Bad Schandau, Pirna, old spa towns, / Half-timbered houses, impossibly run down, / Sanatoria, coming to life again / After half a century ...'

His work accumulates like that, with ease and grace. A good part of Clifton's rage at recent Irish poetry has been his disgust at shoddy writing, at careless making, as well as a righteous anger when presented with much of the Irish sentimentality that is given a free pass by reviewers. While he himself might be accused of misplaced feelings, or displaced feeling, all sentimentality has been thoroughly rinsed out of his work. In general sentimentality like patriotism is a communal feeling, a memory of excreted experiences. Poets should always be deeply suspicious of this communal temptation to write what is instantly recognizable or shared. Remaining at the periphery of these communal Irish feelings is part of Clifton's equipment: his poems believe in being far away the way Yeats's poems believed in fairies.

Dublin Review of Books,
January 2015

August Kleinzahler and the American World

If Irish life is basically about being stuck in a field of mud, the mud of history, then American life is mainly about moving furniture, the furniture of one's personal life. The vast distances Americans must travel, the continental drift that divides an American life lived in Maine from an American life lived in Los Angeles, is what makes personal adjustment a momentous journey for American writers. Unlike a move in Ireland a move in America is always full of the possibility of never going back. It is not miles, but time zones.

This is why I love the work of August Kleinzahler, its lethal, capacious energy and its epic catalogue of dislocations, though the poet did admit to his *Paris Review* interviewer that he was unusual among American poets in that he always seemed to have the option to 'go back' from San Francisco to New Jersey ('The Art of Poetry, No.93', 2007). August Kleinzahler is the great contemporary poet of disturbance and movement, 'movement' being a word particularly associated with Thom Gunn. In *Cutty, One Rock* (2004/5), his intense memoir, he remembers the enriching nature of that movement, the city buses of San Francisco and the Bay Area:

> 'What I remember, and will remember, most vividly about our friendship was travelling around town with Thom on public transport. Neither of us had cars. We were more often than not heading for a movie, and the prospect and the adventure of getting to the cinema seemed to put Thom in high spirits. To travel with Thom was to participate in an erotic mapping of San Francisco out of the bus window. I was reminded of the early Renaissance maps in which significant sites

> like the cathedral or castle are wildly out of proportion, or the Mappa Mundi, in which Jerusalem is placed at the center of the world and given space equivalent to its spiritual or political importance, not its actual physical size and geographic situation.'

And elsewhere in the same book he writes: 'The poet Ezra Pound once wrote that the life of a village is narrative and the life of a city is cinematic.' August Kleinzahler then lives his life and makes his art in that dynamic, disturbed territory, three thousand miles wide, between life as narrative and life as cinematic. Each day has in it the signposts of a possible poem, and the days when they reveal themselves in his poetry have the abrupt and sharp nature of his music reviews:

> 'The brilliant and innovative Avakian, whose fingertips are all over the American record industry from the 1940s through the '70s, had come up with the record industry's first 'concept' series in the 1940s with his Hot Jazz Classics. This Mosaic reissue, Piano Moods, was to be his baby, as well.'

And in 'Music LXVII' from *Music I-LXXIV*, he wrote:

> 'The last major musical event of the 20th century was not, as many might think, the revival of the musical career of Carlos Santana, but, instead, the world premiere of Elliot Carter's Symphonia sum fluxus pretium spei, *with Oliver Knussen conducting the BBC Orchestra.*'
>
> (Pressed Wafer, Boston, 2009)

The fact is that August Kleinzahler is everywhere at once, both there and here, and in the best tradition of American displacement, isolation, expulsion and anxiety. There are certain American poets who seem in permanent exile, disturbed voices like Frank O'Hara, Robert Duncan, Robert Creeley, Carolyn Forché or Terrance Hayes. They are the outsiders who give Europeans a certain ear for the music made by American life, a non-European music that is not following norms, a poetry as distinctively American as Jazz. It's true that those who feel they don't belong describe best what they can't belong to. With Kleinzahler it's been years of moving furniture, or hearing movements:

> You can feel the rumble of the trains
> vibrating up the steel of the hotel's frame.
> They move only very late at night, from three or so
>   until dawn,
> north along the river and then west.
> There is going on just now a vast shifting inventory
> from the one place to another. I can feel it, inside my
>   head.

This is how he puts it in the title poem of his hugely impressive *The Hotel Oneira* (2013). That 'vast shifting inventory' of American life is his target:

> There goes another plane
> Its engines reverberating in the clouds
> Now sirens, too
> Very like the sirens we heard only yesterday
> Beside themselves, tearing their hair out
> Screaming past us
> In that other city . . .

he writes in 'Over Gower Street', a cinematic riff on cities, journeys, waiting and arrivals. And in 'Tranter in America', another poem in the retrospective *Sleeping It Off in Rapid City*, he writes of 'knock back a codeine between gulps of fries as the TV overhead / shows a rerun of Kojac you saw a decade ago in a Canberra motel. / You are drifting, drifting

August Kleinzahler and the American World

even further from Frank O'Hara's Lower East Side flat . . . '
It is John Tranter who was O'Hara's 'green Buick of sighs', and Kleinzahler makes common ground, or shares imaginary fries, with a hero who also seemed dislocated except in online poems. Everywhere in Kleinzahler there's chrome and cold winds, car horns along Fulton and a dog Stolz as well as a spring-like day on Anderson Avenue. The pen is always going somewhere, resting briefly, leaving only trails of ink behind, that fading ink of emotional encounters or emotional entanglements that seem to be as regretted as missed buses. The fact is that he wholly loves his American condition, that he knows no other condition, and that he will traverse the tundra of this condition to the end of every poetry book. He is not Paul Engle, nor would he wish to have been that Iowan, but he can admit when he's beaten emotionally, an admission he makes wholeheartedly in 'Across the Land', like Yeats loitering in Dublin's Municipal Gallery, in one of his loveliest books, the Griffin Prize-winning *The Strange Hours Travelers Keep*:

> *What I can't seem to get past*
> *In the school band's September rehearsals*
> *The tubas, drums and clarinets*
> *Carrying our way from a distant field*
> *The good beefy children playing their hearts out*
> *Braids, buttons and epaulets*
> *In that heat*
> *American as cleanser, as 1958.*

Facebook,
2019

Peter Fallon: Poet, Publisher, Translator, Editor
Richard Rankin Russell (ed)

It is difficult to know where to begin with Peter Fallon. He is a distinctive and important presence, a quiet spiritual equal of Wendell Berry and, if you like, Patrick Kavanagh, but also a crucial translator and publisher. His Gallery Press is the living fulcrum around which the swarming life of contemporary Irish poetry rotates. He has spent a publisher's lifetime trying to recover half the lost sheep of the Irish Pantheon, carrying the one shepherd's hook of critical judgement and no dogs, it might be said, while at the same time assisting at the birth of some of the most brilliant new careers in Irish writing. He has adapted Kavanagh for stage, but he has, much more crucially, translated *The Georgics of Virgil*, an act brilliantly interrogated by Joseph Heininger in an essay in the present volume, which concludes thus: 'In my view and that of many others, Peter Fallon's translation of the *Georgics* gives the freshest and most satisfying contemporary rendering of Virgil's poem by producing passages of poetry marked by thematically rich, musically distinctive, and memorable lines.' Fallon, therefore, has made good art while delivering lambs and become crucial to Irish publishing while searching for stray eggs. He has, in a very real sense, lived the full life that was promised to us in the Whole Earth Catalog when we were young, and he has done all of this without the assistance of the California sun.

Fallon's is a truly extraordinary Irish life, and it goes on still, unabated. Russell's book is an ambitious attempt to praise the gifts of this complex creature as well as to set down an historic marker: yes, Liam Miller's Dolmen Press died, but contemporary Irish poetry didn't die. It just moved to Loughcrew in County Meath.

It was while awaiting matriculation into Trinity, following his schooldays in St Gerard's Bray, and Glenstal, that the teenage Fallon, together with Eamon Carr, started the Meath Poetry Group and founded the magazine *Capella*. Thomas Dillon Redshaw, another tireless shepherd in the wild commonage of contemporary Irish poetry, provides the key to that nearly post-Dolmen era in his meticulous essay, 'The Dublin Arts Festival, 1970: *Capella, The Book of Invasions*, and the Original Gallery Books'. Here we first meet Fallon, tyro-poet and tyro-publisher: 'These readings Peter Fallon and Eamon Carr arranged at a tangent to the festival's administration proper.' The series ran the week of April 6, 1970. Lunch-hour readings happened in the Gallery of the department store Brown Thomas . . . Fallon also organized the readings under the flag of Tara Telephone Publications during the second Dublin Arts Festival, in March 1971.

Jim Fitzpatrick, working from his studio, Two Bare Feet, 'provided the cover art for the two Tara Telephone publications: the broadside series titled *The Book of Invasions* and the little magazine titled *Capella*.' Music, popular culture, a Liverpool beat, youth and the unlimited future: its atmosphere also spilled from Richard Ryan's UCD broadsheet, Hayden Murphy's *Broadsheet*, *Icarus* and Paul Funge's *Poetry Broadside*. The Gallery Press, proper, started in February 1970 with the publication of *Answers* by Des O'Mahony and Justin McCarthy. The Gallery journey had begun, all heaven broke loose.

But how was Fallon the poet doing, this rock star undergraduate who was already implicated in the poetic ambitions of others? Generally it is not a healthy thing to be a poet-publisher: the attrition of others' needs and ambitions can shred one's personal poetry. One can see the wearying action of that responsibility on publisher-poets like Peter Jay of Anvil Poetry, Michael Schmidt of Carcanet, even James Laughlin of

Thomas McCarthy

New Directions. This publishing habit that could bury any publisher-poet psychically seems not in the least to have limited or discouraged Fallon's own sense of a unique poetic self. If anything, publishing, like farming, has braced and broadened his talent. Seamus Heaney, always an astute judge of people, spoke about Fallon's essential character in a wise Abbey Theatre speech, now printed in the present volume:

> *'Essentially he reveals the link between the growth of his poet's mind and the responsibilities as well as the rewards of keeping going as a publisher. Care, company, community have been fundamental concerns of Peter's writing in and about the world: care for people and place, for planet earth and the poetry of earth, for the values espoused by Virgil in the Georgics . . . '*

As the late Dennis O'Driscoll noted in 'Peter Fallon Revisited', 'Peter's energizing omnipresence lit a neon torch for a generation that had had its fill of staidness . . . ' O'Driscoll quotes Fallon approvingly, as many other commentators here will do, from *Winter Work*:

> *. . . All I approve persists,*
> *is here, at home. I think it exquisite*
> *to stand in the yard, my feet on the ground,*
> *in cowshit and horseshit and sheepshit.*

These words may haunt him but their persistence is proof that his voice has found purchase and attached itself permanently to the tradition. A poet becomes what he's remembered for. What Fallon created in the long stretch of lively solitude from *The First Affair* (1974) to *The Company of Horses* (2007) was a journal of the poet's hungry eye; he literally ate the pattern off the royal plate of rural Meath. A Beatle became a Berry, as Dennis O'Driscoll records — 'As two poets with practical farming expertise, unafraid to get their writing hands dirty — even dungy — or to lend them to cow-milking as well as lyric-making, there is a natural affinity between the Meath writer and his Kentucky elder.'

It would be a mistake to overemphasize the Berry bit, as I've just done, but critics always search out the neat synchronicity, the apparent associations. Richard Rankin Russell's essay, 'Nature's News: The Place(s) of Peter Fallon's Poetry', sums up the relationship brilliantly and might indeed serve as the final word on this matter, one of emphasis and temperament where both poets because of the reality therapy of day to day farming successfully resist the ideal, the bucolic and the nostalgic in rural life. Justin Quinn in 'The Obscenities and Audiences of Peter Fallon' takes a cold, wide look at the act of pushing the city away while tumbling into a common human darkness. Quinn brings a studied shrewdness to bear upon Fallon's communal and personal antennae, examining the evidence of poems like 'Carnaross 2', 'If Luck Were Corn' and 'A Part of Ourselves' to find a hinted at paedophilia, suicide, infanticide, and, lastly, the downpour of personal grief at the death of the adored John Fallon:

> *a word first whispered months ago*
> *and longed for longer tripped on the tongue,*
> *a stammer, now a broken promise.*

Even when discussing the *Georgics* in Fallon's oeuvre Quinn cleverly climbs in by the back window of Irish Latin, offering a different view, or at least another way of viewing the same material. It's a joy to read such prose from a poet of really heightened alertness. There are other essays here of equal power. Poet John McAuliffe rotates his critique outward from Martin Gale's photorealistic landscapes to embrace that poetic duet between Paul Muldoon's *Quoof* and Fallon's method in *Winter Work*, the star books of 1983. Ed Madden's 'Fellow Feeling: or Mourning, Metonymy, Masculinity' sets out to question the 'constitution of emotionally pivotal female figures — beloveds, wives, mothers, grandmothers — ' (to use Patricia Coughlan's words from her essay on Bog Queens in Montague and others) in Fallon's work. What is that meaning of a 'hoard' of women, how is the suffering mother a metaphor, how has the poet attached himself, or not, to the 'unsaid' stories? 'Whether the standing-with of fellow feeling is effective or not as political or emotional strategy the wife's cry returns to gender difference, figured here as geographical (and emotional) distance: "miles away".' As a reading of Fallon's great elegy, 'A Part of Ourselves', this work is simply majestic in the writing, where a new method extracts new insights from settled material.

Bryan Giemza, probably the leading expert on Fallon's work, provides a summary of the Fallon-Berry philosophical arc, that view of theme and rhythm as an act of repossession in the deepest ecological sense. The Fallon poem is a prime space of recovery, a space where 'Learning to love life, to find it in the midst of death' is the lesson.

The final section of this book is a Gallery anthology, the best poets gathered in homage to their shepherd. From John McAuliffe's shed to Bernard O'Donoghue's dark room, from Medbh McGuckian's 'Os of all sizes' to Michael Coady's 'Given Light', all the poets seem to perfectly fit, breathing their slim envelope of communal air. Two poets, still young, who have begun to burn very brightly, Vona Groarke and Alan Gillis, are here in homage. They are the two poets whose work has given me the greatest pleasure in recent years, and because they continue to write I check the Gallery lists every springtime. I would never have encountered them had they not met a poet and publisher called Peter Fallon. This book, well edited by Richard Rankin Russell, is a handsome reminder of that Fallon harvest.

Irish Literary Supplement,
Spring 2017

Sinking Ships
R.M.S. Titanic *by Anthony Cronin, with an Introduction by Paul Durcan*
41 Sonnet-Poems 82 *by Anthony Cronin*

There's a general feeling abroad that Anthony Cronin has found his generation. After more than thirty years of thought his mind has recently flourished across the accessible surface of many books: memoirs, fiction and, now, poems. Apart from his *Irish Times* column his talent had been hidden or misrepresented for far too long. Cronin is a rare bird in that he is a truly political poet. We have had many poets of politics, of political manners, but none or few intellectually committed writers. Cronin's work springs from the social concerns and political perceptions of a Charles Donnelly or a Bertolt Brecht. Yeats writing about Kevin O'Higgins or Denis Devlin remembering Michael Collins are politically stillborn compared to this poet of:

> Sick in the bilboes of the world of the poor
> Cling to each other, but the rich cling no more
> Closely to the cruelty that prevents
> The dissolution of the modelled stance.

Cronin learned his gifts elsewhere. He learned his lessons in the dosshouses, among the literary poor. It's his commitment, then, to the fair play of socialism that is the dynamo at the centre of all his work. Paul Durcan in an astringent Introduction to *R.M.S. Titanic* responds particularly to this aspect of Cronin's muse, and perceives it as of Johnson's 'general massacre of gold'.

Thomas McCarthy

This long poem was first published in the magazine *X* in 1960 and was subsequently published in the *Penguin Book of Longer Contemporary Poems*. In an Afterword Cronin says that the immediate inspiration for the poem came from the film, *A Night to Remember*. The method that the author uses is the juxtaposition of images from the night of the disaster (or the night of the film) with images of settled rural peace:

> *Turf smoke is chalked upon the darker blue*
> *And leaves a sweet, rich, poor man's smell . . .*

or

> *Church bells and baking smells . . .*
> *A Protestant hymn vibrates in the musty sunlight.*

Through a careful positioning of images over twenty-one sections Cronin succeeded in turning his apparently narrative poem into a millenary socialist text.

'The central political fact for every poet is his own position in the world, and if he expresses his feelings about that accurately, he is doing as good a political job as anyone else,' Cronin wrote in his essay in *Envoy* more than thirty years ago. The *41 Sonnet-Poems* are a natural extension of his long poem on the *Titanic*. In the former he found the perfect embracing metaphor for the doom of society, while the sonnet sequence is a loose, subjective retelling of the world's story. It lacks the unity of *R.M.S. Titanic*, that catastrophic suction which draws our attention, yet it is kept tidy by Cronin's socialist viewpoint:

> *Connolly wrote that all was held in common*
> *That all were equal holders in the clan*

or

Sinking Ships

> *The guiding principle of the world was not*
> *How much it's worth, but whether it's worthwhile*
> *And worthy and worth doing and of worth.*

Cronin uses a staccato phraseology in most of the sonnets, briefly retelling the essential images out of any era — 'The arming and departure of the knights', 'The great crown . . . surmounted by a cross' or 'Byron the first of the open-necked shirt brigade / Breast bared to bullet . . . ' The poems come off the page like telex messages from an arena in crisis. The impression, sometimes, is one of fragmentary appeals to the habitual reader and keeper of literary history. When the sonnets don't work they merely read like telegrams from a Mel Brooks' film lot. And some don't work because they are still part of Cronin's encyclopaedic reference library, still part of a private mythology that can't be unlocked by the ordinary reviewer. Among the most satisfying sonnets, lyrically, are those that deal with the period 1901-18, with Marconi, Chesterton, Lloyd George and Bleriot:

> *A quarryman who was placing charges looked*
> *Up at the vibrant sky and saw come in*
> *A monoplane irradiate with rain.*

These two volumes should re-establish Cronin on the contemporary poetry scene. Through Raven Arts Press he has been given a megaphone with a new battery. One hopes that he will continue to use it loudly, lengthily, and well.

The Irish Times,
January 1982

John Keats by Nicholas Roe

For those who care to remember him the poet John Keats is remembered as one 'whose name was writ in water'. He died at the age of twenty-five after a frustrating and painful struggle with tuberculosis. The same disease had killed so many members of his family that he felt particularly cursed and hunted by TB from a very early age. His study of pharmacy and medicine can be seen as a truly obsessive act in defiance of this highly contagious killer of the beautiful and the young. Keats was an accomplished medical student at Guy's Hospital and was rapidly appointed a surgical 'dresser' to his master surgeon. As with so many other medical men, from Somerset Maugham to A J Cronin, Keats's mastery of detail and that surgical capacity to retain vast quantities of information created a brilliant predisposition towards literary work. As Nabokov once observed literature arises from an obsession with the 'blessed particulars' of reality. And poetry more than anything else is the story of the suffering body keenly observed.

This sensuous orphan, son of a very successful livery-stables owner and a wilful and sensuous mother, wrote some of the most beautiful odes in the English language. His use of the sonnet form was masterful, his reimagining of the Middle Ages (in 'La Belle Dame sans Merci' and 'The Eve of St Agnes') was uncanny and his epic *Hyperion* created a sensation. How a poet so young could have made such an impact so quickly is the key narrative thread in Nicholas Roe's new biography. Roe's book is nothing less than a restoration of Keats to his tumultuous early nineteenth-century context. Keats was a kind of Picasso, a prodigy who learned his art early, a poet whose flame burned intensely and scorched

John Keats by Nicholas Roe

everything around it. Nicholas Roe brilliantly recreates the political atmosphere of the Keats era: his learned contextualizing is brilliantly done. He traces the influence of Leigh Hunt, a much maligned and misunderstood literary personality, who was a conduit of the poetic liberalism of the age. The achievements of revolutionary and seditious Coleridge and Wordsworth survived through Hunt's advocacy to reach the isolated medical student in his boarding school and lodgings. Roe rescues Keats from the soft focus of romance and restores stars, brooks, fields and seasons to their anti-classicist politics of the nineteenth century. In doing this the book is a major work of literary rescue.

Leigh Hunt was the influential founder-editor of the weekly *Examiner*, a paper whose prestige and circulation rose astronomically when the editor was sent to prison for two years. The paper was edited from the jail cell that Hunt had splendidly wallpapered, repainted and fitted with a piano. A succession of illuminati, including Lord Byron and Thomas Moore, visited the editor in jail and wrote letters of support. It was in the *Examiner* that Hunt invented a new cult in publishing, the cult of the very new, that has its continuing life into the present day through new poetry prizes and young poets anthologies. Hunt published 'On First Looking into Chapman's Homer' along with poems by Shelley and John Henry Reynolds and boldly announced 'a new school of poetry rising of late'. It was at Hunt's home that Keats met Shelley, author of 'The Necessity of Atheism' and 'An Address to the Irish People'. Under the spell of Hunt and encouraged by his brother Tom Keats became convinced that he could make a living from poetry rather than surgery. That might seem a daft calculation in the present era but in the early nineteenth-century literature was still an occupation for gentlemen while medicine most definitely was not: 'My last operation was the opening of a man's temporal artery. I did it with the utmost nicety but, reflecting on what passed through my mind at the time, my dexterity seemed a miracle.' Roe, the biographer, writes movingly of this moment in Keats's life: 'As Keats swapped his lancet for a quill, his hopes for poetic glory were part of a conversation with his dead parents to whom he could speak in no other way.'

But tuberculosis soon took his brother, Tom. Feeling hunted by death, and medically aware of the process of dying, Keats fled from the egotistical sublime of Wordsworth's generation. He suddenly became aware, in a Joycean epiphany, that 'What shocks the virtuous philosopher, delights the camelion Poet.' And then there was Fanny Brawne. While still nursing his dying brother he met this sixteen-year-old who, he wrote, 'is I think beautiful and elegant, graceful, silly, fashionable and strange . . . ' In subsequent letters Keats would characterize Fanny as a minx, as ignorant, as monstrous, but always as having a penchant for acting stylishly. Smitten, Keats was only registering Fanny Brawne through the effects she wished to create. But Brawne was already a fan of Lord Byron's work, the way Mary Colum was obsessed with Yeats, and Roe warns in this book, 'Fanny Brawne's considerable literary intelligence should not be judged at her own self-deprecating estimate.' Keats was still young and their romance was a Victorian one of letters, walks, books and poems. While still working on *Hyperion* and romancing Fanny Brawne, and while still keeping his options open with a number of eligible women, Keats suffered the return of an habitual sore throat. Tuberculosis had begun its work upon yet another Keats. The rest was a swift decline, mollified by laudanum and claret. At Guy's Hospital laudanum had been dispensed liberally: it was opium, an effective but deadly painkiller. Stilled by it he wrote with visionary indolence the great odes with their intricate, interwoven stanza forms. 'I have seen your Comet!' he wrote to Fanny, and thus began the immortal poem:

> *Bright Star! Would I were steadfast as thou art!*
> *Not in lone splendour hung amid the night . . .*

John Keats by Nicholas Roe

But the persistent sore throat became blood on the pillow, arterial blood that Keats, the surgeon's apprentice, recognized: 'that drop of blood is my death warrant — I must die,' Keats said to his friend, Brown. He died in Italy where he is still honoured by a little museum at the Spanish Steps. Keats's early death reminds us that in the last two centuries the true friend of artistic genius has been neither tradition nor individual talent, but an aminoglycoside called streptomycin.

Irish Examiner,
November 2012

Michael D Higgins, Poet

Michael D Higgins is the poet-President of Ireland, having been elevated to the Presidency with the largest popular vote ever achieved by an election candidate in Ireland. Neither the nineteenth-century Irish Liberator, Daniel O'Connell, nor the iconic Eamon de Valera, achieved such phenomenal popular success. Higgins' popularity and his life in poetry are intimately bound together, animated at the very core of his being by that sense of 'emotional honesty which in turn impels him towards a stylistic candour, a simple, deep resolution to say difficult things in clear language', as the poet Brendan Kennelly wrote of him twenty years ago. With Michael D Higgins it is foolish to try to distinguish between the private agony of poems and the public advocacy of Irish politics. In Ireland public feeling is honoured in poetry in the same way that a sense of irony is honoured in the British poetic world. Reticence and irony have no particular stature in the Irish narrative imagination, whereas boldness of gesture and the voice of honest indignation both carry immense literary power: as Yeats wrote in an earlier era, 'I thirst for accusation.' In coming to politics through that trust in humane feeling, and maintaining his dual career of poet and politician, Higgins has maintained a powerful Irish and Celtic tradition, from the aisling poets of the seventeenth century to the Fenian and IRB poets of the nineteenth and twentieth centuries. Higgins has always been conscious of the private realms, as well as the public realm, that give rise to poems. In 'When Will My Time Come?' he writes in nervous anticipation of that moment in his life when he can admire only the scenery, the senses, the memories of a private world:

Michael D Higgins, Poet

And, if there is healing,
It is in the depth of a silence,
Whose plumbed depths require
A journey through realms of pain
That must be faced alone.
The hero, setting out,
Will meet an ally at a crucial moment.
But the journey home
Is mostly alone.

It is interesting to note that the above poem has been subjected to periods of additions, revisions and excisions over the last twenty years, as if the poet was enduring a constant struggle to find that one adequately described place of silence. His instincts and impulses are Yeatsian, yet more democratic and, certainly, more demotic in the manner of George Seferis — and Seferis's intimate political relationship with the political destiny of his country. Higgins' work is always a reflection upon the world, but a reflection combined with a call to action. In his writing career he is very much in the Western Ireland tradition of the novelist-socialist Peadar O'Donnell or Douglas Hyde — Hyde is another Western Ireland scholar-poet with whom Higgins shares the distinction of the Irish presidency; he is most like Hyde in his combined sense of public duty and private passion for poems. In Hyde it was a life of translating Irish-language texts, whereas in Higgins we see another act of translation at work — a bold socialist effort to translate into literature the unheard cries of excluded communities and tribes. His most famous early poem, 'The Betrayal', is one such act of translation. The writing of this work, dedicated to his father, was a moment of catharsis in the poet's life; having written it he knew he'd brought the *un*described, unheard world of the Irish rural poor into the realm of literature: in other words he had transcribed the hieroglyphs of the suffering poor and carried his transcriptions to the bourgeois literary Dublin audience:

Thomas McCarthy

Nor did you speak too much.
You had broken an attendant's glasses,
The holy nurse told me,
When you were admitted.
Your father is a very difficult man,
As you must know. And Social Welfare is slow
And if you would pay for the glasses,
I would appreciate it.
It was 1964, just after optical benefit
Was rejected by De Valera for poorer classes
In his Republic, who could not afford,
As he did
To travel to Zurich
For their regular tests and their
Rimless glasses.

The poem contains a feast of references that are purely Irish and local, yet the sense of outrage and honest indignation is something that crosses national boundaries. It is the poetry of a common humanity, poetry as both voice of feeling and witness document. In method and cadence it is sometimes reminiscent of the 1980s poetry of Paul Durcan or Brendan Kennelly, but it is the unmistakable voice of the Galway socialist, Higgins. His verse structure and narrative stance, that preliminary gait as the poet stands to address the lone reader, is shared with other poets like Rita Ann Higgins, Moya Cannon, Nuala Ní Dhomhnaill, Joan McBreen: all poets of the 'Galway method' or 'Galway Rhetorical' style in contemporary Irish poetry. It is a method much derided by the traditionalists, the neo-Conservative verse makers, but it is a poetic method and rhetorical stance that is now deeply embedded in Irish poetry making.

Michael D Higgins was born in Limerick in 1941. He was educated at the National University of Ireland, Galway, as well as Indiana and Manchester. For many years he was a lecturer in Sociology and Political Science at NUIG, becoming Mayor

Michael D Higgins, Poet of Galway and Labour Party Dáil Deputy for his Galway constituency. His first collection of poems *The Betrayal* (1990) was followed by *The Season of Fire* (1993), *An Arid Season* (2004) and *New and Selected Poems* (2008). He has also written essays, collected in *Causes for Concern: Irish Politics, Culture and Society* as well as film narratives. In 2011, presenting himself to the people as a lifelong socialist and intellectual, he was elected President of Ireland by an overwhelming and unprecedented popular vote.

Poetry International Rotterdam,
2015

A Rebel Act
Michael Hartnett's Farewell to English *by Pat Walsh*

So much water and so many words have gone under the bridge since the early to mid 1970s that it is almost impossible to recreate the atmosphere within which the much loved Limerick poet, Michael Hartnett, made his decision to write only in Irish. In this new book Pat Walsh has created a Boswell-like chronicle of those days, mapping Hartnett's thought processes and cultural anxieties through the interviews, essays and broadcasts of that time. Hartnett's *A Farewell to English* caused a sensation, not so much for the strength of its texts alone but for the associated cultural and political questions amplified by his very public act. At the time his decision to abandon the English tongue seemed a particularly local, and a distinctly Irish, decision. Yet by late 1978 I'd met two other established poets at Iowa University who had made a similar decision — R Parthasarathy, an Oxford UP-Delhi poet, who had decided to write in his native Tamil and abandon an Oxford Poet's career in India, and Alfred Yuson, a poet of the Philippines, who was determined to write poetry only in Tagalog, the everyday language of his native Manila. Around the same time, also, the great Kenyan writer, James Ngugi abandoned his published colonial Christian name and reverted to the correct 'Ngũgi wa Thiong'o'. It was Ngũgi in his seminal *Decolonising the Mind* (Zimbabwe Publishing House, 1987) who distinguished between language as communication and language as a carrier of culture. Hartnett also understood this distinction and decided to do something about it. Pat Walsh has done a terrific job of work in *A Rebel Act* in uncovering the mental weather of that era,

A Rebel Act

as well as offering a narrative of the politics of literary reactions — the latter achievement of his book is something new in Irish literary chronicles, or a mode of retelling that he has rediscovered for our generation. One would have to go back to W P Ryan and his early twentieth-century chronicles of the mainly London-based Irish Literary Revival to find a similarly easygoing and yet thorough chronicle of Irish literary life.

At the heart of these other writers' decisions was not the Plantation of Munster, but the dropping of napalm in Vietnam and the bombing of Cambodia. That was a series of events from which another Irish poet, Caitlín Maude, was already receiving signals. Maude knew that what was a sideshow for the West was the death of entire tribes and communities for these African and Asian writers. Hartnett, though he may not have known it, was in tune with Caitlín Maude's internationalism, acting in solidarity with a post-Colonial or anti-Colonial feeling. The dispute over territory and natural resources had entered the verbal domain. In a real sense Hartnett's *A Farewell to English* completed a project of political reflection begun in the singing and theatrical work of Maude. Caitlín Maude's early death may have ignited two other quite distinct poetic careers, the Irish Hartnett and the exiled Ní Dhomhnaill. Although we, as readers, may not have known it at the time, Michael Hartnett in Templeglantine was all over the zeitgeist. As Ngũgi stated in a 1967 interview, 'I have reached a point of crisis. I don't know whether it is worth any longer writing in English.' In Pat Walsh's wonderful chronicle you will find much despair as well as the stuff of cultural dreams. He has been shrewd and illuminating about Hartnett's class origins, the working-class Hartnett household in the poorest housing of Newcastle West, the tea in jam jars and the dry toilets. There has been a crying need for proper class analysis in Irish poetry and Walsh may have started something he didn't wish to unleash into the literary discourse of the pub and festival. As the son of a working-class father I've often marvelled at the audacity of well-heeled poets masquerading as social victims or outcasts. The license granted to poets has been flagrantly abused by many poetic myth-makers in our own time and Pat Walsh's insightful social writing about Hartnett may open a new line of enquiry in Irish criticism. In the closing chapters of this study Walsh creates an emotional map of the poet's decisions: Rosemary Hartnett's reactions to her husband's Irish adventure are tellingly quoted:

> 'Michael's decision to write only in Irish shut me out from his work. I had been accustomed to being the first to see his new work. I had tried to learn Irish but found it impossible . . . a series of Irish-speaking visitors called to the house and spent the whole evening with Michael conversing in Gaelic. Any attempt to enter the conversation in English was rebuffed. I retired defeated and angry from my struggles with the language.'

It is a telling witness statement, with Hemingwayesque consequences. Hartnett had gone big-game hunting and had left his wife in an English tent without a gun. As a metaphor of marital decline it is heartrending. When *Adharca Broic* was published the poet had achieved his aim, an integrated Irish being, a life without adjectives. Yet the world he'd entered was not a happier place. Within months he would be writing 'And when I read today's poetry / I laugh forests of pens / And cry tears of ink.' Hartnett grew increasingly bitter with critics, despite his own reviewing for *The Irish Press, The Irish Times* and *Hibernia*. He was quickly replaced by Seamus Deane as presenter of *Poems Plain* on RTÉ Radio. Around this time I met him in John Montague's house in Cork. That night he told me that he was hoping to get a job as a night watchman with CMP Dairies. Then Aosdána happened, with its *cnuas* payments like a modest civil list pension. It brought some relief to the hunted creature, the wood-kerne escaped

A Rebel Act

from the massacre of the English language. But the demon, the great demon of Irish writing, alcohol, pursued him to an early grave. Into death he followed the only poet who ever brought out the competitive edge in his character, Caitlín Maude. Pat Walsh follows through to the decline, death, aftermath and legacy. *A Rebel Act* is a marvellous biographical study of a poet both familiar and strange. Every Munster poet, and any poet thinking of giving up drink or giving up English, should read it.

Irish Examiner,
2012

Memoir and Celebration
Selected Poems *by John Jordan*

John Jordan was certainly a brilliant man. Listening to him expound upon the varying merits of Flann O'Brien, Anthony Cronin or John Montague in the Long Valley Bar in Cork many years ago I remember being startled and overwhelmed by his trenchant memory, his insistent mischief and the diamond-edge nature of even his most casual opinions. It must have been good to be alive when these guys were undergraduates. He was as colourful as Micheál Mac Liammóir, but formally educated, with the robust insights of a good scholar, 'Would you ever check in those library records of yours and see if there were ever Wilmores resident at Cork', were his parting words to me at Glanmire Station. Except that he didn't part. He must have got off the train because he was back in the Long Valley snug when I returned that evening. He was searching there, I guess, for the one good bowl of soup:

> *Among the blazing azaleas*
> *Of the Parque del Campo Grande*
> *I perceived the true, sophisticated*
> *Marxist point of view:*
> *Let the people have duck soup . . .*
> 			('For Julius Henry Marx (1891-1977)')

So well educated was he, indeed, that unhappiness and pain had to be expressed in a complex way, in a manner of Austin Clarke:

All the rest of it is maculate:
Clerical quip and liberal mind,
Perspectives of eternity which we're told
Art can find . . .
                    ('Homage to the Pseudo-Jansenius')

He was part of that generation most enriched and most damaged by the conditions of Catholic Irishness. Never before had a generation of intellectuals come to maturity when the Irish Catholic worldview held such sway. There was a complete orthodoxy and social tidiness, an insanity of completion that bordered on spiritual tyranny. Yeats was too recent then, the detritus of his last arguments was still hanging around the foyers and Joyce, even the Joyce of the *Portrait*, was hardly absorbed. Help was on the way. America would open as a possibility, but too late for Jordan, as for Clarke. Jordan's poetry, therefore, is a splintered and damaged literature, with huge lumps of flesh knocked out of his possible genres and aesthetic from battles with that overwhelming orthodoxy, Catholic Dublin. As with others his poetry inside the great Archdiocese would have to live on lack, as Austin Clarke put it. 'I have my nuances and Chekhovian glooms', Jordan wrote in 'Second Letter: To Patrick Swift', and such glooms were personal, sexual and political. There is more than Dublin wit; there is something profoundly sad in:

Dixit: I don't like the use of that word 'bottom'.
Dixit: It's about time we
Learnt that the heart's no pincushion.

And then, you know, he put out the light,
And they went to bed and were unhappy everafter.
                    ('A Seduction of the '40s')

But there you have it: that struggle to have a personal life, a personal imagination. In Jordan you have a poet conscious of the general malaise that pervaded Ireland and post-War Europe as well as a civilized man's considered statement to the moment. John Jordan was all of these things and more. He had limitless potential, like Dublin itself. His voice was so clear and beautiful, a cornet solo above the noise of mere opinions. When he spoke it was always so meaningful and oracular. It is impossible to believe that he has been gone these twenty years.

Poetry Ireland Review,
October 2008

Speckled Bird of the North
Rain *by Don Paterson*

After huge critical and market success of *Landing Light*, winner of both the T S Eliot Prize and the Whitbread Prize for Poetry, expectations must be extremely high for any reader picking up a new book by the Scottish poet Don Paterson. The last book was simply astonishing in its emotional toughness and its cleanliness and poetic precision. *Rain* is a different kind of assembly, a broader verbal church, a book of many kirks and weathers, rain included. There is definitely something different about the air in Dundee; it produces great poets and Paterson is one of that elect assembly. In the first poem here — 'Two Trees' — the poet gives us ample warning, to be alert, to eschew sentimentality:

> They were trees, and trees don't weep or ache or shout.
> And trees are all this poem is about.

Following which, even John Ashbery would be afraid to approach a tree again. This tone is developed through the book, as if the poet stayed up late merely to 'collect the dull things of the day / in which I see some possibility'. A key anxiety of the poems, a sort of dynamic myth, is the yearning to collect or re-collect the 'dull hours'. The book, therefore, is a metaphysical assembly, anxious with explanations and riddled with human understandings blown off tangent in different ways and in different scenarios. Sometimes, we are in the territory of a fiction by Stephen King or a painting by Martin Gale:

Thomas McCarthy

> *for all the child was barely there*
> *and for all that we were over*
> *I could not weigh the ghosts we are*
> *against those we deliver*
>
> *I gave the empty seat a push*
> *and nothing made a sound*
> *and swung between two skies to brush*
> *her feet upon the ground*
> ('The Swing')

There is no punctuation here. I doubt if the editor was asleep. The reader is also challenged not to be. It is language, here, that swings between two skies. The poet runs deeper and deeper into this disturbed territory. In 'Renku: My Last Thirty-Five Deaths' he writes of 'my birthday in the Void' as well as 'At least I leave the world I lost / an ounce more real for one less ghost.' In 'Correctives' he watches his son steadying his own left hand and thinks, for us disciples of Donne, that 'the whole man must be his own brother / for no man is himself alone.' He continues in this thoughtful, thought-swallowing rather than thought-provoking vein, through a series of elegies and conversations. In 'The Day' he writes of the night sky, of galaxies into the future, but with less of ecstatic celebration as in MacDiarmid's 'Birth of a Genius Among Men' and more of a Puritan and Calvinist anxiety, where a partner is lonelier than she thought she was:

> *We are not chosen, just too far apart*
> *to know ourselves the commonplace we are,*
>
> *as precious only as the gold in the sea:*
> *nowhere and everywhere. So be assured*
> *that even in our own small galaxy*
> *there is another town whose today-light*

> *won't reach a night of ours till Kirriemuir*
> *is nothing but a vein of hematite . . .*

Rain is dedicated to the late Michael Donaghy and a brilliant sequence, 'Phantom', tests most of the anxieties and chilling perceptions against thoughts of the dead poet. Here we are with the Yeatsian shades, in rooms where the mirrors are 'switched off' and where a white cup of memory leads over the page into a meditation on Zurbarán's 'St Francis in Meditation' where 'something had passed between / the man and his interrogated night'. Elegy here becomes an illuminated testing ground, a mirror of speculations:

> *One night when I was lying in meditation*
> *the I-Am-That-I-Am-Not spoke to me*
> *in silence from its black and ashless blaze*
> *in the voice of Michael Donaghy the poet . . .*

The end of it all is the nocturnal perception that 'We come from nothing and return to it.'

The title poem 'Rain' begins 'I love all films that start with rain' and ends 'and none of this, none of this matters.' It is a script adapted from the original play, as Paterson says. The dead poet, the poet's friend, was part of that script, as fixed as the stars over Kirriemuir. This collection is much more than the brilliant words, precise phrasing, metaphysical perceptions: it is a work of art, full of lifeblood, erected in memory of Michael Donaghy and the companionship of poets. It is high art redeemed by life. Here, despite himself, Paterson teaches us that everything matters.

Poetry Ireland Review,
March 2010

Desmond O'Grady and Federico Fellini

When that gifted young Kinsale-based poet Adam Wyeth, with Keith Walsh, captured the late Desmond O'Grady on film in *Life in a Day of Desmond O'Grady* (DVD, 2005) he was rendering a final cinematic tribute to a poet who was no stranger to cinematic high art. Nearly half a century earlier O'Grady as a young Irish poet in Rome had been captured forever in Federico Fellini's brilliant and disturbing *La Dolce Vita*. Desmond knew Fellini well and had a Roman condescension towards him: 'Of course, I knew Fellini well, McCarthy. Fellini was a provincial, from Rimini. I introduced him to Roman society,' said Desmondo to me one day over a glass of vino in the Long Valley. Strange as this may seem Desmondo was probably telling the truth, as he had hung around in that circle of the Princess Caetani and Rome's diplomatic aristocracy, as secure and as at home in Rome as any Irish boy educated privately by the Cistercians of Roscrea in the 1950s. In that pre-Vatican II time the mental formation of any bourgeois Irish Catholic would have allowed them to slip seamlessly into Italian living. Desmondo was no exception, taking to Italian life like a duck to water, though in his case it was an Irish duck taking to Orvieto and Amarone della Valpolicella. O'Grady arrived in Rome with the necessary passport, a full collection of poems, *Chords and Orchestrations*, published at McKerns Printing Works, Limerick, in 1956. He began with rhapsodic lyrics, and the rhapsody of his charmed life continued unabated, the rhapsody captured so well by Adam Wyeth in 2004 and 2005. But Federico Fellini, sharp and shrewd provincial that he was, knew a good thing when he saw it. Desmond O'Grady was

Desmond O'Grady and Federico Fellini

the real thing at that moment, a true poet of the Gael, a Wandering Celt, a poet blessed with charm and youth. A foil to the dissatisfied, troubled fraud, Marcello of *La Dolce Vita*. Desmond was as sure of himself as the gossip-mongering and immoral Marcello was insecure. Desmondo rode with the higher paparazzi, Ezra Pound, Denis Devlin, the lingering whiff of Yeats's grandeur, the very certainties of being an Irish poet at that moment in time. Everything could seem effortless in O'Grady's life: beautiful companions, a friendship with Pound, a festival at Spoleto, a Harvard thesis that became the exquisite and rare Dolmen Editions book *The Gododdin*, even a speaking part in a Fellini film.

I watched *La Dolce Vita* again last night just to see young Desmond in his youthful prime. He plays a crucial, inciting role in that marvellously composed and 'framed' succession of *mis-en-scènes* in Steiner's house, in an elegant library/drawing room with its lovely Morandi painting. (Morandi was still alive in Bologna when his painting was inserted into this scene by Fellini. Marcello will talk longingly about Steiner's Morandi painting.) The scene begins about an hour and seventeen minutes into the long film, after the brilliant Apparition of the Madonna sequence, at 1:17:11, when we glimpse Desmond in Steiner's room, then ten seconds later we see Desmond cheerfully lighting a cigarette. At 1:20:09 as the famous Italian poet guest 'Iris' speaks oracularly (she calls herself 'the alcoholic oracle') Desmond gestures to her with familiarity. Fellini captures Desmond laughing in recognition and gesticulating as she says, 'The thing is to burn and not to freeze,' Desmond listening and puffing his cigarette. At 1:20:50 there's a full shot of Desmond at the centre of the frame as Iris says, 'I like the three big oblivions: drinking, smoking and going to bed,' and while saying this and after saying it she reaches back to Desmond who takes her hand. They clasp each other's hands in poetic recognition. Suddenly, at 1:21:18 and for the next fifteen seconds, Desmond leaps up and shouts, 'Quiet! A moment please! Dialogue between feminine wisdom and ... um ... masculine uncertainty.' He switches on Steiner's professional-looking tape recorder and we hear the sound of thunder filling the room, startling the guests. Steiner is disturbed: the sounds, his recording are an indiscreet baring of his soul, a prophecy of more terrible things. Steiner insists that his tape of nature sounds be stopped, but the guests are so moved by it all that they ask him to let the tape flow. As we hear the sound of recorded waves crashing Desmond reappears, occupying a third of the screen, looking elegant and elegantly dressed, and he recites Caliban's words to Stephano and Trinculo in *The Tempest*: 'Sounds and sweet airs that give delight and hurt not.' A beautiful shot, then, of Desmond leaning against the long bookcase, smoking still. At 1:22:52 Desmond moves to behind the couch where the listening women sit. He puts a book back on the shelf and sits on a fireside stool beside the women, including Emma, Marcello's long-suffering companion. This is a beautifully composed shot with Desmond at the centre of it, like one of Bill Brandt's high society photographs. How I'd love to have a print of that. At 1:23:30 the spell of the sounds is broken as Steiner's two beautiful children come into the room, frightened by the sound of the thunder. At 1:24:20 Desmond appears again as Steiner talks about his clever daughter. At 1:26:06 our poet Desmond is now seen sitting in another position, at a table on the left by the window as Marcello moves through the French windows to join Steiner on the balcony. Marcello, moved by everything he's experienced in the room, says to Steiner: 'Your house is a real refuge. Your children, your wife, your books, your extraordinary friends. Me, I'm wasting time, achieving nothing.' It's after this encounter that Steiner moves to check on his again sleeping children, that moment in the film where he delivers a long soliloquy on the darkness of the world and his terror of the future — this darkness will lead to the most shocking event in the film.

This 15-minute scene where Desmond plays such a key

role is almost a film-within-a-film. Had it been shown as a short it would also have won all the prizes. It was certainly one of the greatest moments in Desmond O'Grady's life. To be at the centre of high European Cinema, how could anything in life ever again live up to that? He must surely have understood how important that film would become, and what a compliment Fellini had paid to him and their friendship in including him in such a world-class event in cinema.

The presence of O'Grady in such Irish character in world cinema is also culturally important for another reason. It is a reminder of why we like Europe. In the English language at that moment in cinema Irishmen would be the talking fools of Disney's *Darby O'Gill*. Later Irishmen would be the violent, drunken mobsters, thugs, robbers of further British and American cinema. Later they would be the terrorists. That is the only narrative available to an Irish film maker who wants to sell cinema product in the Anglophone world. But here was Fellini, who listened, who heard what an Irishman could say. With honourable exceptions like Huston's *The Dead* this would hardly ever happen again. Wisdom, elegance, certainty: Such things should be allowed to Irish character in films. For showing us how it can be done we should celebrate Desmond O'Grady.

Facebook,
2020

The Last Cold Day by Sara Berkeley/ *Company* by Tom French

Hospice nurse and poet Sara Berkeley's new collection begins in urgency, the first urgency that will not be the last urgency before we reach the end of this breathtaking and breath-demanding book. The first two poems are interconnected, in that the first commemorates a CNN report of the lost Icelandic glacier, Okjökull, a victim of global warming, and the second, 'Let's Pack All Our Clothes', charts an escape from fire into the refuge of a hotel room. The collection begins, therefore, with a sense of change, flight and getting away. 'Rings Off' pictures a new beginning, or at least the casting off of an older attachment:

> *My rings are off, they are in*
> *the tiny silver box I set aside for them*
> *and here come the twelve bands of light*
> *all the way from ultraviolet to infrared*
> *taking me from utter darkness . . .*

'Let me be done with the business of doing / and the work of love, let me go down / to the lake with a pen, some champagne . . . ' she writes in 'Morning Number One', setting us up, as readers, for a new narrative in her life, a new beginning. This new beginning leads her across the great continental mass of America in a time when winter is broken, when the poet is 'sure / it's love' that pulls her to the other shore of the US. By page 24 the collection has begun to feel like a good, very intriguing road movie, a narrative of new beginnings, complete even, in the poems 'Hanuman' and 'Grace', with the poet swimming cinematically in the Manby gorge:

The Last Cold Day by Sara Berkeley/Company by Tom French

*I lay in the river, the river didn't care
what brought me there,
it flowed on over me
washing my clothes, my hair,
moving my memories like river weed.*

This is the set-up. But the poet could not have anticipated what was about to happen in the America of that springtime: Covid-19 would soon take over the task of writing the script of all her following days. Soon she will be in the thick of the battle, more involved professionally than writer Vera Brittain of an earlier era, more medically needed in that moment. Landed in upstate New York she is soon overwhelmed by the great life and death struggles that develop along the pandemic-saturated Hudson valley:

*When I show up for death
I take off my thousand pound weight*

*so I go in light
and I wait*

*there by the bedside
for death to look up.*

'After I lay down my cloak / for the dying man,' she writes, explaining then how she hears a son calling out 'Dad!' but knows the father is at an end in that Elysium of drugs and absent pain. Sometimes, as in 'Strangers' Doors', she arrives at the house of the dying, like a nineteenth-century fever doctor: one house, where Mozart's *Requiem* is playing:

*I stand witness
in the bethel of their suffering
and in the sanctuary of their ease.*

Thomas McCarthy

After days and months of this, in 'Early Morning Call', she has become tired of stories of dying, exhausted by the needs of families as well as patients, yet maintains that human connection, that instinct of a great nurse. When two daughters make a shirt for their dying father, 'World's Best Dad', she manages to slip it over his head to complete the gesture of need and attachment. As she looks at the dead patient she thinks, 'I felt he was there, / that wherever he was / he saw.' Few Irish poets of the modern era will have ever carried such a load. Berkeley's bravery is magnificent, her palliative courage remarkable. She gets back to Ireland the following February, not angered by exile but estranged like Beckett after Saint-Lô. She has simply experienced life and death at such ferocious intensity that conventional notions of Irishness and exile are simply inadequate:

> *Terminal Two:*
> *we taxi down the runway,*
> *the roots that were nourished in this soil*
> *are coming loose,*
> *takeoff rips them free, the wrench*
>
> *in the chest, the heart crossways*
> *and salt rime, every time,*
> *as the plane banks steeply over the Poolbeg twins*
> *and the melancholy wails to be let in . . .*

Maturity, detachment, profound wisdom about life's frailty, all of this permeates the work in poem after poem, making *The Last Cold Day* one of the most important collections of this contemporary era. Life throws us side-balls and quicksands and Sara Berkeley has been through an exile's Inferno that very few of us have been called to witness. Her sanguinity about these matters is magnificent. Through its urgency and artfulness her collection illuminates the whole of life with an extraordinary and shocking loveliness.

The Last Cold Day by Sara Berkeley/Company by Tom French

Kilkenny native Tom French may seem to have written of less urgent business than our gifted hospice poet but he also explores and interrogates the various predicaments of life. Shortlisted for the *Irish Times* Poetry Now Award and winner of an O'Shaughnessy and Dermot Healy Award his is now a fully matured and highly esteemed poetic presence in Ireland. Despite this incremental build-up of honour he has remained faithful to his Public Service desk in the Local Studies Department of County Meath Libraries. But even in this library perch he has been shaken by life's wilder tragedies. In 'To Distance' he, also, writes about our bleak pandemic era, but with a different edge, a different insight:

> *I do what I have never done —*
> *remove my wedding ring*
> *because it 'harbours infection',*
> *and find, printed beneath,*
> *its pale reflection.*
>
> *Even my very skin is married.*

This poem, a lengthy sequence, is placed towards the end of the collection, not clouding the atmosphere nor allowed to determine the book's tone. French spent part of Covid-time planting ten varieties of trees, including three kinds of birch:

> *It will be years before they touch;*
> *still, we plant them ten feet apart.*

The knowledge that things will come together again is one of the strengths of his sequence. The collection more properly and formally opens with an impressive and sustained meditation on the paintings of Emma Schrock, a painter that he credits his publisher Peter Fallon with introducing into his orbit. It was a fruitful encounter, propelling French into a sinewy, formalist ekphrastic fugue of lyrics based on Schrock's paintings

Thomas McCarthy

of Mennonite life. His method here, his easeful formality as a poet, is now an important aspect of his aesthetic signature. His use of quatrain, tercet, couplet, and his choice of form in relation to apt materials, is superb:

> *The mill is canopied, like an altar on wheels.*
> *They'll work by moon until the stooks are cleared.*
> *The artist's hands are yellow. The stubble shows*
> *how rich the harvest was. Her palette glows.*

Masterful timing and phrasing are common characteristics of the work. In poems as widely different as 'Agnes Moran's, Mornington' and 'Communion, Western Front' his formality and skill is as fine as anything by Richard Murphy — the indented lines in the latter poem, for example, are as effective as any mid-century poem by Robert Penn Warren or John Crowe Ransom. Neither is Tom French afraid to work with very large nails and huge bolts of textile, whether in poems like 'The Ayreshire Cattle Breeders are Holding a Meeting . . .' or 'At the Bishop's Palace'. He is in complete command of his materials, which is a kind of definition of a master, and this skill and high knowledge of the art of the poem is one of the many reasons why *Company* is such a solid, enduring achievement. 'This patch of grass is the altar in the dews,' he writes in 'Still Life, Chancellorsville, 1863' and follows thus: 'This is the glory and the gospel loosed.'

Dublin Review of Books,
2022

Acknowledgements

The author wishes to express his gratitude to the wonderful Catherine Coakley. Also, much gratitude to my brother, Kevin McCarthy, at UCC, whose computer skills often rescued a lost text.

Thanks to all the editors of the journals and newspapers who encouraged or provoked me into writing these reviews and essays over the last half century.

Deepest gratitude to Peter Fallon, to Suella and Jean, of The Gallery Press, for the prodigious work involved in the publishing of this book, and in particular to Peter without whose guidance and direction this book could not have happened. His confidence in my sometimes tangential and obscure subject matter became the *anima mundi* of all my working hours in 2023-24. Thank you, dear poet.